"*Let's each* buy what *we want,* and have a little *fun*"

Louisa May Alcott
Little Women

Books for little women,
big men,
and everyone else besides
at Waterstone's

BIG MEN

51

GRANTA 51

AUTUMN 1995

EDITOR Ian Jack
DEPUTY EDITOR Ursula Doyle
MANAGING EDITOR Claire Wrathall
EDITORIAL ASSISTANT Karen Whitfield
US EDITOR Ann Kjellberg

CONTRIBUTING EDITORS Pete de Bolla, Will Hobson,
Liz Jobey, Blake Morrison, Andrew O'Hagan

FINANCIAL CONTROLLER Geoffrey Gordon
ADVERTISING AND MARKETING Sally Lewis
CIRCULATION Lesley Palmer
SUBSCRIPTIONS Kelly Cornwall
OFFICE ASSISTANT Lila MacMahon

Granta, 2–3 Hanover Yard, Noel Road, London N1 8BE
TEL (0171) 704 9776; FAX (0171) 704 0474 SUBSCRIPTIONS (0171) 704 0470

Granta US, 250 West 57th Street, Suite 1316, New York, NY 10107
PUBLISHER Rea Hederman
US PUBLISHER Matt Freidson

SUBSCRIPTION DETAILS: a one-year subscription (four issues) costs £21.95 (UK), £29.95 (rest of Europe) and £36.95 (rest of the world). Subscriptions telephone: (0171) 704 0470.

Granta is printed in the United States of America. The paper used in this publication meets the minimum requirements of American National Standard for Information Sciences—Permanence of Paper for Printed Library Materials, ANSI Z39.48-1984. ∞

Granta is published by Granta Publications Ltd and distributed by Penguin Books Ltd, Harmondsworth, Middlesex, England; Viking Penguin, a division of Penguin Books USA Inc, 375 Hudson Street, New York, NY 10014, USA; Penguin Books Australia Ltd, Ringwood, Victoria, Australia; Penguin Books Canada Ltd, 10 Alcorn Avenue, Toronto, Ontario, Canada M4V 3B2; Penguin Books (NZ) Ltd, 182–190 Wairau Road, Auckland 10, New Zealand. This selection copyright © 1995 by Granta Publications Ltd.

Cover design by The Senate. Photographs: Hulton Deutsch, Douglas Brooker

ISBN 0-14-014110-3

CORMAC McCARTHY
the crossing

VOLUME TWO OF THE BORDER
TRILOGY WHICH BEGAN WITH
All the Pretty Horses

'A superb and moving
work of art which stands
head and shoulders above
most contemporary
fiction ... There
are parts of this
book I know I
shall never
forget'
JOHN BANVILLE

NOW IN
PAPERBACK

PICADOR

CONTENTS

Andrea Ashworth Our Mother's New Man   9

Gitta Sereny My Journey to Speer   47

Dear Adolf   73

John Sweeney Hitler and the Billygoat   85

Caroline Alexander Plato Speaks   91

Blake Morrison Bicycle Thieves   109

Douglas Brooker LA Women   125

Lindsey Hilsum Where is Kigali?   145

Edward Blishen Trouble at the Waterworks   181

Claire Messud The Professor's History   193

Clive Sinclair The Lady with the Laptop   215

Harold Pinter Girls   253

Notes on Contributors   256

BIG men

GRANTA

ANDREA ASHWORTH
OUR MOTHER'S NEW MAN

My father drowned when I was five years old. A picture of me, framed in gold plastic, was fished from his pocket and returned to my mother with a soggy wallet and a bunch of keys. The keys were to our new terraced house, now paid for with his life insurance.

Outside our house, my father's mini-van sat undriven. Weeks before his death, he had stencilled its sides in bright yellow: ANTHONY CLARKE: PAINTER AND DECORATOR. TEL: 431 7677. Occasionally, newly-weds called up to have their homes decorated. My mother explained that the man they needed was dead.

On the way home from his last paint job, he had stopped to take a pee, my mother said. He slipped in the mud, landed on a rock and drowned face down in a shallow stream.

'Less than four inches deep,' she told people.

Strangers dropped by to mourn over tea and biscuits.

'Such a handsome young feller,' they sighed at my father's photograph on the sideboard. 'What a waste!'

My mother lost a lot of weight. Her veined hands took my three-year-old sister, Lauren, and me through the sooty streets of Manchester. Scuffing along the pavement, my red sandals jumped the cracks by heart. I glanced up every now and again, from the shoes of strangers who had stopped in the street to stare at my mother and her daughters. My eyes floated past hedges and chimneys to purple-grey clouds, bellies full of rain, waiting to bucket down.

'What bee-yutiful girls!' ladies exclaimed over our caramel faces, gasping at my mother, 'You don't look old enough, love. You truly don't!'

My mother was something of a celebrity on our street. A twenty-five-year-old widow, she had long lashes casting velvet shadows, and dimples that danced about her lips when people swore she looked like the Gorgeous Natalie Wood.

'Oh no, *she's* a beautiful woman!' My mother laughed over the compliment every time, blushing and waving it away. Her laughter sounded the same as ever, though it came out of a thinner face.

11

By the time I was six, my mother's stomach was swollen full of a third child. A looming, red-faced man was introduced to Lauren and me as our new daddy.

'I used to be a sailor,' he told us. 'In the merchant navy, like, on the big ships.'

I suspected he was around to stay when large paintings of ships, sails billowing, began to line the staircase. My pregnant mother strained on tiptoe to hammer the winking brass hooks into the wall. A new wedding snap squatted on the sideboard in a heavy wooden frame: my mother was standing big-bellied in front of a brick building (not a church) with the tall new man.

I skidded to a halt one afternoon when the headmaster called me by a strange surname.

'Andrea Clarke-Hawkins!'

My name wagged its ugly new tail, creating whispers behind my back until the home bell rang. My mother wasn't there to explain the new name; she was in hospital to give birth to our new sister, Sarah, who came out blonde and screaming.

Sarah's eyes were sky-blue marbles. She lay blinking, pink, dusted with talcum powder. Her yeasty cheeks made me think of chewing. Wheeling home from school, people stopped the pram to coo over her face while Lauren and I stood by, fingering the spokes in the wheels.

'The little angel,' they tutted and sucked. 'Doesn't look like your darker ones, though, does she?'

'Different father,' my mother explained.

During the day, my mother stewed Sarah's dirty nappies in a bucket in the kitchen. When it threatened to rain, she rushed out into the backyard to unpeg the laundry: the clothes smelt of other people's chimney smoke; the clothes-pegs were wooden people with whom Lauren and I played while our mother clanked pots and pans and steamed up the kitchen.

Every night at the same time, my stepfather's keys rattled at the front door. Boots brushed and scraped on the doormat, and in came Peter Hawkins, a red face sticking out of wide blue overalls smeared with car grease. Before tea, my stepfather scrubbed the oil from his face and hands at the kitchen sink. He combed his black hair flat against his skull and flicked the dandruff from his shoulders. Under the soapy scent, we caught faint whiffs of petroleum when he smacked our cheeks with kisses.

Tea was ketchup with chips and things out of tins, baked beans or spaghetti. We ate it without a word while our stepfather sat chewing and staring over our heads at the television. After tea, my mother washed the dishes, washed our faces and changed into a stiff green dress that zipped up the front. Then she folded into her car—a battered blue Princess whose rust patches she was forever daubing with metallic paint—and drove off to look after dying people until dawn. She worked the night shift at Manchester City Council Home for Geriatrics.

'It's at night that they pop their clogs, that's the worst part.' She described the toothless corpses to my Auntie Janet. 'Their faces are smiling—sort of floating up—but their legs feel like lead.'

While she swept corridors and bathed worn-out brows, my stepfather watched over Lauren, Sarah and me. Lulled by soap operas, his eyelids drooped over a warm can of beer. Sarah slept cradled on his dozing belly, calmly rising and falling, while Lauren and I played in silence behind the dining table. We were allowed to play with Lego, but only if we stuck the bricks together without any clicking sounds. Our heads were crammed with helicopters and red Lego dinosaurs, but we put all our bricks into building ships to please our stepfather. He slouched on the sofa while the television's light flickered electric over his features, now blue, now red.

'Da-daa!'

We stuck our ship, portholes and all, under his nose. He rubbed his eyes and sat up to let a smile break over his creased face.

'It reminds me of me navy days. When I was a lad: no kids to feed; no cars to fix neither.' My stepfather took a long look at the yellow plastic ship.

He had gone through a whole family—wife and babies—before he ran into my mother. One afternoon, while he was at work, his old wife had rung up to tell my mother a thing or two. My mother's face fell while the telephone rattled its high-pitched story into her ear. She knew nothing about any ex-wives with babies to feed. When she replaced the receiver, my mother and Auntie Janet had to go and brew a pot of tea in the kitchen. Behind the glass door—clicked shut—they mouthed and made

13

faces. Broken noses, affairs, and drained whisky bottles whispered through the see-through door.

Before Peter got home, my mother changed her face and wiped it smooth, her fingers tucking at the temples where creases might show. My stepfather scraped his boots and elbowed at the sink to soap the car-grease from his face. A pale, hairy stomach peeked out of leather-belted jeans. My mother smiled and murmured through his kissing compliments.

'House looks spotless, love. Me trousers dry? Fried mince for tea? Smells great. Really great. Christ, I had a bugger of a motor to fix this afternoon! Let's go down the pub tonight, eh? I'll ring the babysitter.'

My mother said nothing about the strange phone call. It was kept in the teapot, to be poured out and sipped in the afternoons between her and Auntie Janet.

We ploughed through the nightmare of cabbage and mince that my stepfather loved. After scrubbing the dishes, my mother pulled on her black silk dress, blooming with painted roses. It was the same dress she used to slip into every Friday night when my real father came home from pasting flowered paper to people's walls. With the week's housework done, she set her old Motown records spinning under the needle and swished about hypnotically. The songs were all about love and leaving, but my mother just smiled and smiled and sang along. My father used to come home in his baggy white overalls, splashed with bright paint, to dance with her before tea.

Now my mother fastened a straight brown coat over her dress to step out into the rain with her new husband. He didn't like music, so there was no swishing, but sweet musk wafted in the hall as the door closed behind her.

My mother kissed us goodbye at the school gate and wheeled off with Sarah in the pram. When the bell rang for playtime, I rushed out to find my sister in the crowded playground. We touched hands for a second, then ran off with separate groups of coloured faces. My eyes scooted along the school railings: sometimes, our mother was standing there on her way home from the shops, peering into the crowd for Lauren and me. She wanted to give us a packet of Opal Fruits each before she went home to sleep. We took the shiny yellow packets through the iron railings and kissed her hand before she pushed off into the traffic with Sarah's pram.

I gave up a green sweet to a red-haired girl who was taller than me. She wanted a pink one, but I was saving those.

'Why's your mum wear sunglasses all the time, then?' She asked the playground as well as me. 'Even when it's raining.'

When I got home I tried not to stare at my mother while she vacuumed our trodden green carpet in her dark glasses. Rain tapped at the windows. My mother put the kettle on. Auntie Janet came round to show off the snaps of her new council house. In the photographs, my mother stood out like a beetle: every shot caught her smiling in sunglasses. My aunt and she laughed, but when my mother lifted the shades, her face was full of green and purple bruises. Sarah's dimpled fist reached for the colours; my mother winced.

Behind her teacup, Auntie Janet asked, 'Does he hit the girls too?'

'God, no!' my mother was adamant: 'He'd not lay a finger on them!'

I looked at my mother's swollen eyes. She knew nothing about the night my stepfather had knocked me unconscious with the back of his hand.

Sarah had made a stinking mess in her nappy. My stepfather didn't know how to change it. He pinched his hairy nostrils and rolled the dirty nappy into a ball. When he went to fasten the clean one, he couldn't find the pin.

'Where the f—?' Biting his lip, he sent me upstairs to find it.

I couldn't find the pin anywhere. The nappy was loose, Sarah was screaming, but I couldn't find it anywhere. My stepfather came upstairs, spraying spittle.

'Where is it then?'

I couldn't say. My stepfather smacked me across the face, and I fell against the door jamb. My head hit the hinge.

When I woke up, Sarah had stopped screaming, and my stepfather was crouching over me, a chocolate bar in his fist. His black hair was dripping: he had gone out in the rain to buy it.

Pressing the Milky Way into my hand, he said,
'You're not going to tell your mum, are you?'
My throat was tight, but I ate the chocolate to show that I
was not going to tell. My stepfather watched me swallow before
he stood up tall again. Then he took the bright Milky Way
wrapper and buried it in the bin, underneath the potato peelings.

My mother waited for her swellings to go down before she
took off her sunglasses and drove us to see our
grandmother. Granny Chadfield lived on the eighth floor of
Circle Court: a concrete tower of lonely old people in the middle
of Stretford. On Sunday afternoons, grandchildren hijacked the
lifts and buzzed pensioners' doorbells before legging it. After
chasing each other down the echoing corridors, we gathered for
Gran's meat and potato pies. They glowed in the middle of the
table, gravy sizzling through forkholes, with glazed pastry leaves
whose veins had been etched in, one by one, with a knife. Wolfing
down my wedge, I begged through stuffed cheeks for seconds.

After Sunday dinner, Gran collapsed the table's mahogany
wings and pressed it back against the wall. During the week she
ate packet meals from a tin tray on her lap. Stuck on the eighth
floor, she sat by herself, looking over the city and thinking while
cars roared past on the motorway below.

'I don't ever want to live cooped up lonely like that,' my
mother murmured on the way home. 'I'd rather be dead than so
alone.'

I imagined living cooped up with Gran's wallpaper,
patterned over with orange and yellow cubes. One moment they
seemed to stick out from the wall; the next they were sucking in.
I asked, 'Do they go in or out, Gran, these boxes on the wall?'

'That depends on your perspective,' she said.

'What's that?'

Gran gave my hand a veined, skeletal squeeze.

'It's the way you choose to look at things.'

My grandmother had been forced to look at things differently
when her second husband left home with her eldest
daughter and the new refrigerator: Grandad and Auntie Val

moved into a semi-detached in Bury, where they had three children. Every week, my grandmother trudged across Manchester to take the pies she had spent hours baking to her grandchildren who were also her stepchildren.

'Flesh and blood,' she said, when neighbours raised their eyebrows at the dirty scandal. 'They're my own flesh and blood, come what may.'

My mother still woke in the night sometimes, crying because her family had been mangled. Still, we drove out to visit my Auntie Val on the odd Sunday afternoon. Our car strained up the hill, chugging, then Lauren and I peeled ourselves from the sweating vinyl seats to go dashing across the back fields with our cousins. At teatime, we came in from the cold and crowded around the kitchen table, noses red and feet kicking underneath. Auntie Val pulled a steaming sponge cake from the oven.

'Want a piece, Andy, love?' Her huge bosoms beckoned behind the cake. 'It's vanilla.'

I looked up at my stepfather to see if it was all right. The furrow cut deep between his brows said it was not. We were not allowed to accept treats when we went visiting with our stepfather. The cake loomed there, a delicious pillow, until my aunt took a knife and cut eight hot slabs from it.

Plenty. I breathed in sweet vanilla, sweet vanilla.

When I looked up from the crumbs, my stepfather's eyes were so dark the pupils had disappeared. He motioned to the door; I swallowed and scraped back my chair. The carved sponge was still steaming in the middle of the table.

'What have I told you about being greedy?'

It was cold outside, and I shivered.

'I wasn't being greedy, Dad: I was just being polite.'

'You don't go wolfing down cake to make me look bad!' My stepfather pulled at my hair to press my head back against the stone wall. 'You want them to think I don't feed you properly?'

The stones of the wall cut into my head.

'I just ate it to be polite, Dad, after Auntie Val had baked it for us.'

He lowered his face to mine, his eyebrows meeting in the middle.

17

'You know fucking not to.'

His spittle was in my face. The stones were cutting in. I began to cry. My stepfather pressed his moist hand hard over my mouth.

'Shut it: shut them tears up before I give you what for.'

I shut them up behind my damp, hot face and he slid his palm from my mouth.

'Now go inside and be quiet.'

I went inside and was quiet.

It was the same whenever we went visiting with our stepfather. Biscuits and cups of tea were stuck under our noses; we always said no. We had to sit still and be quiet when he was in the room.

On Sundays we had to be especially quiet. My stepfather snoozed in front of the gas fire while the television droned through church services or football, and the rain slapped a wet, grey curtain against the window. I lay on the carpet under the dining table, reading the new book my grandmother had saved up to buy for me out of her shopping money. Fairy tales: hard-backed and expensive. Lauren pulled a ball out of our toy basket and rolled it across the carpet; I sat up and threw it back. It made a small rubber thud. Peter stirred and peered at us over his white belly. He spotted the ball through the legs of the dining table.

'Put that bloody thing away before you break summat.' His face twisted, irate for a moment, before he sank back into the sofa's cushions.

I stuffed the ball back into the basket with a sigh, 'God, I hate Sundays.'

The words escaped him, but my stepfather caught the tone.

'What was that?' He sat up.

Dropping 'God', I told him, 'I hate Sundays.'

My stepfather stood up, tightening his belt a notch.

'You said you hate me, didn't you?'

'I said I hate Sundays, Dad, not you.' I squeezed affection into the word 'Dad'.

'You said you hate me, Andrea. Admit it!'

Behind the hardbacked fairy tales I denied it.

My stepfather grabbed the book. He was going to have to teach me a lesson. Gripping the first page in a hairy fist, he said,

'Admit that's what you said: you hate me.'

My lips opened, but nothing came out.

My stepfather ripped out the first page and crumpled it in his fist. He tossed the pale paper ball on to the carpet. After that I admitted nothing, because I knew the book was gone. He tore out every single page to the end, to the empty spine and the cover that still said *Fairy Tales*, though the endings had been scrunched into paper fists and scattered over the carpet.

Without his jacket, my stepfather stormed out into the rain. The door shuddered behind him. My mother made me wash my face while she washed hers. The day was in shreds, and it was time for our weekly bath.

My mother used washing-up liquid on our hair. She clipped our toenails and our fingernails and trimmed our fringes sharp and high across our foreheads. She kissed me, and I went to bed knowing that Gran would never hear where her precious food money had ended up.

When my stepfather staggered home smelling of whisky, ceramic hit the wall. We got used to the smash and the next-day stain, but eventually the wallpaper began to fade, and my parents resolved to change it. Every wall had to be stripped of the old flowered paper my father had pasted up before he drowned, and we set to with clumsy metal scrapers.

During the renovation, my parents fixed a date at the domestic court where Lauren and I were to be adopted by Peter Hawkins.

'A proper, legal family we'll be then,' my mother imagined.

At court, Lauren and I stood holding hands and trying not to gawp at the lion and the unicorn rearing up in gold on the wall above our heads. An official woman wearing a silver badge took us into a side room for questioning. She closed the varnished wooden door on our parents and asked:

'Would you say that you are happy with your stepfather?'

I looked at the official woman, who smelt of apples. Pearly buttons ran straight up her shirt into a dead white collar. Her pen was poised above her clipboard, and the silver badge blinked on her breast.

Yes, I said, we were happy with our stepfather.

19

The door opened, and we were ushered into a larger court room. My stepfather signed some papers, and my new name was pronounced: Andrea Hawkins. We went home in our Sunday dresses to eat spaghetti on toast. My mother sprinkled cheese on top and melted it under the grill until it bubbled up, golden.

Lauren and I were zipped nose to nose into an itchy sleeping bag on the sofa while our bedroom was stripped and renovated and painted a minty pale green. A hollow, plasterboard wall now divided it in two, with a sliding door to shut Lauren and me off in our bunk bed from Sarah in her cot. When my stepfather's mother, Nana Hawkins, came for tea, she shook her head in admiration:

'You've done a smashing job, Pete love,' she bounced Sarah against her bosom. 'It's nice for our Sarah to have her own room, separate from the other two, like.'

Because we were darker than Sarah, Nana Hawkins didn't consider us her proper grandchildren. When we stayed with her, she powdered her face in chalky layers before dragging us round the Bramhall shops and tutting over her purse at the extra money she was spending to feed us. Other blue-rinsed ladies, coming out of the shops, raised their eyebrows,

'They're not yours are they, Joan?'

'They're our Pete's adopted,' she explained. 'Proper little Pakis, aren't they?' They laughed over our heads, flashing pink dentures.

Nana and Grandad Hawkins lived in one of the council houses that huddled in a low, grey ring around a concrete playground. When Lauren and I went out to play on the swings, older kids shoved us off, calling us dirty Pakis. We insisted we were grandchildren of the Hawkins at number seven, the ones with the brass lion knocker, and explained that our real, dead father had been a quarter Italian, a quarter Maltese and half English.

'Yer wot?' A skinhead stuck his broken nose into my face.

I explained that I was dark-skinned because I had some Mediterranean blood in me, but that, actually, I was English just like him.

'You're not fucking English!' The pale boy backed into his

crowd of skin-headed friends, swigging the beer in his fist. I was only eight, skinny, and a girl; they smashed a few bottles and left.

My attention was drawn off the street and back into our house when my parents began to speak to one another in code, spelling things backwards so that I wouldn't understand. A-D-A-N-A-C. I said nothing while I worked out that my mother was planning to visit her sister-in-law in Canada. After a treat of beefburgers for tea, it came out of her mouth the right way round.

'I'm going to visit your Auntie Beryl in Vancouver,' she said. 'Your Dad'll look after you for a couple of weeks.'

My mother promised suitcases of souvenirs to make up for the looks on our faces: a fortnight with our stepfather, alone!

When the black cab finally came for my mother and her small vinyl case, my stepfather was actually very sweet. Chocolate crept into our daily menu to keep us quiet, and everything was fried, fried, fried. Eggs, bacon, sausages: men's food. On the fourth day without our mother, Dad made a few phone calls, then handed Lauren and me a new canvas bag each. We all packed: my stepfather, Lauren and me, with an extra bag for Sarah's nappies and things. I was beginning to see snow-peaked mountains and towering evergreens like the ones that arrived bashed on the back of postcards from Auntie Beryl in Vancouver.

By evening, my dreams of aeroplanes had fallen back to earth: our stepfather dropped us at Auntie Val's house before driving off to the airport. The minute she closed the door, Auntie Val was on the phone to Auntie Lynne.

'Can you believe it? Just like that—rushing off after her as if she can't breathe by herself! After wiping all them old people's bums for this one holiday of her own; she'll be furious!'

If my mother was furious, it didn't bring her home any sooner. The fortnight dragged itself out while Lauren and I wandered in the back fields all day, missing our school, which was miles away. A ten-pence piece swung in my pocket like a pendulum, rolling back and forth, back and forth, until the church bell gonged three and I ran down the hill to the sweet shop and bought two ounces of rainbow sherbet and a stick of liquorice, the hard kind, for sucking not chewing.

Dipping my liquorice stick in the sherbet, I trudged back up the hill and lingered around the red telephone box at the top. When the street was clear of grown-ups, I slipped into the stinking, smoky box and, because I had no number for my mother in Canada, I dialled strange numbers until the ringing tone began to purr in my ear. If anyone answered, I slammed down the phone while the pips were going off. After that, I walked back to Auntie Val's house for tea, secretly full of sherbet and liquorice and the choking, smoky calls.

Before my teeth rotted, my parents came home, breathless and full of plans they no longer bothered to spell backwards. We would be emigrating to Canada.

'As soon as we find a buyer for the house,' my mother told Auntie Janet. Clutching her cup of tea, my aunt asked enthusiastic questions about this part of green, sun-soaked Canada that my parents swore was so full of amazing opportunities.

'The standard of living's fantastic, Jan.' My mother's eyes lit up. 'You don't have to be loaded even if you want to build your own place. Right from scratch!'

Under her perm, Auntie Janet's eyes were brimming, afraid that cups of tea at our house were about to dry up. She patted her frizzy hair and laughed nervously,

'Who'll do my perm when you're gone?'

My mother had spent all morning chopping hot dogs and cheese for the relatives we were about to fly from.

'It's a lovely spread you've done, Lorraine.' Fat aunts complimented her buffet through mouths full of egg mayonnaise, watercress straying at their lips.

'Well, you have to put on a bit of a do when you're leaving so many people behind, don't you?' Where others nibbled sandwich triangles, my mother clutched a burning cigarette. The smoke swirled about her gaunt features. Suddenly, she stumped out her cigarette and grabbed my hand.

'Tell you what,' she bent so that her hair fell silky in my face, 'why don't we put on a bit of Motown and have a quick dance?'

My mother led me by the tips of her fingers, spinning me under the arch of her arm like a tree, a weeping willow whose branches sway down to meet you.

'Lorraine!' My stepfather called my mother away to refill people's glasses.

By now, I was hot behind the ears and down my back, twisting my hips in small, smooth circles like my mother's.

'That's enough dancing, Andrea,' my stepfather told me.

'Oh, let her twist, Pete,' Auntie Thelma laughed, tipsy. 'She's doing no harm.'

The music was still playing; people's feet were tapping in time; my sandals twisted and shuffled against the carpet's dull green until hot breath whispered into my ear:

'Upstairs!' My stepfather's anger was hidden from the party under the music, the flushed chatter, and clinking glasses.

On the stairs, my stepfather pressed a large, cold hand against my back, shoving me up into the bathroom. Inside, he locked the door and twisted the taps until the water gushed noisily into the sink and was sucked, belching, down the plughole. The cascade drowned out the sound when his hand came down to slap my face.

'Don't you dare defy me!' My stepfather's lips moved while my ears rang full of the slap and the water and the party downstairs. I went to say 'I won't Dad,' but the words were muffled under my stepfather's hand, pressing down to stifle my tears. Faint petroleum seeped from his palm, choking me.

When my eyes bulged, my stepfather peeled back his palm and washed his hands before twisting the taps shut. Everything stood still in the bathroom. The mirror was steamed over, reflecting nothing.

My stepfather took a flannel and wiped my face with a shaking hand.

'Now then, go on downstairs to the party.'

I went downstairs, where the party was still brimming with smoke and chatter and spilling drinks. Bubbling with wine, people asked me to twist for them. I pressed my back against the wall, smiling out of sore eyes.

'I'm tired of dancing,' I told them. The music sounded flat

and tinny, and I stayed close against the wall.

When people finally gathered their coats to leave, some of them were in tears: 'You'll be thousands of miles away,' the wine reminded them.

'Good luck, love. Take care!' Car doors slammed. Aunts, uncles and lifelong friends chugged off down the street. At the corner, yellow indicators winked before the cars turned and were gone. I finished waving on the doorstep, then climbed the stairs to wash the tears and lipstick kisses from my face. Our bedroom light went out at eight o'clock, but I read by the light of the street lamp until I fell asleep.

O ur suitcases sat bulging at the locks. 'All our worldly goods!' my mother laughed. Later, while we waited for our taxi to the airport, my mother cried on the telephone, squeezing in a few more goodbyes to my grandmother and Auntie Lynne.

'I'll write, Mum,' the sobs came up from her chest. 'The minute we land, I'll write to you.'

I was glad when the taxi arrived and my mother had to dry her eyes to face the driver; her tears made me feel dizzy and small.

At the airport, my stepfather stood at the window with Sarah in his arms and Lauren by his side, watching the planes take off into the night. My mother and I sat at a red plastic table, sipping Coke in tall glasses through straws. She reached her hand across to squeeze mine tight, saying,

'We can always come back, Andy, love—anytime you say so, if you get frightened or homesick or anything.'

Before then, it had not occurred to me that I might feel frightened or homesick or anything. I said,

'I'll tell you, Mum, if I'm not happy.' Then I puckered my lips back around my straw and sucked at my Coke until it was time to pass through the metal detectors and board the plane. An air hostess buckled me into my seat, and I sat looking out of the window and thinking about what my mother had said. I mulled it over and over until the engines roared, my stomach shot up into my mouth, and Manchester dropped out of the picture.

It was like being shut up in a spaceship with our stepfather, pressing our faces out at the world. Not in the clouds, where smiling air hostesses hovered under helmets of hair and made us suck mint after mint out of crinkling silver wrappers, while he sat strapped into his seat licking their legs with his eyes. Not in the clouds—but from the moment the plane shuddered down, and our stepfather unbuckled his seat belt, clutching the passport with all our names in his fist. He slipped it into his shirt pocket, flat against the nipple, and a look slid across his face, like a glass door shining shut. No more Gran or aunties to keep their eye out or stick their oar in.

Down a long fridge tunnel, Lauren reached to grip my mother's little finger. 'My legs've gone funny.'

'Move it.' Our stepfather grimaced behind the trolley full of luggage.

'Damned heatwave,' Uncle Vern drawled when we came out into the glare to load into his truck. The air boiled in slow waves so that the smile slithered leery over his face. I wanted to ask my mother if she remembered that summer in Manchester when the ladybirds landed and landed on our arms, then crawled drunkenly through the hairs, sucking the sweet sweat, while the air rippled up off the tarmac, and old people melted slowly down the street. But her face was fixed over my head in a smile set to spoil if I tugged on it.

While my stepfather swore, wrestling with suitcases, and my mother mopped up Sarah's tantrum, Auntie Beryl slipped a jar of something strange into my hands.

'For you and your Lauren.' It looked like golden glue oozing with light.

'Honey!' Auntie Beryl laughed, 'out of a beehive.' She explained through her smile how the honeycomb had been ripped out of the beehive and squashed into the jar with the lid screwed down.

'Oh.' Inside, at the heart of the honey, glistened a world of boxes that bees had spent their lives building out of the faces of flowers. I piled into the back of the truck with the suitcases and Lauren, letting her stroke the glass but gripping the lid jealously in my fist, to keep the sweetness from spilling.

While we were homeless and resting on hospitality, we kept our lives squeezed up in plastic leather suitcases too crammed to risk opening properly. My mother unzipped just a corner, and whatever she pulled out we wore.

'The buggers'll never shut back up,' she said when Lauren and I urged her to hunt out the twin red dresses whose halter necks would let the sun melt like toffee down our backs. She chipped her nails shoving stockings and dumb woollens back through the zip jaws.

'This is bloody ridiculous!' We saw the half-moons spoiling and stopped clamouring for our favourite clothes.

Some nights, after the whitest hot days, our mother let other things spill out behind the bedroom door. She pulled us to her and buried her salty face in our hair, crooning, horrible but delicious, *It wasn't meant to be like this, it wasn't meant to be like this,* until our stepfather sozzled in off the porch, and her eyes dried up.

'Don't fret, Lol.' He patted her thigh and fell into bed, slurring, 'We've wads of cash. Have our own pad in no time.'

Before the end of our first week, my stepfather had blown a wad of cash on a fat red Cadillac that he screeched us about in to see the sights. Lauren, Sarah and I clung to the back seat, gulping pine and soil and sun-grilled grass as it smacked through the windows to fill our faces and set our hair screaming. Our mother sat in the front, her face dead under dark glasses, while mountains whizzed by.

At night, our mother soaped the days off our faces with a warm flannel. We watched our stepfather feasting with Uncle Vern on steak and white bread dipped in hot gravy, while we chewed rubbery air out of tinned hot dogs. Our jaws cycled slowly, taking care not to scoff, until the men jerked back their chairs and left the table to bite the heads off cigars. The doors slammed on my stepfather's red Cadillac, and they growled off in search of bars.

I hung about my mother's chair, milking her for after-dinner kisses. While my stepfather was out, she gave up her cheek— creamy Ponds spiced with Craven A slims. She let me twist her newly permed curls in springy tubes around my thumb. But her smile snapped when I tried resting the tip of my little finger in the fleshy groove where her eyebrows met, to furrow over milky coffee growing cold and losing its froth.

Something fisted in my belly when Auntie Beryl scraped off the plates, forking chunks of still-warm steak into the dog dish. My mother helped her rinse blood and gravy off the plates, then they boiled up more milk and bowed their heads close at the table. Their perms mingled into a single frizzy bush as they whispered over the two milky coffees. Whatever they had on their minds was drowned under the miraculous splash and whirr of Auntie Beryl's new dishwasher. I stood next to it, 'Wishwishwishwishwishwish,' gobbling bits about jobs, big houses, bruises and the bloody fortune just blown on that damn car.

The house clenched up, tense. Uncle Vern and my stepfather had not staggered home at their usual hour, and something was up.

'Bloody fools!' Auntie Beryl kept saying. 'Bloody fools! They could have been knifed, or shot even, the dives they end up in.'

My mother rasped a match to light one more cigarette, half closing her eyes at the first puff, then flicking her wrist fast to snuff out the flame. She kissed the tip with a slow pucker, and her thoughts were her own.

When gravel crunched in the drive, she stubbed out her smoke in the ashtray brimming with dead dimps. They came in laughing, my stepfather and Uncle Vern, holding one another up in a stinking cloud of cigars and stale spirits. We scattered as they fell on to the settee, muddying the velvety cream.

'Lolly, love,' my stepfather gagged on his own tongue. His face kept twitching and twisting, trying to sort tears out of the drunken, strange laughing that had taken over his insides.

'Lolly, love,' he got out, 'something . . . ' Then his face let go and there was an avalanche of tears, worse than sick. We froze, fascinated.

'Lol,' a bloodied hand groped for my mother's. 'It's me car. The Cadillac. Down the ditch, an accident—tell them, Vern.'

I saw my stepfather's wide, red Cadillac smashed in the murk of a ditch, back wheels dead in the air. A truck had come steaming round the bend—lights too low, no bloody horn—and there was nothing for it and that was that, one almighty swerve and they were lucky to get out alive, goddammit and sweet Jesus.

My mother boiled up cold coffee and made my stepfather sip like a baby to still the trembling and stop the tears. He moaned low into the mug, slurping, 'Lolly, Lolly, Lolly.'

But you could see through the steam it was his smashed up Cadillac he had in mind.

'Vern's found work for me, under the table, like.' My stepfather spoke with bright, wet eyes. 'Few months is all it'll take me to get me act together, then we can think about building our own place, Vern says. How about that, then?'

His hair reeked of smoke and spirits, but my mother smiled straight into the face of my stepfather's dreams.

'Smashing, love.' She stroked his hair. His black curls sweated at the roots.

'A pad of our own,' my stepfather sighed. 'How 'bout that, Andy, love?'

It was bloodshot but rare, the smile my stepfather tossed me. I saw the Cadillac nearly killing him and thought of kissing his hands where they sprawled on his tired denim knees. The knuckles lay hairy and grooved, resting, I imagined, after a lifetime of hoisting sails and fixing cars. Under the nails lurked ancient oil stains and dirt out of nowhere.

'We'll have a garden, won't we, Dad?'

My stepfather's fingers flexed, promising to pull a house out of the ground, with ironed lawns and a wooden fence all around.

'Yes, love,' my mother whispered. My stepfather had slipped into one of his drunken snoozes.

'There'll be a huge garden,' she said, watching him snore.

There was a huge garden. A huge, leafy jewellery box sprouting yellow melons and golden squash. Pumpkins perched like swollen footballs, with a crowd of strawberries crawling tendrils and pouting ruby kisses luscious along the fence. Canada. Our eyes devoured it all, while our mother and stepfather retreated for a moment out of the sun. They had to leave Lauren and me on the veranda with Mr Ranjanpul, the owner, while they stepped inside to make their decision. In private.

'We'll take it.' My mother smiled hard, as if she had been slapped, when they came back out.

'Very good,' the Indian man said, touching his turban. 'Very good.'

My stepfather shuffled green notes into the man's hand. They fluttered in the breeze. Rent.

'Just a month for now, mind.' He frowned at the man's bright purple turban. 'We'll be buying our own place any day.'

'Very good.' Mr Ranjanpul made a fist of the money. Then he waved it over the garden: 'Not included, you understand?'

He left us on the veranda, held up on stilts, over the empire of fruity colour.

My stepfather zoomed us to garage sales and flea markets on desperate quests for furniture. We sloped home with no mirrors or pictures to let the walls breathe. The curtains, from the cheap end of the rack, were a dull red-orange, like a rotten sunset. To ease my mother's migraines, we had to pull them tight and put up with the putrid light seeping through.

'The heat here can be cruel,' my mother wrote to Gran on the back of shiny mountains or pioneers smiling in front of forts. Going to play her favourite record one morning, she found it curled up and melted on the turntable under the window.

'Why didn't you pull the curtains?' She gave me a look and yanked them across so that the room swilled orange and my stomach turned over. I watched her cursing the sun and crying over the shrivelled black disc. Now the voice was trapped in the warped vinyl lines, and the song was dead.

Nobody had warned me about the wrong kind of sun. In England, it made you feel more alive, glimmering out from behind the clouds and then slipping back in before you'd had enough. In Canada, it made you think of dying.

The moment I saw it shining to kill, I went to lie in the shade of the porch, resting my face on the cool stone steps. I closed my eyes, and the sun was a different yellow. Under my lids, the sky bulged full of purple clouds, like bruises, swinging in sooty circles over slate roofs and chimneys and concrete lamp-posts. There were horses in the clouds and strange faces, like God's. Like Gran's.

The battered red Cadillac still clogged up the drive, its front end a mangled silver smile hauled out of the ditch. The house sat sweating behind its sour orange drapes. My stepfather slouched asleep in the only armchair, snoring at the ceiling. His head lolled back, baring his neck white where the sun never licked.

I held my breath to keep him like that.

He had woken once, when I wandered into the dark orange room, and pulled me into his lap.

'Here Andy, give us a kiss.'

I brushed my stepfather's bristly cheek and went to get out of the chair, when his denim knees gripped. Holding my head like a melon between his hands, he slid his tongue into my ear. A black shudder went through me, all down one side.

'Now, you kiss me.' My stepfather turned his face away and pushed back greasy curls: 'In my ear.'

My thighs were bruising between his knees; I stopped wriggling and looked into the ear.

'No, Dad.' Hiding panic under a giggle, 'It's too hairy!'

Nails scratched my face when my stepfather grabbed my hair, 'Come on, Andy, love.'

'No!' My voice threatened to break out of its whisper, with all the hammering inside: 'I've got to go and wake up Mum, Dad—Mum's asked me to wake her up.'

The knees slackened and my stepfather shoved me off his lap, 'Go on, then.' *Little bitch*, he added under his breath. 'Go on, then.'

I wanted to go to my mother. I knew she would be lying in her room with the covers fastened over her face. Our house was baking, baking, but still she hid under her heaviest blankets. She had to have her sleep. There had been fights—screaming and smashed ornaments—over money and booze and indolence. Afterwards, our stepfather would slam out and rev up his car to go drinking. My mother disappeared into her bedroom, where she shut herself in with her cuts and bruises. The knob clicked once and there was dead quiet behind the door. I boiled up the kettle, stirring mugs of weak coffee to wheedle my way in.

'Coffee, Mum.' My ears strained to make her breathe through the wood.

Sometimes, a muffled groan rose from the blankets. My mother was conscious and might let me in to grip one clammy hand while she sipped from the other, trembling one. More often, a murky silence seeped under the door. A sly twist of my kirby-grip slid open the lock. Her face was buried under the blankets, and I had to peel them slowly back, holding my heart down.

No splits or gashes. All the bones where they should be.

I let myself breathe. Around her eyes the skin puffed veiny blue with bursts of purple, then sagged, yellow-green and hollow, under the cheekbones. Where they used to dance, her dimples carved shadowy holes deep into the cheeks.

I bent to kiss the smell of my mother's messed up face. Woody perfume came from her hair, rich with hours of sipping muddy coffee and kissing cigarettes in her pink housecoat and green fur slippers.

'Andy, love?' Her eyeballs shifted under bluish skin lids.

I hovered—*wake up, wake up, wake up*—over the closed eyes.

My mother's head lolled in the damp pillow. Her groaning faded and slowed. She sank back into bruised sleep, and I let her be.

When our mother was what she called recuperated, the door would creak open. The toilet flushed and gurgled, and she flapped down the hall in her slippers to cook tea: mountains of mashed potatoes—no money for meat.

While my sisters and I ate, our mother stood at the window, smoking and staring over the garden bursting full of Mr Ranjanpul's fruit. Letting out a long, smoky-blue sigh, she glanced her fingers over her face, then wound her sleeves up tight to do the dishes. I hovered close to her hip, wiping plates hot and lemony out of her hands and trying to swallow the bitter orange pill she made us suck on a Saturday, to be sure of our vitamins.

When the phone rang, her face frowned painfully, and she fumbled to kill the bubbles between her fingers.

'Hello?' Nobody ever rang us in the evenings. People were too busy feasting in families over tea and television.

It was a stranger at the other end, making our mother sing cheerful, tight as a wire, down the line.

'Yes, that's us,' she said, then folded into a chair to chat. Lauren and I stood by, riveted. We watched her back melting, and the lines unravelling out of her forehead into the phone.

'We'll be waiting.' My mother laid the receiver in its cradle. 'Well, kiddlywinks'—she touched her face round the edges— 'we've somebody coming to see us. Tomorrow, first thing.'

We went to bed with jam butties inside us instead of water. We had a name, too, to chew on. Auntie Dorothy, distant cousin of Great Auntie Joan in Manchester. It's lovely, I wanted to tell my mother, when your stomach lets you lie down without that hole squelching full of water while you're trying to sleep.

When we woke up, our mother was a new woman. She threw the curtains back wide and drew a slick of lipstick glossy across her mouth. Instead of the exhausted pink housecoat and green slippers, she came out in royal blue slacks with the seams pressed sleek up her legs. We marvelled at curls springing out of their rollers, where yesterday our mother's hair had been dead black straw clinging to the skull.

She let Lauren, Sarah and me press our noses against the nets to look out for our visitor. We were glued to the glass when a wide silver bonnet purred up our drive.

A lady's Cadillac.

She stepped out glazed, her skin tanned: Auntie Dorothy.

Gold earrings dangled money around her face. I kept my eyes on them, trying not to stare where her eyebrows had been plucked to death then pencilled back on, too high, in skinny wings of surprise.

'You're all so pretty!' she laughed, though her eyes skated politely to avoid the colours bruising my mother's face.

She was tall, and her knees made delicious cracking sounds when she stooped to give us kisses and biscuity stars baked out of gingerbread and dipped in pink icing. Where once I would have burnt to wipe it away, I let the lipstick kiss linger, sticky, like a pearl on my cheek.

Auntie Dorothy gave us ice cream and barbecues and a garden growing wild—grass under our soles and pine trees to look up to. Her silver Cadillac whisked us to a white wooden house only a moment from the sea, with an outdoor pool that made our mother gasp: 'Azure!'

Life was too short, Auntie Dorothy had discovered over the years, to be anything less than sweet.

We stripped off and skinny dipped in the blue, before sinking our teeth into beefburgers that burnt our eyes: smoked over charcoal, sizzling with cheese and oozing spicy tomato relish out of sesame seed buns.

'Little gannets!' Auntie Dorothy laughed, and my stomach seized up in the sun.

But he was miles away—we had left him buried, snoring, under the covers.

She smiled over us, 'It tastes better with your vests off, doesn't it now?'

Afterwards, Auntie Dorothy stuck us under her Power Shower and let us loose with her perfumed soaps in the bathroom full of mirrors and fancy bottles. I could have stayed in there forever, with the water pummelling my back and steam rising behind the swirled-glass door that you could lock, without a sound, from the inside.

'It won't run out,' Auntie Dorothy insisted, when I worried about the water. At our house the tank never heated all the way, so the taps dribbled lukewarm before gushing out icy. The electricity cost a fortune, and we had to conserve all our hot water for dirty dishes and for our mother's long and silent soaks, locked in the bathroom with pink ointments after another bloody to-do.

Auntie Dorothy pressed a white furry towel into my arms, and rubbed my toasted back.

'Little wings,' she traced my shoulder blades, 'Little wings, sticking out to fly.'

'Get summat on,' our stepfather tutted when his car growled up and he caught us spurting cherries and spitting bloody stones in our Fruit of the Loom knickers.

My arms folded over my nipples, suddenly prickling.

'No.' Auntie Dorothy spoke as if she were royal. 'It's good for them, a lick of sun on their backs.'

Our stepfather's eyebrows met in the middle, but his mouth sat still.

'Now, Peter honey,' Auntie Dorothy's nails shimmered, bronze lacquer, against a green bottle, 'What would you say to a beer with your burger?'

Our stepfather left us bare-bellied under the sun, to run in white knickers through the sprinkler's rainbowed webs. But things were beginning to cloud over, and my mind was on my vest. The wildness was gone.

Under Auntie Dorothy's influence, our mother marvelled, her Pete was a reformed character. Instead of sponging up game shows and days full of soaps, he heaved out of his armchair to face the mirror over the sink.

'Time for a shave, methinks.' He slit his eyes and peered at himself, lost in the lather.

Our stepfather sped us like lightning to Auntie Dorothy's garden, where he could preside over the barbecue, talking money and motors with her rich but shrunken husband. Uncle Bob was the shakier side of sixty, making his hair white and his words few and slow. They stood across the garden, spearing steaks and making men's talk in the curling, meaty smoke. I kept my eye on them—swigging gold beer from green bottles, with the sun going down—and wondered how long the barbecues would last.

Although he still smelt of smoke and men's spirits, our stepfather was not unpleasant to be near, now that Uncle Bob had secured him work fixing the odd motor here and there. 'Soon adds up, the odd job does.' Some nights, he swaggered home with iced doughnuts in boxes and passed pink sugared almonds and stray green notes into our mother's hands. Other nights, he staggered home empty-handed, carrying only sick whiffs of whiskey and dirty, clinging smoke. With no engines to fix, our stepfather went prowling to kill the hours. On the rampage, our mother called it. Empty days brought him home sagging, though he might puff himself up on tales of wild cars and vile men toting guns in back alleys. Every so often, he turned up in mad debt, having squandered a fistful of cash on a telly or a stereo or some other dodgy deal. We were torn between biting our lips for our mother and smiling for our stepfather when he tried to pass off his drunken disasters.

'Here, kids.' It could be anything from a bashed-up bike to a radio that nearly worked. 'I got this for you.'

Our mother fumed and cried, but there was no getting the cash back.

'We've sod all to eat, and you're still frittering it away!' She clenched her jaw and the bones stood out like knives in her neck. 'What in Christ's name are you thinking of?'

In the evening he might stay in, watching horror movies and dipping peanut-butter cookies in tea. The tang of peanut butter made my teeth shriek, but I sucked the soggy cookies in order to be part of the family. We huddled around the TV, letting the blood and gore scream across the screen while we watched quietly, behind cushions, with the lights turned low.

'Monsoons,' our mother breathed, when hulking black clouds came wheeling in off the Pacific to dump the ocean in silver sheets over our heads. Every morning was the same, opening the door on the wet world outside and having to swallow—not sadness, but a hole where happiness had been, before stepping into the road.

Gran had been there, under our roof, with Auntie Lynne and Uncle John and our cousins, Robert and Stephanie and Laura. They had come on a plane and slept in sleeping bags on the floor just to be with us. It had been all phone calls and kerfuffle and paradise flashing under our roof. Now it was gone. But we had the photographs to prove it. Two pure weeks.

'More like two minutes.' Our mother sifted through the photos, with Sarah on her knee. Lauren and I stood behind, stroking her back and devouring them over her shoulders.

There was one that made me shudder when it came to the top of the pile. Our mother and Auntie Lynne were posing in pinnies in front of the sink. But, where Auntie Lynne was alive, her round cheeks lit up from inside, our mother looked like death. Despite the big smile, she definitely looked like death.

My mother looked at herself laughing and started to cry.

'Pull yourself together,' our stepfather tutted, catching us all in the kitchen, 'miserable bloody cow. Pull yourself together.'

It was almost worse when our mother pulled herself together and acted as if everything was fine and dandy while scabs sat on her cheekbones, bleeding when she caught them with her hairbrush.

'Mum?' Lauren cringed when the skin seeped scarlet.

Our mother kept up her smile: we watched it gleaming with the eyes, frighteningly bright. She was letting nobody in. She had built up a wall of invisible stony bricks, and she was stopping on the other side.

Auntie Dorothy was off defying the wet weather and cruising the Caribbean with Uncle Bob and his arthritis. The neighbours refused to see anything.

'Howdy!' They kept everything packed behind their eyes, in fat looks that I strained to weigh up.

The only person to share our mother's bruises was Auntie Beryl, who had a face full of her own. Something strange was happening in her house, the huge one Uncle Vern had built out of raw timber with his bare hands, to show the sheer size of his love. Under her perm, Auntie Beryl's face was swollen like our mother's: they sat like twins, sipping coffee and looking livid.

Three weeks later, Uncle Vern was dead.

'Stone cold dead.' My mother could not believe it. 'A brain tumour.'

Auntie Beryl came to our house to heave through the days.

'I thought it was just the booze,' she sobbed, 'and his godawful temper. How was I to know?'

She wept through eyes still puffed blue-green in the wake of Uncle Vern.

'Ssh, love.' My mother laid Auntie Beryl's head on her bony chest, stroking her devastated hair. 'You weren't to know, Beryl. Who could have known?'

I was desperate to ask someone about brain tumours.

'Do you get them from drinking?' I wanted to know. 'Are they catching?'

I thought of all those nights my stepfather had strolled off and rolled back, shoulder to shoulder, swaying and singing, with our dead Uncle Vern. I caught myself in the mirror and it was written all over my face—what I was thinking—ready to sell me down the river the minute I opened my mouth.

When Auntie Dorothy picked me up in her silver Cadillac, I tried to flash things at her out of my eyes. My stepfather would kill me if I breathed a word, but I strained under my eyebrows to let Auntie Dorothy in—to let on, without words, what had been happening inside our house while she was off cruising the Caribbean on a luxury liner.

'OK, sweetie-pie?' Her eyes danced between me and the rear-view mirror. 'Been doing OK?'

'I can't make it this week,' my mother phoned from her pillow to cancel their Saturdays. I heard myself donated to Auntie Dorothy: 'Oh yes, our Andy would love that.'

At Auntie Dorothy's it was just me and the TV: she cooked things up in the kitchen while Uncle Bob lay in bed, looking to put some life in his bones. There was nothing I might do to help her—no dishes or polishing or sweeping up or anything.

'In this house, we relax,' Auntie Dorothy insisted. 'You just sit back and don't fret, till I call on you to appreciate my cool-a-nerry talents!'

It was at the dinner table that the feeling came over me. I had to go home. I had to get home to my mother and Lauren and Sarah, all stuck in our house without me.

'It's asparagus, honey,' Auntie Dorothy said, when she saw my face chewing strange.

'It's lovely,' I said, but I couldn't bring myself to swallow the third grassy finger.

Hiding it under my tongue, I looked at Auntie Dorothy and asked, 'Can I be excused?'

In the bathroom, I let the mush out of my mouth and flushed it down the toilet. It was divine, the white-green taste under my tongue, but I had to spit it out. My mother and Lauren and Sarah, my stepfather and the insides of our house had all seeped into my mouth and spoilt it.

Black stars crowded across the bathroom, blotting out the mirrors.

I called, 'Auntie Dorothy.'

It was like nothing before. Smashing and thudding yanked me out of sleep, and I sat up in bed at the same time as Lauren. Something hot and edged ran up my spine.

'You bloody bastard!' our mother was screaming in the kitchen.

'Get out of the fucking way!' We heard our stepfather shoving to get past our mother into the hall. 'Where is she, the stirring little bitch?'

Lauren reached for my hand in the dark.

'You keep away from them,' our mother was saying. It came out twisted, as if through locked teeth. Then a clattering metal smash and she screamed, 'Peter!'

We leapt out of bed and ran down the hall, blinking at so much white electric light after the sleeping dark. In the kitchen, the table had been knocked flat on its back, smashing dirty plates and oozing cold gravy with peas. Under the sink, our stepfather had wrestled the cutlery drawer off its runners and on to the floor. The silver lay skewed and glinting against the tiles.

'Dad!'

In his hand, our stepfather had the carving knife, shining, with its varnished wooden handle and the long silver blade edged fine for slicing beef. Our mother was standing against the wall, her back pressed into it, away from the beef-knife hovering and gleaming along her cheek. Her eyes looked through the blade into our stepfather's.

'Put it down, Pete,' she said softly, over the trembling. 'Put it down, love.'

My stepfather shifted his eyes at me.

'You let that little bitch feed people a pack of lies about me,' he jerked the knife, pointing.

'This isn't about the girls, Pete.' Our mother's voice was like a lullaby. 'Let's put down the knife and talk about it, why don't we?'

Our stepfather was sweating.

'Get rid of the fucking kids, then.'

Thick, whitish drops welled, shivering, in his nostrils.

Lauren and I held hands in the hall, barefoot and glued to the carpet. Our eyes were riveted on the blade, glancing to take in food spurted up the walls and plates smashed against the tiles.

'Back to bed, girls,' our mother whispered.

'Go on,' she slid steel into her voice when we failed to move. 'Back to sleep, the pair of you.'

We stood for a moment, swaying and saying nothing, then turned and padded back in the dark to bed.

My stepfather forbade me from fainting outside our four walls, and put a flaming end to those luxury weekends—swanning off as if I was somebody in that silver Cadillac.

'Spoilt fucking brat!' He used his words as well as his hands to bring me down a peg or two.

Instead, Auntie Dorothy came to us, and my mother let her in, whatever the state of her face. Although we tried not to get up our hopes, she was often there, complete with just-baked surprises, when Lauren and I loped home from school.

'Auntie Dorothy!' We spotted her silver fender, and our legs broke into a sprint, bursting in on hot cookie dough floating with chocolate chips in our mother's clouds of chain smoke.

I became convinced I had magic powers, predicting which Cadillac would be waiting in the drive when Lauren and I came around the corner from school. I took the corner hard, concentrating over the pounding in my chest to conjure the right number plate. When the silver bumper met us, our hearts rose up and ran; they weighed down with slow blood whenever it was red.

Our stepfather would be in his armchair, glaring at the walls and cracking his knuckles into the quiet.

He stumbled in early one evening, before our mother had finished her nap. Lauren and I had decided to take care of ourselves and our Sarah, by creating a marvellous macaroni cheese tea. Lauren snipped the corners off the cheesy powder packets; I balanced the water on to boil; the front door rattled and in he strolled.

'What's all this bloody nonsense?' Our stepfather found us alone, cooking at the stove, with Sarah perched on the counter to watch.

'Lorraine!' he bellowed and our mother came flapping down

the hall, fumbling where her housecoat flashed open on sagging white skin.

'What's up, love?' Her eyes were red and watery with sleep.

'What's all this shit?' he wanted to know. 'Where in Christ's me dinner?'

'I'll make it now.' Our mother trembled, rolling up her sleeves. 'You're back early, love.'

'I bloody well am, aren't I?' Our stepfather smashed the heel of his hand into the table. 'Got the kids cooking behind me back now, have we?'

Just out of bed, our mother's creased face screwed into a pale question mark. It jumped, frightened, from the great pan of water gurgling on the stove, then back to Lauren and me.

'We were meaning it as a surprise, Dad,' I said. 'Mum didn't know.'

'Shut it,' he said. 'And don't you be defending this slag— she's a bad mother, she is, lazing on her arse when she should be up and cooking.'

Our mother stiffened her shoulders, bubbling up red. 'That's bloody evil,' she gritted. 'What've you done for them lately, you greedy sod, except guzzle the food money so I can't feed them like I should?'

Our stepfather lunged to slap her.

'Cheeky bitch!' He missed her face, but tore the silver butterfly earring out of our mother's pale lobe.

She winced and put her hand up over the rip.

'Get to your bedroom, girls.' She spoke without looking at us, eyes fixed on our stepfather. They stood facing one another, anger simmering in each of their faces, like a mirror.

Our mother was flaming livid. Our stepfather was flaming livid.

'Get to your bedroom,' she said again, in a strange, mannish voice.

Thinking of punches and slaps and the beef-knife flashing in our mother's face, my stomach churned to leave them alone. My voice cracked when I dared,

'But we've not eaten yet.'

'Get into your room and lock the door!' Our mother screamed

when our stepfather grabbed the pan of boiling macaroni off the stove, swinging around to face her. I stood frozen, gripping Lauren and Sarah by the hands, until my mother shoved me.

'Get to your room. Call Auntie Dorothy, then lock the door,' she said.

We stood our ground. The pan was bubbling and spitting in our stepfather's fist. Our mother looked naked in the face of it.

'No, Mum,' I found myself crying. 'Please, Dad, you're frightening us.'

Lauren and Sarah took on my tears: we had all three of us seen our mother's face smacked scarlet and punched to blue-purple, but the water was something else.

Simmering. Scalding.

Our stepfather looked at us, then turned away.

'Oh, Jesus!' He flung the boiling water and macaroni against the window, letting the pan clang into the sink. Pasta slithered slowly down the pane and over the sill.

'Christ, what am I doing?' Our stepfather grabbed his hair in his fists and scrunched his face tight red. His eyes were wet slits. He opened them and looked at us all, crying,

'I'm sorry. Jesus, I'm sorry.'

Fluttering letters were as close as we could get to Gran and Auntie Lynne and anyone else on the other side, since the price of a transatlantic call was astro-bloody-nomical. My mother used to scribble her heart out in secret, until our stepfather discovered a bit of blue tissue in with his dirty underpants and socks. The envelope was addressed to our Gran, but he tore straight in to see just what our mother had to say about him. Our mother was too careful to write anything bloody, but the letter gave out how homesick she felt—enough to sell up and go home.

'What do you think you'll sell then, smart-arse?' our stepfather demanded. 'We've got nothing, so you keep telling me.'

I looked at my mother, wondering where on earth the money might come from to get us back over the Atlantic, home.

'It's just pie in the sky, Pete,' she sighed. 'Wishful thinking. We're not going anywhere.'

'Dead right you're not.' Our stepfather grabbed our mother's face between his fingers and thumb, twisting the skin the wrong way and ruining the bow of her lips. His grip was so tight she could only speak with her eyes through his fingers.

'You're not going anywhere without me.' He slid the words, with bits of spittle, straight into her ear. 'Don't get any fancy ideas, Lorraine. You're not leaving me, bitch.'

Our mother snuffed out the light in her eyes and, when our stepfather let her face go, she said in a dead flat voice,

'Don't worry, Peter, I've got no fancy ideas.'

But the snuffed look in her eyes let on differently. Behind them were some very fancy ideas that no shouting or beating were about to wrench out of her.

Our stepfather drew back his hand and brought it slamming into her cheek. The skin gave a quick shout then turned a deep, slow red, but our mother's face stood still.

He booted a hole straight into the wall and stormed out.

When I ran a facecloth under the cold tap, my mother let me press it against her cheek.

I touched her hair. 'Don't you want to cry, Mum?'

A tear welled and ran from her left eye, but it came from the slap, not from inside.

'No.' She stopped my patting hand and held it still in hers. 'There's nothing to cry for now, Andy. Nothing at all.'

My mother squeezed my hand hard, and I went to bed. Jammy Dodgers and iced Bakewell tarts sifted into my dreams. Custard creams, teapots and drizzly days.

In the light of the next morning, I asked my mother, 'Is that the only way to get back to England, then—in a plane?' I had to stamp my voice flat, to sound casual.

We were alone, polishing the fireplace with baby oil, and she put down her rag.

'Not a word,' she said, and lifted a ball of newspaper out of the hearth that cost too much to light. Wrapped in the faded news lay dangly diamond earrings, a ruby ring and an old, old watch wrought in dull gold.

'They're your Gran's,' she told me. 'She's said to sell them to get us all back.'

A blue tissue letter was folded up in the chimney, and my mother pulled it out to show me. From miles away, in gorgeous loopy writing, Gran was begging Mum to sell up and fly.

'Can you, Mum?' I tried not to get my hopes up in front of her.

'They were supposed to be heirlooms.' My mother sighed over the jewellery in the murky print. 'They're all we've got.'

'We can get more heirlooms, though, can't we?' I pressed my palm against hers. 'In England?'

To keep her eye on the cost, our mother set the clockwork oven-timer ticking when she picked up the phone.

'Hello? Mum?' She spoke loudly and quickly over the ticking to squeeze everything in before the bell went off. The timer was set to ring in twelve minutes, and everything seemed sorted, when our stepfather sauntered in from his afternoon revels.

Our mother went white. Our stepfather saw it all.

'You scheming bitch!' He lunged at our mother and tore the phone out of the wall. The line to Gran hung dead in his hand, ripped from its socket and dripping bits of plaster.

'Peter!' Our mother shielded her skull when our stepfather raised his fist.

'No, Dad!' I ran to my mother and wrapped myself around her. Lauren and Sarah hurried to do the same. The four of us stood clinging to one another in front of our stepfather.

'Christ!' he screamed, 'What are you trying to do to me?'

'Out of the way, girls,' he told us, but we all three held on to our mother. I felt her ribs sticking out brittle where I had seen them kicked by a boot on the bathroom floor, late at night under fluorescent white light.

'Move!' Our stepfather grabbed the teapot, steaming full, off the table. It was fat and round, with a sharp ceramic spout curving out to pour. He held it up to throw.

'Daddy!' Sarah began to cry, and our stepfather's arm stiffened.

'You bitch,' he said to our mother, very quietly. His pupils glowered and grew. 'You fucking bitch.'

He looked our mother deep in the eye, then brought the

43

teapot and its spout crashing into his temple. Blood and tea trickled down our stepfather's face, oozing out of the hairline, past his ear and into his collar. Staring at our mother, he pulled back the teapot and smashed again, this time cracking off the spout and howling.

My mother peeled my fingers from her arm and shoved me towards the back door, keeping her eyes on our stepfather.

'Fetch the police.' Her voice was hoarse. 'Run.'

I pelted into the street in my socks, heading for the house on the end where a family with a pool table and a stuffed moose head lived. Their car was gone from the drive. I panted back the other way to the old couple who gave us white chocolate on weekends. The curtains were pulled tight. There was nothing for it but to knock on a stranger's door.

I came back with a policeman and the man with the gammy leg, who had agreed to make the call.

My stepfather was sitting on the kitchen floor, in all the exhausted chaos, holding his face in his hands and moaning. When the strange men came in from outside, he looked up and wiped his nose. Blood was beginning to crust in his hair.

'That's my dad,' I explained.

My mother moved out of the corner where she had been sheltering Lauren and Sarah, braced behind the table for his next move.

'I'm sorry, Officer,' she said, 'I'm afraid we've wasted your time. We're working things out for ourselves.'

'Well, folks, if you're sure . . . ' I watched the two men turn and shuffle to get out of our house, clearing their throats and forgetting things fast.

'Go and call your Auntie Dorothy.' My mother gave me a dime. I ran back into the street, this time in my sandals.

Auntie Dorothy and Uncle Bob turned up with age sagging in the ripples of skin under their eyes. In front of them, our mother and stepfather looked like children, lost and dirty, with rips in their clothes and their hair sticking out.

Auntie Dorothy shook her head at the bloody mess spewed across the kitchen and down my stepfather's face. Her gold earrings rocked.

'This has got to stop.'

No words, only sniffling, came from our parents.

'You can stay with us,' she told my mother. 'I'll help you and the girls till you get back to England, if that's really what you want.'

'It is.' My hand grasped Auntie Dorothy's leathery one, loaded with sparkling rings.

'It is,' my mother said, looking at my stepfather and his bleeding head. She moved to bathe it, but Auntie Dorothy caught her arm.

'Help the girls pack, Lorraine.' She held my mother gently by the wrist. 'You've got to make up your mind what you're taking with you and what you're leaving behind.'

GRANTA

GITTA SERENY
MY JOURNEY TO SPEER

Gitta Sereny, aged fifteen, as a student at the Reinhardt drama school in Vienna

Albert Speer touched my life before I even knew of his existence.

My father, who died when I was two, was a passionately Anglophile Hungarian, whose greatest ambition for me was that I receive an English education. And so it happened that in 1934, I was travelling from my boarding school in England to my home in Vienna when the train broke down in Nuremberg. I was an eleven-year-old girl, on my own, wearing my English school uniform—brown, as it happened, though I don't really think it influenced subsequent events. The German Red Cross, or its equivalent Nazi organization, quickly took charge of me; within an hour, to my amazement and, it must be said, pleasure, I found myself in a spectator's seat at the Nazi Party Congress.

I was overcome by the symmetry of the marchers, many of them children like me; the joyful faces all around; the rhythm of the sounds; the solemnity of the silences; the colours of the flags; the magic of the lights (these, though I didn't know it, Speer's creation). One moment I was enraptured, glued to my seat; the next, I was standing up, shouting with joy along with thousands of others. I saw the men on the distant podium and heard their hugely amplified voices. But I understood nothing; it was the drama, the theatre of it all, that overwhelmed me. (Forty-four years later, Speer described to me his own feelings that day and said, resignedly, 'To think that when I'm gone, *that's* what I will be remembered for: not the buildings I designed but that—*theatre*.')

A few weeks later, back at my peaceful school near the Kentish downs, we were given the subject for our first essay of the new term—not surprisingly, 'The Happiest Day of my Holiday'.

What else could I, not yet twelve, have described other than that experience in Nuremberg? Although my essay was not chosen to be read out to the class (that honour fell to a lovely description of the birth of a foal), my teacher, Miss Hindley, told me that it was 'a very good piece of work'. She had a strangely formal way of speaking which I found very beautiful, and I thought her a marvel of erudition and adulthood. In fact she was in her early twenties, a slight, delicate, rather shy young woman, with a fine English complexion. She had a quiet sense of humour, was passionate about books and drama and had the wonderful

49

gift of imparting that passion to her pupils, however cloddish.

'I think you need to understand what you were seeing,' she told me. 'Anyone who comes from your part of the world needs to understand.' And she handed me a book. 'Read this, or as much of it as you can.'

The book was *Mein Kampf*, and I did read as much of it as I could. Years later, when people told me they had found *Mein Kampf* unreadable (in Speer's case, he said Hitler had told him not to bother, that it was outdated), I never understood what they meant. It was hard going, true enough; I skipped large portions, and certainly I wished that it had more paragraphs. But I understood what Hitler was saying and, above all, that his vision of a new Germany, a new Europe, could not be realized without war.

Was I particularly prescient? I don't think so. Throughout those hundreds of densely written pages, he repeated, again and again, Germany's need for *Lebensraum* in 'the East'. I knew nothing about politics and very little about the geography and tortured history of Eastern Europe, but it seemed to me obvious that no country would voluntarily give away any of its territory. How could anyone doubt that?

I also knew very little about anti-Semitism. 'Why does he keep talking about "the Jews"?' I asked Miss Hindley when I returned the book.

'He hates them,' she said. And, as she so often did with all of us, she left me to think it out on my own.

I did not succeed. I knew, of course, that there were, in the school of my early childhood in Vienna, three classes of religious instruction—Catholic, Jewish and, my own class, Protestant—but I was not really aware of who among my classmates belonged to which group. This must sound strange, but I have since asked Viennese friends of my own age, from similar backgrounds, about this, and they too, I found, had little awareness of religious difference—which is perhaps a tribute to our schools.

For a privileged child like me, Vienna was paradise. I lived with my mother, who was beautiful and much courted, in a large flat overlooking St Stephen's Cathedral. She had been an actress when she was young, and her life revolved around the theatre, actors, playwrights and drama. Was St Stephen's cathedral, with its powerful smell of incense, its monotonous singing and its silences, its bleeding or smiling statues, just drama to me? I don't know, but until I was sent to England, I went in there every day on my way to or home from school, leaving my irritated governess outside while I knelt there in a curious pretence of—or perhaps wish for—religious fervour.

My other passions were more prosaic: my mother, for her looks; a few of her gentleman friends, for their charm and elegance; the countless books I read, many on the sly by torchlight under my bedclothes at night; teachers—there was always a special one—for their cleverness and, as I was mostly lucky, kindness; the theatre, which obsessed me from my first visit at the age of four; and Vienna, because it was Vienna.

By the time I was fourteen, I had left my English boarding school and was back in Vienna, studying at the Max Reinhardt Drama School. Although I had not inherited my mother's looks— I was a little girl with puppy fat—I somehow never doubted that they would give me a place, and for some reason I was accepted on the spot, as was another girl my age. She was delicate, with a cloud of silky, dark hair, and was most appropriately named Elfie. We were inseparable from that moment on.

The Max Reinhardt Drama School was a wonderful place, housed in the extraordinary setting of the Imperial Palace of Schönbrunn. Reinhardt, the greatest director of his time, who had had to leave Germany and his school in Berlin because he was Jewish, made a speech on the day the school opened in Vienna which was reprinted in a brochure we were given: 'Use this place. Walk in the park on your own, think on your own, speak on your own, dream on your own: before you can know anyone else, in life or on the stage, you must know yourself!'

These were powerful words for young minds, and both Elfie and I followed his advice, conscientiously taking long walks on our own, speaking aloud as he advised, expressing our thoughts, our longings, our anger, on occasion, and our dreams.

Most of Elfie's and my life was spent together. We would meet every day halfway between our homes, by the statue of Johann

Strauss in the park. We would go together to our fencing or dancing lessons close by, or attend rehearsals at Reinhardt's theatre, the Josefstadt. Later on, we would take the tram to Schönbrunn and most nights—often very late, because many of our teachers were directors and could only take classes in the evening— we would walk home past the park, down the immensely long Mariahilfer Strasse and finally along the Ring with its beautiful trees and baroque buildings. When we reached the Opera, we parted, Elfie turning right and I left. No one ever bothered us; despite its many political conflicts and frequently violent demonstrations, Vienna was a strangely safe city for children.

This innocent, or insouciant, life ended shockingly and quickly in March 1938, when Hitler invaded Austria. At about nine-thirty in the evening on 11 March, Elfie telephoned me. 'Meet me at the statue,' she whispered.

'Why are you whispering?' I asked.

'Just come,' she said, and hung up.

While I waited for Elfie in the dark, deserted park, I heard for the first time a sound that was to echo around Vienna for weeks: the rhythmic chant of many voices shouting words I had never heard before: *Deutschland erwache! Juda verrecke!*— Germany awake! Jews perish!

When Elfie arrived, we stood stiffly in the darkness, listening. Then she said, 'My father—'

'What's the matter with your father?' I asked, and then, to my own surprise, added, 'Is he a Jew?'

Elfie looked at me helplessly. 'A Jew?' she said, confused, her voice tight. 'He is a Nazi. They told me tonight. He's been an illegal for years. He said I was never to speak to any Jews at school, and that anyway'—her voice sounded dead—'the whole place will be . . . *disinfected* from top to bottom. What shall I do?' She sobbed, holding on to me. 'How can I not talk to Jews?' Then, for the first time, she put into words the subject that had never touched us, reeling off the names of four of our teachers whose criticism or praise had dominated our lives for over a year.

I was almost speechless. 'But why?' I asked, and then, immediately, 'How do you know they are Jewish?'

'*He* knows,' she said, tonelessly. 'He says they are *Saujuden* and that they will all be got rid of.'

'Got rid of?' I repeated stupidly, and she cried out then, furiously, 'Didn't you hear what I said? *Disinfected*, he calls it, the schools, the theatres, everywhere'—she spat out the word—'*disinfected*.' The chanting from the street went on and on as we stood there under the trees. 'What shall I do?' she said. 'How can I live with them?'

She could do nothing, of course; well-brought-up teenage girls in Vienna did not leave their families. (In the end, happily, she did manage to escape; by the time she was sixteen, she had become a big star.)

Two days later, I stood in a crowd underneath a hotel balcony and heard Hitler speak.

I had become terribly, achingly aware of wrong, wrong in my small world and in the world beyond it. But I don't remember Hitler saying anything outrageous; he was just lauding the Austrians for welcoming the Germans. And indeed, huge numbers of Viennese, and Austrians all over the country, did welcome them, and the air was full of excitement and joy. What I remember most clearly—to my horror—is how excited I felt myself as, part of this seethingly emotional crowd, I listened to that man. Four years earlier, in Nuremberg, I had sat high up in the stands and found myself shouting with joy. Small as I was, I was aware that my pleasure derived not from any person or words but from the theatrical spectacle. But now? I had heard the Austrian chancellor Kurt von Schuschnigg announcing the plebiscite of 13 March, his voice breaking at the end: 'Austrians, the time for decision has come.' I had heard Elfie crying about her father's betrayal. I had heard those raucous voices, *Deutschland erwache, Juda verrecke*. And here I was, standing before this man whose orders had sent troops into Austria and who had followed those troops so as to seal the deed with his presence. What was it that made me join the mindless chorus around me, welcoming this almost motionless figure to our Vienna? What was it in him that drew us? What was it in us—in me too, that day—that allowed ourselves to be drawn?

The next day, Elfie and I went for a walk around the city. On the Graben, one of Vienna's loveliest streets, we came across a band of men in brown uniforms wearing swastika armbands, surrounded by a large group of Viennese citizens, many of whom were laughing. As we drew near, I saw that in the middle of the crowd, a dozen middle-aged people, men and woman, were on their knees, scrubbing the pavement with toothbrushes. Horrified, I recognized one of them as Dr Berggrün, our paediatrician, who had saved my life when I was four and had diphtheria. I had never forgotten that night; he had wrapped me again and again in cool, wet sheets, and it was his voice I had heard early that dawn saying, '*Sie wird leben.*' (She will live.)

Dr Berggrün saw me start towards one of the men in brown; he shook his head and mouthed, 'No,' while continuing to scrub with his toothbrush. I asked the uniformed men what they were doing; were they mad?

'How dare you!' one of them shouted.

'How dare *you*?' I shouted back, and told him that one of the men they were humiliating was a great physician, a saver of lives.

Stunningly beautiful, her trained voice as clear as a bell, Elfie called out, 'Is this what you call our liberation?'

It was extraordinary: within two minutes, the jeering crowd had dispersed, the brown guards had gone, the 'street cleaners' had melted away. 'Never do that again,' Dr Berggrün said to us sternly, his small, round wife next to him, nodding fervently, her face sagging with shock and exhaustion. 'It is very dangerous.' They gassed them in Sobibor in 1943.

(When I told Speer, forty years later, that I was in Vienna in March 1938 when he too, as he had told me, was there to prepare a hall for a rally at which Hitler was to speak, I asked him whether he had seen the shop windows marked in white paint with the word 'Jew', or noticed Nazi brutalities. He said no: 'I saw nothing like that; I wasn't there long. I did my work . . . I stayed at the Hotel Imperial. I strolled along the Ring and the old streets of the inner city, and had a few good meals and lovely wine. And I bought a painting—that was nice. That's it.' He hadn't known that people, Catholic and Jewish patriots, were being arrested in droves by then and that the first wave of suicides, mostly elderly Jews, had started? 'No, I knew nothing about that. I still know nothing about that. Suicides?')

The schools and colleges reopened within days. I have tried to recall the changes in our lives. The main one, at least for me, was a sudden awareness of feelings I had not felt before, an excitement that I didn't understand, and didn't really want to feel.

Though Hungarian by nationality, I loved Austria and above all Vienna; even now, having lived in cities all over the world, I cannot recall ever having been so joyfully aware of the changing of the seasons as I was there. Is there another city in Europe where the scent of lilac lingers so heavily over the streets in May, or the leaves of the trees in the parks turn so golden and red in October, or the snow lies so thickly on roofs and streets in winter? I remember as if it were yesterday the hard, clean feel of the pavement under my shoes once the galoshes were put away: childhood memories of unimportant things that mattered. All this probably didn't change, but my awareness of it did. It was a warm and beautiful March, but I don't remember the sun or the buds on the trees or the smell of the lilac later that spring. It is people I remember: the first day we returned to school, two students wearing swastika pins, and a few days later, the school administrator too, a man of great importance to us all, appointed by Reinhardt himself.

By now, we knew of course that there were three categories of people who were in real danger: Jews, communists and Austrian patriots. For the rest, life could go on more or less as usual, although foreign embassies sent small pins in the national colours to their citizens, urging us to wear them. My mother and I received small Hungarian flags, and I wore mine not so much for protection as to separate myself from those at school who wore that other pin.

In the weeks that followed, people began, slowly, to disappear: one of my teachers, a small man of quite incredible kindness to fumbling young drama students, killed himself by jumping out of a fourth-floor window; two others left for the United States. Elfie and I no longer walked home; her parents and my mother forbade it. We no longer went to theatres, for rehearsals or performances. All of us came and went in groups, orderly, quiet and, in many cases, suspicious of each other.

A few months before the *Anschluss*, my mother had become engaged to Ludwig von Mises, one of the country's leading economists. He had been living and teaching in Geneva for several years, spending only his summer holidays in Austria, where he and my mother indulged their passion for mountain-climbing.

Among my mother's many other admirers was a high-ranking German diplomat. One evening in May 1938, he appeared at our door and told her that the Nazis intended to arrest her and hold her as a hostage against von Mises's return; being both Jewish and a prominent intellectual with dangerous ideas, he was high up on their blacklist.

I don't know whether the Nazis would actually have taken my mother hostage, but she believed it, and so we had to go. By eleven o'clock that night, she had packed our cases and arranged for friends to send on to Switzerland my father's collection of paintings and other valuables. Austrians, by then, needed exit permits for travel abroad, but we had our Hungarian passports and we left the next morning for Geneva.

I don't think I was bitter; just as Elfie could not leave her family and live on her own, I could not stay behind by myself in the political cauldron of Vienna. But having experienced the adult freedom of drama school, I was both sad and furious to find myself in a finishing school near Lausanne. I developed a particular loathing for the headmistress when, just weeks after my arrival, a little German Jewish girl was suddenly removed from the classes and our luxurious accommodation and sent to work in the kitchen; her parents, it transpired, had been sent to a concentration camp, and there was no money for her fees. My mother and my new stepfather, together with the mother of my co-conspirator, a wealthy New York socialite, came up trumps; they threatened not only our removal but the most unpleasant publicity for the school unless the child was immediately given a free place.

This incident, which demonstrated that the Nazi poison was not limited to Germany and Austria, along with Elfie's carefully phrased letters, which clearly conveyed her unhappiness, convinced me that an expensive finishing school was not the place for me. At dawn one lovely Sunday, when I knew my mother and stepfather were away for the weekend, I ran away. I confided in two slightly older American girls who thought the plan mad but romantic, and gave me a large sum from their considerable hoard of pocket money. I packed a small bag; my American friends agreed to lock the door behind me (they also promised to telephone my mother that night, having told the teachers at Sunday breakfast that I had joined my parents for the day); and without great difficulty I got to Geneva in time for the early-morning train to London via Paris.

I knew nobody in London, having only been there on brief excursions from my school in Kent years before, but I had a plan. Either I would obtain a place at the Old Vic Theatre School, where I would complete my training; or I would audition for Alexander Korda, Britain's top film producer, and get into films. Of course, neither plan worked. At the Old Vic, the suspicious school secretary, having seen the address I had written down of a fleapit hotel in a less than salubrious part of London, asked whom I was staying with and then added kindly, 'It's none of my business, but don't you think you should go home, wherever home is?' Fellow Hungarian Alexander Korda, upon learning my name and that I came from the Reinhardt school, granted me an audition and talked to me for a long time about what was happening in the world, about books and about music. By the time we got down to my audition, his wife, Merle Oberon, had joined us, and he had managed to extract a lot of information from me. 'You have some talent,' he said, after hearing my Juliet (I had played the part in Vienna in a special English performance for the Duke of Windsor and Mrs Simpson). 'I'll help you here, if you really want, but I suspect this is the wrong direction for you. You are too young and you are uneducated. I advise you to go away, grow up, study— then come back and see me in a couple of years.'

Merle Oberon then took me to lunch, lent me a handkerchief when I cried and arranged for me to telephone my mother.

By early autumn, I was living in Paris with two young academics, sister and brother, in a wonderful old flat off the avenue Henri Martin. I had a pass for lectures at the Sorbonne, had signed up for a typing course at Pitman's and was taken on as a pupil by one of the most generous and awesome actresses in Paris, Madelaine Milhaud, the wife of the composer Darius Milhaud. Vienna, the *Anschluss* and the Nazis were suddenly very far away. I was caught up in a passion for all things French and above all Paris; my life was wonderful, and I was learning what it was to learn.

When war broke out on 3 September 1939, I was in Les Baux en Provence, at that time not even a village, more a settlement of about fifty people who lived in caves dug out of rock on top of a mountain. There was one extremely basic hotel, the Reine Jeanne, which the conductor Pierre Monteux took over for a few weeks every summer for a seminar to which, that year, thanks to the Milhauds, I had been invited. There were about a dozen of us, French and American. We had been immersed in music for two weeks when we heard on the wireless that the Germans had invaded Poland and that France and Britain had declared war. French mobilization was incredibly swift—the young men in the valley were gone within days—and a request arrived from the mayor at the foot of the mountain that the maestro's young students should come down and help with the grape harvest.

The weather was glorious; it was fun to wash our feet and legs with rough country soap, rinse them in a stinging, green disinfectant and then walk, jump and dance on the grapes. We held hands and made a ballet of our first war-work. On the last evening, Monteux conducted his student orchestra in a piece by Brahms; '*N'oubliez jamais*,' he said at the end, '*lui aussi était Allemand.*'

My mother and stepfather ordered me to return to Switzerland. When I refused to go, they stopped my allowance in an attempt to force me. But I was sixteen and in love—with an English boy, with France and with my studies. Nothing would have made me leave and, after a few weeks during which I slept on friends' sofas, ate very little and walked wherever I had to go, they relented, at least for the time being. I was not an easy daughter or stepdaughter; I suspect that they were almost relieved.

My return to Geneva soon became a moot point. Five months into 1940, the Germans, with almost unbelievable swiftness, occupied France. Thousands of refugees streamed into Paris, among them many children whose parents were dead or lost.

For the next year, I worked as a volunteer nurse for an aid organization called the Auxiliaire Sociale. It established reception centres for abandoned children in Paris and homes for them in châteaux all over occupied France. I went to Villandry, one of the great châteaux of the Loire, which belonged to the American mother of Isabelle de la Bouillerie, the president of our charity. There were two young volunteers and one paid nurse to look after about twenty children between the ages of three and fourteen in a hastily converted stable block. Downstairs was the kitchen with one tap, a huge, old, wood-burning stove and a long table with benches; upstairs was a dormitory with twenty-odd iron bedsteads. I had a tiny room off the dormitory; the other helpers and a number of refugees from Paris, Isabelle's friends and staff, some of them, incidentally, Jewish, were lodged in the château; we all ate together with the children.

My mother and stepfather had gone to the United States, and I had no money at all except for pocket money Isabelle sometimes gave me, particularly after I became her interpreter in negotiations with the Germans. It was an important function, given our desperate need for documents to facilitate the running of the centre and food for the children and, as a well-brought-up Viennese Hungarian, I was peculiarly qualified for it.

I was, of course, passionately Franco- and Anglophile and—mainly, I suspect to give myself an identity—furiously anti-German. As time went on, there were a few opportunities for minor practical acts of opposition—hiding a few shot-down British airmen, smuggling out documents—but there was not much opportunity for subversion; the most one could do was treat the visiting Germans with disdain. Hundreds of—rather polite—Germans, mostly officers, who came to see Villandry on their rounds of the châteaux of the Loire, were received very coldly indeed.

There were two in particular who came quite often, one an army doctor, the other a supply officer who had been a schoolmaster in civilian life. Both took an immediate interest in our children and helped us obtain medical supplies and food. They were—though I refused to see it at the time—good men and, I suppose because of that very fact, allowed themselves to be targets for my fury. For months, they accepted my railings and Isabelle's more elegantly phrased criticisms without demur. And then, without warning, they disappeared. The doctor, I later discovered, was soon sent to the Russian front, where he died within weeks; the former teacher, older and not very fit, was sent to a concentration camp. They had both been devout Christians and opponents of the regime.

We had never known. They hadn't told us; they had just tried to express it by showing affection to the children and helping us to care for them. Indulging our own feelings, we had abused their kindness. We had never sensed their pain and their dilemma, or that they desperately wanted to be—and indeed were—our friends. (Three years later, when France was liberated, Isabelle de la Bouillerie was imprisoned at the Santé, accused of collaboration—principally on the basis of her friendly relationship with those two Germans; she died there.)

It was another German who, some months later, undoubtedly saved my life. He was a Prussian aristocrat, head of military intelligence in the nearby city of Tours. He had helped me get assistance from official quarters for the children and had become something of a friend. I had suspected for some time that he was an anti-Nazi. One day, getting no reply when I knocked on his office door, I opened it. The room was empty, but the door to his living-quarters was open. As I walked across the room to announce myself, I heard the radio, tuned to the BBC. For the average German, listening to the BBC was a crime. Perhaps this rule didn't apply to officers, but even so, he was startled when he saw me.

'You see,' he said, spreading his fingers in a gesture of surrender, 'I'm in your hands now. Will you spare me?' He was a charmer.

One night, about six months later, Marie, the oldest of our children, who had appointed herself my friend and assistant, tiptoed up to my bed and whispered that there was an officer in a car at the gate who had asked for me by name.

It was just before dawn; the air was sweet. I ran out to the gate. 'You are going to be arrested this morning,' he said very quietly. 'Get dressed quickly. Don't say goodbye to anybody. Hurry.'

Gitta Sereny, right, as a volunteer nurse with Auxiliare Sociale at Villandry

Not long before, we had hidden a British airman for a week or so, after which, disguising him with a nurse's cape and veil (he was very young and thin), I had driven him in a horse-drawn buggy Isabelle had lent me to a rendezvous from where he would be taken to safety. I had been stopped by a German security patrol, but the Auxiliaire passes I carried—issued with the help of the officer who now waited for me at the gate of Villandry—plus my Hungarian passport, got us through, and I had thought myself quite safe.

I sent Marie back to bed, swearing her to silence; dressed in my uniform; packed nothing except soap, a toothbrush, a change

61

of underclothes, a spare shirt and my papers; and left. I had no money, but he gave me all the French currency he had and drove me to Orléans, where I got an early train to Paris.

It sounds dramatic, but it didn't seem so at the time. I was grateful, but not that surprised he'd come to my aid—I would have come to his, had the opportunity offered itself. As I rode on that train, it was a beautiful day; Paris, a few hours later, was still Paris; I had very good friends. Two days later, still in my nurse's uniform, I was taken over the Pyrenees by a mountain guide, and walked out of France and into Spain.

(When I told Speer about this German, I asked him, 'If it had been you, would you have helped a young girl like me?' He thought for a long moment before he answered. 'I don't know,' he said, finally—he always tried to be honest, though he didn't always succeed. 'I really don't know. Thank God, the question never arose.' I said that wasn't quite so, that a number of people at risk, for political or 'racial' reasons, had been offered a safe haven in his ministry. 'True,' he said, 'but that was my ministry, not me: I knew, but I didn't *have* to know or do anything myself.')

Although I was sad to leave, and quite determined to return as soon as possible, I was also glad. I had many friends of my age in the growing French *maquis* who already knew of Gestapo cellars, particularly in Paris and Lyon, where people were subjected to appalling tortures. I fear I was not a heroine; I was afraid of physical pain.

The next three years I spent in the United States. This period has never seemed quite real to me; amid the incredible plenty and—even in wartime—peace, I never stopped feeling guilty and ashamed: guilty for having left Europe, ashamed for being safe. Everyone tried to make me feel at home—I had never experienced such kindness and generosity—but the only way I could deal with my grinding homesickness, which wasn't for one particular place but for all the places in Europe I so loved, was to work at things connected with my life there and so remain a part of the struggle from which I would otherwise be excluded.

For my first eighteen months in the United States, I travelled across the country, lecturing in schools and colleges on the war and Europe's children. Still practically a child myself, and trained for the stage, it was not difficult for me to communicate with the thousands of young Americans I met. I gave, on average, three lectures a day, driving from town to town and city to city, travelling through about twenty states in all. It allowed me to get to know the country, and I grew to love it too. New York was electric and exciting, but it was the rest of America that touched, fascinated and also frightened me: that extraordinary mixture of innocence and chauvinism, kindness and incipient violence was utterly different from anything I had known before.

I learned, when giving my lectures, that the most effective way to engage people, whether they are children or adults, is through emotion. This was a great lesson. I often had to remind myself to hold back, to go easy when, standing on stage in an auditorium, I felt waves of emotion coming from my audience in response to my accounts of what was happening in Europe. Even in these circumstances, I grew to understand that people's need to feel must never be abused. Many years later, when Speer explained to me how Hitler had exploited people's emotions, I remembered my own temptations on stage in America, and was glad I had resisted them.

For the rest of my time in the States, I worked at the Office of War Information, writing anti-Nazi propaganda and broadcasting it, via England, to German troops.

Four months before the end of the war, I finally managed to return to Europe. I had joined the United Nations Relief and Rehabilitation Administration as a child welfare officer, working in the displaced persons camps in what would become the American zone of Germany. I had arrived in the States in the navy-blue uniform of an Auxiliaire Sociale nurse; I left just over three years later in the khaki uniform of UNRRA.

My very first assignment in the field, which lasted only two weeks, was the care of child prisoners from Dachau concentration camp. For someone like me, arriving with only the shortest of briefings, it was traumatic. There was, I now know, no comparison between the condition of the prisoners at Dachau and those at Bergen-Belsen and Buchenwald (and of the camps in Poland we knew absolutely nothing, not even their names). But

Dachau was bad enough those first few days—especially meeting those people who had been force-marched south for weeks from other camps, and then, of course, the children. Was it thinkable that they would have sent children to these places? It was: children of all ages, all religions, many nationalities, including Germans.

There were very few Jewish children—most of them, we found out later, had been killed—but many from Eastern Europe: young children who had been taken away from their mothers when they were sent for forced labour; older ones who, even during that last year of the war, had been taken away from their countries to work in Germany and who, at the end, had been marched south to end up in concentration camps. And then, perhaps more incomprehensible still, were the German children who, curiously isolated from the others, looked less worn but were, if anything, the most helpless of all. These were victims of the *Sippenhaft*, the imprisonment of families accused of treason, frequently the children of high-ranking officers and diplomats, some of whom had doubtless attended Nazi élite schools. Heaven only knows how they coped with their reversal of fortune, with the brutalities of their jailers, with their co-prisoners, almost all of them from 'races' and nations they had been taught to despise.

My job was to help the American army authorities to get all the children out of Dachau as quickly as possible, to their homes, if that was feasible (it almost never was), to hospitals if necessary but in most cases to the UNRRA reception centres and camps which were being set up all over Germany in expectation of many thousands requiring care.

I would eventually work in three camps, the first in Neumarkt, a small town in Bavaria not far from Nuremberg, looking after six thousand Poles. After that, I was sent to Regensburg, to a camp which housed about twenty thousand Ukrainians. Most of these people had been slave labourers, but hidden among them were men who had served as SS auxiliaries in the worst of the Nazi camps. This was an immense installation which, over the years, would turn into a loosely fenced-off township with its own, highly politicized administration, its own churches, schools, playgrounds, meeting halls and thousands of barracks, where men and women would live, court, marry and

Albert Speer with Hitler, Weimar, 1936   HULTON DEUTSCH

have children. These people, most of whom had been brought to Germany by violence, now didn't want to go home, where they feared more violence awaited them.

My third assignment was the finding and care of children from Eastern Europe whom the Nazis, having decided that they were 'racially desirable', had kidnapped from their families and brought to Germany to be brought up as Germans. I found forty-seven such children and, in the summer of 1946, was able to return thirty-eight of them to their families in Poland. By this time, I was about as deeply immersed as anyone could be in the misery the Nazis had caused. My wish—indeed my need—became more intense with every day to find out how it could have happened.

It was at the beginning of that year that a friend of mine, George Vassilchikov, one of the first two simultaneous interpreters in the world, obtained a visitor's pass for me to attend the Nuremberg trials.

This was the first time I saw Albert Speer. I knew nothing about him and only noticed him among the twenty-one accused because, then forty years old, he looked young and, with his smooth face and strangely shaped, bushy black eyebrows, startlingly handsome. In contrast with many of the other

65

defendants, who pretended to be bored or asleep, or who read or fidgeted endlessly, he always sat very still, listening intently, his face immobile except for those dark, intelligent eyes.

'Who is Speer?' I asked Georgie one night at the Grand Hotel where we were dining and dancing.

'The second most important man in Germany,' he said, leading me, a rather bad dancer, expertly around the floor. 'It was because of his requests for ever-more workers that the people you are looking after now were shipped to Germany as forced labour.'

I remember feeling an odd sense of surprise. It was hard to reconcile the terrible treatment of the slave labourers with the interesting, chiselled face I had become aware of in the dock.

'You mean, he was responsible for the way they were treated?' I asked.

Georgie was always precise in his answers. 'We can't really know yet about the nature and extent of people's individual responsibility,' he said. 'But of course, he had to *know*.'

Later, I learned that if it hadn't been for Speer, Hitler would have had to give up at least a year earlier than he did. A year. How many people died in that year? It was then, I think, that Speer entered my subconscious. The next two times I attended the trial, I looked harder, focused more on that silent figure, that attractive face in the dock.

It was—it seems incredible—thirty-one years later, in the second half of July 1977, that I received a letter from Speer, who had been sentenced to twenty years in Spandau prison and released in 1966. He was writing, he said, because he wanted to thank me for an article I had written for the London *Sunday Times*. He felt he needed to express his appreciation of the manner in which we had approached the subject.

A great many things had happened to me in the intervening years. I was married in 1948 to the American *Vogue* photographer Don Honeyman, and we had had two children; we had lived in Paris and New York and, in 1958, had decided on London as the place where we wanted to bring up our children and work. I had written a novel, *The Medallion*, about a little boy who was kidnapped from America and taken to four-power-occupied

Vienna, and had decided that writing would be my life. I worked as a journalist, and remained passionately interested in two subjects: the Third Reich and troubled children. (In 1969, I was to write a book on the case of Mary Bell, an eleven-year-old girl in Newcastle who killed two little boys.)

In 1967, I went to Germany to attend some of the Nazi war crimes trials which, virtually unmentioned in the foreign press, had been going on for several years. The federal government's office for the prosecution of Nazi crimes had begun its work as soon as the administration of justice was returned to German hands in 1958. By 1967, hundreds of suspects had been found, and major trials were being held in Frankfurt, Hamburg, Düsseldorf and smaller cities. Witnesses—primarily Jews who had been in the camps—were brought to Germany from all over the world to testify.

Despite my experience in the UNRRA camps, I found the testimony I heard during the four trials I attended harrowing. But those six weeks I spent in Germany reinforced my feeling that there was a great deal missing, not so much in our knowledge of the past as in our understanding of those who enacted it. This feeling led to me to write my third book, *Into that Darkness*, the story of Franz Stangl, Commandant of Treblinka, as he told it to me during weeks of conversations in Düsseldorf prison after he had been sentenced to life imprisonment. I wanted to understand how a perfectly normal man with average gifts and of presumably average morality could be made into a monster, and whether, under slow moral pressure, he could be brought to recognize his guilt.

It was an extremely difficult book to write, at times nightmarishly so. And when it was finished, I promised myself that I would stop exposing myself to Nazi horrors. But I never quite succeeded in suppressing my involvement with the Third Reich and its aftermath. I often succumbed when editors asked me to undertake commissions in or about Germany. It was one such commission that resulted in my letter from Speer.

The article Speer had read was written in collaboration with a colleague, Lewis Chester. Its subject was a book, *Hitler's War*, written by the British revisionist David Irving. Irving claimed to have discovered that Hitler had not known about the genocide of the Jews until October 1943 at the earliest. On first reading, his arguments were plausible—just; his proof, in the form of quotes from Hitler, Himmler and others, was intriguing. Revisionists all over the world had for years been trying desperately to clear Hitler of the gas-chamber murder of the Jews. If they could prove that Hitler had not been involved in the order for genocide and indeed had not known for years that such genocide was happening, then they would have succeeded in changing Hitler's image and, with it, the history of the Third Reich.

Our method of investigating Irving's claims was to follow the trail he himself laid. Irving himself was surprisingly helpful: 'This is my Jew file,' he said, pointing to a long box filled with meticulously cross-indexed cards. 'Everything is in it; you can borrow it.' He was so generous and persuasive that I almost thought he might have something.

I spent just under two months talking to survivors from Hitler's circle and checking in German archives every document he had registered in his 'Jew file'. By the end of our research, we understood the devices Irving had employed to support his thesis, and our long article completely discredited his claims.

In his letter, Speer wrote that it was 'ludicrous' for anyone to claim that the genocide of the Jews could have been anyone's idea but Hitler's: 'It shows a profound ignorance of the nature of Hitler's Germany, in which nothing of any magnitude could conceivably happen, not only without his knowledge, but without his orders.' The fact that there was no documentary evidence of such an order from the Führer meant nothing, he said. He knew from personal experience that many of Hitler's most critical orders were issued only verbally. 'From the historical point of view,' he wrote, 'the matter has now, thanks to your exposé, been dealt with. Nonetheless, unfortunately, Irving has provided fodder for the abominable efforts of those whose aim is to create a new *Dolchstoss Lüge* (war-guilt lie), as it was called after 1918, in order yet again to deceive the German people. It appalls me.'

Although I knew a great deal about Speer, had read his two books and had seen him many times on television, I had never wanted to meet him. I had admired his books, the second one, *Spandau: the Secret Diaries*, even more than the first. This story of his twenty years imprisonment—his bitter relationships with at least four of his six co-prisoners; his extraordinary personality change under the tutelage of the French chaplain Georges Casalis; his transformation of the prison yard into a flowering park; the thousands of letters he wrote to his best friend and his children; his organized reading and study programme (he read five thousand books, taught himself English and French and by the end of his imprisonment could probably have obtained degrees in literature, ethics and even theology); and, finally, his 'walk around the world', carefully measured hikes he took daily around his 'park', supported in his imagination by maps and descriptions, walking from country to country and city to city over deserts, plains and mountains until, twelve years after he had started, he had walked just under thirty-two thousand kilometres—all this made it the most extraordinary prison memoir I had ever read; he had been, it was obvious, an extraordinary man.

But none of this had emerged from what I saw of him over the years on television after his release and read in countless interviews where, too glib, too smooth, too sure, he appeared only to repeat himself endlessly, above all in denying that he had ever known anything about the Nazi crimes. He made me uncomfortable; I didn't like him; I didn't want to know him. Then, the day after receiving his first letter, another one arrived. He had forgotten to mention, he wrote, that a year or two previously, he had read *Into that Darkness*, which had caused him sleepless nights. If I was ever in the vicinity of Heidelberg, would I perhaps care to come and talk?

I telephoned him after receiving this second letter, partly to thank him and partly because the letters didn't sound the way I imagined him. His voice came as a great surprise, and was partly responsible for me changing my mind about meeting him. In the interviews I had read—perhaps because the questions and answers had essentially always been the same—his replies and obvious evasions had irritated me; on television, particularly when he spoke in his heavily accented English, he had almost always sounded arbitrary and arrogant. But on the telephone, he sounded hesitant, shy—not of me, specifically, but as a person. What intrigued me most, however, was that I sensed a great sadness in him.

A t the beginning of 1978, the editor of the *Sunday Times* magazine agreed that I could do a profile of Speer, and that Don, my husband, could take the pictures. By the time we went to Heidelberg in April, Speer had telephoned me many times—we had already talked for hours, and my feelings about him had changed: I no longer regarded him with active dislike, though I could not say that I liked him or, above all, trusted him. Even if he had been truthful about everything else in his books and interviews, he was, I was sure, lying about not having known until Nuremberg about the murder of the Jews. But I had no idea what he felt, admitted or denied about Hitler's other crimes; nor did I know about his family, about his friends and enemies during the Third Reich and since, about what his life had been like before the Nazis came to power and when he was a child.

To find out about the background, motivations and feelings of Franz Stangl was one thing. To try to discover how a man of Speer's talent and immense intelligence could have been convinced by the arguments of National Socialism and become— as far as was possible—Hitler's friend, how he could have stood by him until the very end and probably through his efforts prolonged the war by a considerable period, was quite another. But my main feeling, as we drove up to the Speer house in time for tea, was curiosity.

Over the years, I have established a way of dealing with these professional encounters. When I am talking to someone whose past is immensely controversial, my rule is to tell him at the very start how I feel about him. I do not pretend to come as his friend, to help or console him. If he has murdered, I want to find out what has made him do it; if he has cheated, I want to find out why; if he is a ruler of an industrial empire or a country, and I find his rule suspect, I tell him so. In the case of people involved with the Third Reich, I tell them what I feel about the Nazis and how I feel about them personally.

For me, this is a kind of insurance policy: I want none of them to be able to say afterwards that, in order to get him to talk, I pretended to be other than I am. And quite aside from feeling that this is, morally, the right approach, I have also found that making such a statement creates a special atmosphere: people respond to it, speaking more openly, saying, perhaps, things they would not otherwise have said. This was certainly the case with Speer.

Speer's house was large and comfortable but, except for his study, which was full of papers and books about the Third Reich and was dominated by a large painting of his mother, it was curiously impersonal: 'good' furniture, carpets and paintings; ornaments on the tables; expensive curtains and lots of flowers. It could have been the home of any upper-class German family. It conveyed no sense of Speer, or even of his wife, who had lived in it throughout his imprisonment and raised their six children there. It was later, at their house in the mountains, that I got more of a sense of him; he had created it himself, from an old farmhouse. It was very simple, almost spartan, but everything it contained—the old pieces in the bedrooms and the kitchen, and the new ones Speer had designed for the huge living-room, converted from the former stables—was beautiful.

By the end of that first evening, Speer had made friends with my husband. He had almost immediately suggested that they call each other by their Christian names, which is very unusual in Germany. With me, he was, not reticent, but much cooler. It would be some time before we too called each other by our first names.

By the time we left that night, though knowing no details, I knew that Speer had had a miserable childhood and hated the Heidelberg house because it reminded him of it, and that he and his wife and he and his children were and always had been miles apart. I knew that he was deeply nostalgic for Spandau, though I didn't know why; and I knew that he had loved Hitler, though not to what extent. What I didn't yet know, and wasn't to learn until much later, was that he was consumed with guilt about the murder of the Jews. It was a long time before I grew to like Speer, but by the end of our first three weeks together, I fully believed, and loved, that feeling of guilt in him.

Albert Speer died in 1981. By then, we had talked a great deal, and I have often asked myself how I really felt about him. Perhaps my reaction to his death goes some way towards providing an answer: I was shaken, because it happened so unexpectedly, in London, while we were away, and because there was a message from him on our answerphone when we returned, by which time he was already dead. But I was not sad. He had given me a great deal of himself, of knowledge and of understanding, and I was grateful to him for that. No one else could have given me what he did; there was no one else who knew and understood as much as he did. But when he died, I thought that his death was right and, in a terrible way, overdue; fate had given him thirty-five years after the Nuremberg trials, at which he should probably have been sentenced to death, as were others perhaps less guilty than he.

What Speer gave me was a new perspective on Hitler, on his personality, his actions and his goals; a new understanding of the significance, in political events, of human emotions. The book I now wanted to write was the book, I suddenly realized, that I had always wanted to write, ever since finding the imprisoned children at Dachau and the stolen children in southern Germany, ever since learning about the dead children in Treblinka, Sobibor and Belsec. Speer had given me the gift of himself, against whom I could place, consider, deplore and mourn all those events, and all those human beings who had lived and died in my time.

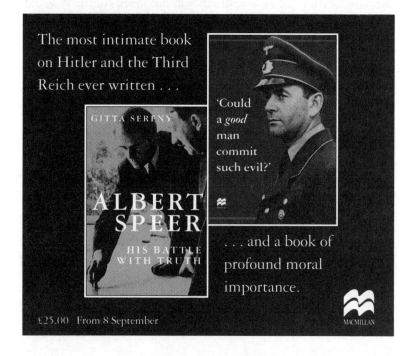

DEAR ADOLF

Hitler with women from the Rhineland at the Ministry of Propaganda HULTON DEUTSCH

In 1946, an archive of personal letters to Adolf Hitler was discovered in Hitler's former Chancellery in what was then the Russian sector of Berlin. The man who made the discovery, Willy Eucker, was a German with a long history of anti-Nazi activity. He had been imprisoned for treason in 1933, soon after Hitler came to power, and during the war was interned in France, from where he had escaped to join, eventually, the US secret service. It was as an officer in the US Military Government of Germany that he made his first trip to the old Chancellery building. It had been badly damaged by bombing, and its floors were strewn with papers—the contents of the filing cabinets which, Eucker was told, the Russians had emptied and taken away. He picked up a couple of letters addressed to 'Our beloved Führer' and put them in his briefcase. From later, unofficial visits—he made between twenty and twenty-five in all—he collected more than eight thousand documents, which he arranged to be forwarded to a friend in the United States. There Eucker took possession of them again when he emigrated in 1947.

Many of the letters conveyed good wishes, and sometimes protestations of love, from ordinary German women to their Führer. Eucker, who changed his name to William C. Emker in the United States, did not want to embarrass their writers, so he kept his archive private for nearly fifty years, until a small German publisher, Verlag für Akademische Schriften of Frankfurt, published a selection in 1994. The letters which follow are the first English translations from that selection.

It is unlikely that Hitler ever saw letters such as these. Officials simply filed them and sent standard replies. A few senders of birthday cards received thank-you cards engraved with Hitler's signature. Others got more formal acknowledgement: 'The Führer thanks you', or 'The Führer thanks you, but due to the pressing demands of the war, is unable to reply in person.' Only the love letters received no answer at all. If Hitler's admirers wrote persistently, the Chancellery informed the police, who gave them a preliminary warning. Correspondents who did not heed this warning could be declared 'mentally unfit' and detained in a psychiatric hospital.

From Miele, who sends cakes

Berlin, 10 September 1939

My dear, sugar-sweet Adolf,

I must write to you, because I'm so alone. The youngsters have gone for a walk. Lenchen is at her friend's, and I'm sitting down and sewing—darning socks and mending laundry. I wanted to go out, but it's raining, and I've got so much to do—always working, isn't that so, my sweet? I look at your pictures constantly, spreading them out in front of me and giving them a kiss. Yes, yes, my dear, sweet, good Adolf, love is as true as gold, and I can't do a thing about it. My sweet, I hope things are going as well for you as they are for me. Now I'm going to turn on the wireless and later I'll listen to the news, then I'll go for a walk for an hour or so and think about you, my darling, and what you're doing at the front. There's no Sunday there, my sweet, but things are going well because our soldiers are so brave, especially when they know you're at the front with them, inspiring such courage. So, my sweet, I'll presume you got my parcel with the cakes and that you liked them. Whatever I send you, I do out of pure love. Now I'll finish. My dear, sweet, good Adolf. Thousands of best wishes and kisses from your dear, good Miele

From Margarete, who has moved to new lodgings

Königsberg, East Prussia, 10 December 1939

My heart's own!

It's already a week since I moved to my new rented room at the address I sent you before. It's not at all easy moving lodgings like this! I took my possessions with me: the bed, the wardrobe, one chest, a coffee service, a Japanese tea service and some glass plates, and I got someone to give me one of those old washstands, you know, my poppet, the ones that open up on top to reveal a hole where the wash-basin fits; and underneath there's a drawer, and underneath that, a big cupboard with a door, where you can put everything you want. There's a colourful jumble in mine: Ata scouring-powder, a tonic called B-Drops (glucose), postcards, a brown rain cape, a cooking-pot, a sewing-basket, perfume, talcum powder, even a box of floor polish. My dear heart's own, you really must see all this for yourself, my dear, because, apart from the laundry chest and a little stove (which I'm sitting on: it's already one o'clock, so it's 11 December now) I've also bought a wicker chair, a round table, a coconut-matting runner and a curtain rail. (I had the dark red bedside rug where I lived before.) I had to bring the wicker chair back here on my own because first, the delivery van had broken down, and second, vans, cars etc. are needed for army purposes.

It's certainly more important that the army should have vans than that we should, my darling Adolf, because they can put them to good use, and it doesn't matter whether the undisciplined masses get the goods they've ordered later rather than sooner, because—can you believe it?—they're afraid of inflation and are already panic-buying anything they can get their hands on, just so they can get their money's-worth. The shops are full of shoppers like this, and so the prices keep going up. Can you believe it, Adolf? I asked about an upholstered chair: seventy-two Reichsmarks. And for two little ones, they were asking eighty-five Reichsmarks. Those are exorbitant prices. But if stupid people want, and are able, to pay them, then let them! It'll make the shopkeepers happy there's a war on, if nothing else. The charming inhabitants of Königsberg are already queuing at the cakeshops, hoping they're in luck and will be able to get marzipan, almonds and so on. Is it like that in Berlin as well? They'll soon be calling this 'famine' abroad again. Then you, my heart, will get it in the neck politically. Even I can see that your life has been really endangered since Munich. England has got its spies everywhere and won't shrink from murder. You're the one whose death would give free rein to their plans for world power. Now, my dear, listen to me: I'm having a front-door key and a key to my room made for you, Adolf. In the next letter, you'll get the first one; and in the letter after that, you'll get the room key. But, my heart's own, your life is at stake, and sadly, the scum—that's the only way to describe these criminals—are resentful (because of the war and just because . . .), so we must be very careful. My heart, come here as early as you can, whenever you want; just ring the doorbell and ask my landlady, Mrs S., a civil servant's widow, if I'm in. If the worst comes to the worst, our parents (because they're yours now as well) have given me permission for you to come to their house at any time, and so we can spend the night together there! We can always stay here until ten in the evening, but it wouldn't be wise to stay longer because, as you know, death lurks everywhere, and that would mean that my life was in jeopardy as well. Poppet, I must stop. Adolf, my darling, at the start of this week, I'll send you a parcel with one of the pillows I've made (the feathers come from my coverlet).

What would Father and Mother say to their Adolf and Margarete? Your Rapunzel kisses you with tender love, and may God the Almighty protect you.

Your woman

From Sch., who would gladly go to the front

Berlin, 15 June 1940

To the Führer of all Germans!
Führer's Headquarters.

Führer! Dear! *Sieg!* Every heart rejoices!
Invasion of Paris!

Ah, how gladly I would come to the front, if only I could. Everything in me rebels when I think that I might outlive the object of my love.

But I'll do as you wish, because you, whom I love, are my soul. I almost feel as though I am a prisoner because I have betrayed so much of my love. My tears have been torn from me by force. But I'm not afraid because right at the start of the war I saw you coming back at the end of it.

What would life be without struggle? A gilded cage, perhaps? But our lives must have their own plan.

The most beautiful thing for me is to be allowed to write: Dear Führer. Now it's as if I'm looking into your grave eyes. No longer isolated and yet so true.

But let's change the subject. May I tell you something about your people? One hears so many opinions about the new era when people come canvassing. One woman said that however much of a National Socialist she was, she still didn't want to give up the lovely old Christmas celebrations. When I asked whether the new Festival of Love wouldn't be even lovelier, I got the reply: Yes, yes, the Führer also wants something like that.

When people talk about the war, I am deeply struck by how pure their trust is in the Führer. Again and again I hear: 'The Führer will sort everything out.'

An old woman, born in 1863, said to me that she still couldn't get used to the new greeting; she is a Berliner and had always been a National Liberal. So I asked her whether the absent-minded 'Morning' was as good, or 'Bye', which you still hear young girls say even now. If you have any longer conversations, everybody expresses such a heartfelt, shy love for you. It wells up when you dare to mention the word 'love'. But some people are far too eager. A young woman with a six-week-old-baby who had been working as a Red Cross nurse wanted very badly to work for the Red Cross again. She planned to ask her husband if he'd look after the child. I have strongly advised her against it and managed to put her off. She seemed to find this the best solution as well.

Führer!

Yesterday on the newsreel I saw again the death-defying sacrifices our soldiers make and the terrible destruction from which you have saved Germany. After that there was *The Woman in the River*. In it a life unfolded as if it were my very own.

Führer! Beloved, best of all, the most beautiful thing I can wish you with all your responsibility is for you to have the necessary peace and rest every day for the next struggle. So I worry when you give up much time for my sake. Every evening I wish you goodnight and long to watch over you so your sleep won't be disturbed.

Full of gratitude for all your trouble and love, I remain, in warmest love,

Your Sch.

Dear Adolf

From Anne-Marie R., who proposes marriage

Chesières, Switzerland, 5 August 1940

Dear Chancellor,

Would it be possible for you to sign the enclosed certificate and return it to me?

Yours most respectfully,

Anne-Marie R.

MARRIAGE CERTIFICATE

I, the undersigned hereby certify that I take Miss Anne-Marie R. to be my lawful wife.

....

From Jose, who wishes he were in her cart

Bad Kreuznach, 30 September 1941

My dear,

My true love, our great Führer and inspired commander, *Sieg Heil, Sieg Heil, Sieg Heil.* The most brilliant victory has brought the greatest war of extermination in history to an end. *Sieg Heil* to our great, inspired Führer and commander, to my beloved Führer, my true love. Let me clasp you to my heart today and give you special thanks, my darling, for all your work and worry. I can only pray for my love and ask the Lord to bless you, my dear, and your great undertaking. All your trouble and worry are for our sakes and for the sake of our great, magnificent Fatherland.

It's still so pretty in our little town. The weather is good, so no one wants to stay inside. For the past few weeks, the A. family have all been here. It's so wonderful the way everyone sticks together. And Carl-August wrote from the East that that's how it should be, that mothers should make sure that families get together, even in wartime. The last of them are off tomorrow, and it will all be quiet again. Then, my dear, your Jose will busily get down to work and think often and long about you, my darling, my happiness, my everything in this world.

Do you think a lot about your Jose? Yes? Yes? Remember me with love, my true love. I'll always be true to you and always be good, you shouldn't worry yourself about me. Today we went on a lovely outing with the horse and cart round Spreitel. There's a lovely forester's house in the wood there. On the way home, we sang songs; there was room for one more in the cart, and I would have been so happy if my love had been with us—but we'll be happy after the war. Yes? Yes? My love. Thank you for all the love and devotion, for all that is beautiful. You are so loving and good to me. This makes me so proud and happy, my great, true love. It pains me often, my dear, that you have so much work to do, but after the war, things will be better for you too, my love. Yes? But what does your Jose know? Darling.

Rudolf's writing is coming on well, but he's only interested in pralines or chocolate—he so loves chocolate. Now, my dear, once again we're bringing our little heart-to-heart to an end. I've told you everything again, let me hug you close to my heart and accept my fondest, most heartfelt wishes, my true love, Adolf Hitler.

Your Jose and the boys

From U., who leaves her door unlocked in case he visits

Triebes, 25 August 1942

My beloved Führer,

At the last rally here, the speaker talked about waiting, the waiting you have learned to do—and about how you are still waiting, even now. What can I say? It's not just a couple of years that I've been waiting for a reply from you—it's seven or eight.

The worries and difficulties with which you struggle are growing all the time—I'm afraid I'll never ever get to see you. The speaker warned us that the English bombers will start striking at the centre of Germany. I'm afraid that air attacks are the greatest danger, and not the least of your worries. If there is more destruction, when the situation isn't very stable anyway, and when the people are so worn down . . .

How badly you have been let down by Brazil, when up till now we'd considered it more or less as an ally. The world is full of deceit. How we have suffered from it, you, my Führer, know better than anyone.

In the meantime, you and your heroic soldiers have won great victories, but against what terrible odds! If only luck could be on our side for once!

I found the enclosed four-leafed clover today, and it made me think of you.

26 August 1942

I was too tired yesterday evening to finish writing, and even today it's already very late. The second and third acts of *The Flying Dutchman* are playing on the wireless. When the first act was announced on Sunday (I didn't listen to it because, as I've said, I was at the rally) I suddenly thought that I had better leave the front door unlocked. I can't do it any more, it puts me under the most humiliating suspicion. After the rally, I waited about an hour for the other occupant of our house to get back so I could unlock the door again after he'd locked it. But for some stupid reason, he had to go out again and realized that the door was unlocked and that I'd already gone to bed. All I can do is leave the key at the agreed place, in case you can't get a definite message to me.

I'm sure, in any case, that you can't get away in the middle of this terrible struggle. Now it's summer, of course, I can't spend the whole day listening to the wireless. There's work to be done out of the house.

You must forgive the bad handwriting. I can't grip very well with my right hand. I've already been told that I'll get an inflamed tendon if I don't look after it. It's particularly painful at night. It's already very irritated and I want to make sure it doesn't get inflamed, but as long as I don't strain it too much during the day, I can sleep at night. At the moment, though, it absolutely refuses to cooperate, so goodnight, my beloved.

27 August 1942

My beloved,

Today, I've decided to post my letter, and also to go to the cinema for the first time in ages. I'd originally planned to go with my son, but nothing came of it. Instead he went off looking for raspberries—the jam I make does him good. It's done me good to have someone close around for the past few months. It's a shame the beautiful holiday weather has gone so quickly. I've been in anything but good spirits, feeling lonely and abandoned. Until now when, once again, anxiety about the state of the whole Reich has taken my mind off my own predicament. Sometimes frightening thoughts occur to me: perhaps we'll live only as long as we fight, as long as our children protect us with their bodies.

Compared with thoughts about survival or annihilation, all other worries and disappointments seem insignificant. It would be much more important for me to know that you had climbed the highest mountain and could breathe freely for once.

In true love,

Your U.

Translated from the German by Will Hobson

The Royal Opera

Myth Art & Magic

Arianna
World Premiere
Alexander Goehr
Directed by Francesca Zambello

Sponsored (1995) by The Drogheda Circle
September October

Mathis der Maler
New Production
Paul Hindemith
Directed by Peter Sellars
November December

The Midsummer Marriage
New Production
Michael Tippett
Directed by Graham Vick
January February

JOHN SWEENEY
HITLER AND THE BILLYGOAT

Hitler has only got one ball!
Goering has two, but very small,
Himmler has something similar,
But poor old Goebbels has no balls at all.

Hitler's missing testicle, the subject of this famous Second World War marching song, has become a modern myth. The world is a less troubling place for us if Hitler the monster can be explained by Hitler the sexual inadequate. But was the song anatomically—at least as far as Hitler was concerned—correct?

The Soviet commission charged with establishing the facts about Hitler's death found that: 'The left testicle could not be found either in the scrotum or on the spermatic cord inside the inguinal canal, nor in the small pelvis.' *Hitler had only one ball!*

Dental records had initially convinced the Russians that they had the right corpse, but the absence of the left testicle made them think again. Did they have a double on the slab?

The defect was not noted anywhere in Hitler's medical records. One of his doctors claimed that the Führer always refused to have a physical examination. But Hitler kept a swarm of personal physicians on his case, and his favourite, Theo Morrell, told Hans Baur, the Führer's personal pilot, that 'so far as his sexual organs were concerned, [Hitler] was completely normal.'

Dietrich Güstrow was a lawyer in Germany during the Third Reich; after the war, he won a prize for his anti-Nazi resistance work. In his autobiography (he died in 1987), he recounts a bizarre episode that happened in 1943.

In the autumn of that year, Güstrow received a telephone call from a pasta wholesaler in Heilbronn. The pasta man told Güstrow that his Uncle Eugen was in some kind of trouble and had been taken to Spandau prison. The family did not know why, and it seemed out of character for their uncle—who, before the war, had been an inconspicuous Bavarian accountant—to have done anything criminal.

Güstrow agreed to take on the case, and went to Spandau where he met Corporal Eugen Wasner. He was chatty, but frightened at finding himself in prison. He told Güstrow a very strange story.

Wasner had been at school with Hitler in the village of Leonding near Linz in Austria. According to him, Adolf had one day made a bet with another boy that he could pee into the mouth of a billygoat. Güstrow recounts Wasner's story:

'I held the billygoat between my legs, and another friend' [Bruno Kneisel] 'opened the goat's mouth and jammed it open with a stick. And Adi peed into the goat's mouth. As he was doing so, the other lad pulled the stick out, and the goat snatched up and bit Adolf's penis. He yelled terribly—there was blood everywhere—and he ran away crying.'

During Wasner's time in the infantry on the eastern front, he had bragged to his comrades about his intimacy with the Führer. He had also gained a reputation as a vociferous complainer, and the company commander warned him about his attitude. After a particularly disastrous retreat, Wasner went too far: 'Ach, Adolf,' he said. 'He hasn't been right in the head since he was little when a billygoat bit off half of his penis.'

The company commander heard about Wasner's story. He interrogated the corporal and tried to get him to say that it wasn't true, that he had made it up, that it was a silly joke. But Wasner was insistent: 'No. It was true then and it's true now.' A statement to that effect was read to him and signed by him. Two days later, he was arrested and sent to Spandau.

Güstrow in turn tried to convince Wasner to admit that it was all a figment of his imagination, but was unsuccessful, even when Güstrow warned him that he could lose his head. Wasner explained that he was a devout Catholic, that he was telling the truth and that, if he had to die for it, then he would die with a clear conscience. He suggested that Güstrow question the Führer about the matter. He also proposed that Güstrow track down Bruno Kneisel, the boy who had put the stick in the goat's mouth.

Güstrow talked to the judge responsible for the case, who was not encouraging. Güstrow argued that Wasner was obviously mentally disturbed, and he asked the judge to approve a psychiatric report on his client. Then, trying a different tack, he said that there had been a witness to the incident. At this point, the judge lost patience. 'For goodness' sake, do you want to get us into trouble too? Maybe you're going to ask me to call the Führer as a witness? This is a totally unbelievable and totally absurd story. Please spare the court such useless evidence.'

Güstrow tried to track down Bruno Kneisel, and discovered that he had died of pneumonia in 1939. Might his premature death have had something to do with his knowledge of the goat accident? Güstrow suspected so.

The court martial was held in secret, because it concerned the security of the state. It was very short. The accused was interrogated and stuck to his story. He added that he had not intended to insult the Führer; he had just wanted to amuse his friends. He now regretted having done so.

The psychiatrist gave his opinion. Wasner was long-winded, had a limited capacity for logical thinking and a stubborn religiosity, but there was nothing to suggest long-term, or even short-term, mental disturbance. Güstrow tried to play down the effect of Wasner's deed: he was an insignificant little corporal who had let the fact that he had had the rare privilege of personal acquaintance with the Führer go to his head. The prosecutor asked for the death penalty.

The judge's deliberations took five minutes.

'The accused Wasner has maliciously insulted and slandered Germany's Führer. He has, through this and other defeatist remarks, undermined the armed forces of the German people. He is therefore sentenced to death.'

Güstrow made a formal appeal to the Führer for clemency, which was unsuccessful. He also appealed to the Chief Justice, a man named Rosencrantz who was not a Nazi and had a reputation for fairness. He told Güstrow that he too had heard about the goat accident when the story was doing the rounds of the casinos, but that he could do nothing to help.

Eugen Wasner was guillotined in November 1943.

There the story might end, were it not for the fact that Dietrich Güstrow (whose real name was Dietrich Wilde) was not quite the fearless anti-Nazi he portrays in his memoirs.

In 1991, Professor Hubert Rottleuthner of the Free University, Berlin, and Dr Johannes Tuchel published an article in *Kritische Justiz*, an academic law journal, entitled 'Who was Dietrich Wilde, alias Dietrich Güstrow?'. The article exposed Güstrow/Wilde's numerous lies, elisions and evasions.

I spoke to Tuchel and asked him about Güstrow/Wilde's anti-Nazi credentials.

'Wilde was a vicious anti-Semite. He wrote at least three articles for a Nazi magazine, giving legal advice on how to evict Jewish tenants, how to sack Jewish employees and how to keep them out of air-raid shelters.'

But was he a reliable witness?

'Güstrow was a fantasist. He describes things that didn't happen.'

Many court records were destroyed when bombs fell on Berlin, but some had been shipped to Prague for safe keeping. Rottleuthner and Tuchel were able to compare just one of Güstrow's stories with the record: the trial of a member of a resistance group in Berlin. Güstrow's account was inaccurate in almost every detail.

So, I asked Tuchel, could the goat story be true?

'Maybe some part of the story is true. But if we don't have the court records, we can't say.'

In Martin Page's indispensable book on the marching songs of the Second World War, he quotes from a popular nineteenth-century American ditty about a trade union leader, which opens:

> *Arthur Hall*
> *Has only got one ball.*

Page also discovered that rumours about the state of Hitler's genitals were circulating in Central Europe as early as the 1930s.

Perhaps tyrants are always suspected of lacking something *down there*. But in Hitler's case, if the Soviet pathologist is to be believed, he really was missing something; and, if the Nazi lawyer is to be believed, some of what he *did* have was bitten off.

CAROLINE ALEXANDER
PLATO SPEAKS

Dr Kamuzu 'Hastings' Banda

I had seen this same room in the pages of the *Malawi Daily News*, in the days when it was the only newspaper permitted in the country. Photographs showed a wood-panelled room, furnished with a long table spread with a leopard skin. They had not shown the stuffed lion that stood to one side of the door, preserved in an attitude of eternal optimism, a sniffing-the-dawn expression frozen on its face; nor had they shown the many photographs on the walls of a small African man in the company of Kenyatta, Kennedy and other world leaders. Now the same small man sat before me in a gilt chair at the head of the table. This was Dr Hastings Kamuzu Banda, formerly the Life President of Malawi, which he ruled for thirty years, and the *ngwazi* or 'saviour' of the people he had led to independence from Britain in 1963. He had been out of office for a year, deposed by Malawi's first multi-party elections.

With us in the room were Cecilia 'Mama' Kadzamira, Banda's helpmate, whose official title as the nation's 'Hostess' belied the fact that she had been its most powerful woman; and Gustav Kaliwo, a lawyer who, in Mama's phraseology, was 'helping His Excellency with his case'. The case dated back to the murder of four government officials twelve years before, with which Mama and four other alleged co-conspirators had been charged, as well as Banda. In deference to his extreme age (perhaps as much as ninety-six) and uncertain mental health (he had had brain surgery in 1993), he had been placed under house arrest rather than imprisoned, and Mama, his companion for many years, had been allowed to remain at his side during his confinement.

Only a week before we met, a panel of doctors approved by both the prosecution and defence had determined that Banda was mentally unfit to stand trial and would therefore be tried *in absentia*. The diagnosis was hypertension and some minor symptoms of Parkinson's disease, but his most obvious affliction was an acute loss of short-term memory. He could not, it seemed, remember the hour or the day or the year before, though he was still capable of lucid, even elegant conversation along carefully selected lines. My meeting with Banda had been arranged by his lawyer, who felt that discussion of certain interests dear to his heart would be stimulating and good for his morale; and this was how it came to be that in the early evening of 7 June 1995, the former dictator and I were discussing the classics.

We had already compared Latin to Chichewa, the language of Malawi, and had agreed that Pompey was less interesting than Caesar, and Banda was now reciting from the latter's Gallic Wars. '*Gallia est omnis divisa in partis tris, quarum unam incolunt Belgae, aliam Aquitani . . . * ' he declaimed with gusto, demonstrating that short-term memory doesn't count for everything. His Excellency had also imparted the surprising information that as a young man it had been his dream to become a professor of classics, a subject he had first encountered as a student in the United States. His voice, with its delicately inflected English, was familiar to me from the radio broadcasts I used to hear when I lived in Malawi in the early 1980s. But the face from those years—the portraits that hung in every office, the likeness that graced calendars, coins and stamps—had changed. Its contours were still much the same, but the formidable, potentially dangerous animus that once informed them had vanished, and I faced a little copper-skinned man with mild brown eyes. He wore his usual dark-grey three-piece suit, brightened on this occasion by a red silk tie and pocket handkerchief, and it was difficult to tell how heavily His Excellency's 'case' weighed on him. His skin was smooth and remarkably unlined—an old age attained comfortably indoors, not in harsh fields or smoky villages. Yet the years had not left him unscathed. A conspicuous dent on his left temple was the relic of his surgery the year before, and he had almost entirely lost his hearing. To compensate for this deafness, he was wearing a set of large headphones that were wired to a microphone which had been given to me. When I spoke, it was as if I were speaking directly into his brain.

Following his conversational thread, I asked Banda if he regretted the fact that as a young man he had allowed himself to be talked into becoming a medical doctor instead of a classicist. Looking at me for a moment in apologetic incomprehension, he turned to Mama: the panel of doctors who had examined him the week before had noted that Banda's hearing was more attuned to female voices than to male, and above all to the voice of Mama

Kadzamira. Now, when my own voice eluded him, Mama discreetly took the microphone from me so as to interpret.

'Having failed to be a professor . . . ' she began in her clear voice.

'Hmm?' Banda interrupted, his expression becoming alert.

'Having failed to be a professor, do they regret . . . ' she continued, addressing Banda, as she had throughout, with what could be termed the royal 'they'.

'Failed?' repeated Banda, his voice now sounding more like the radio speeches I used to hear. 'Failed in what?'

'They wanted to be a professor,' said Mama, regrouping. 'Dr Bailey advised that they should be a doctor. So they did not become a professor. So the lady is asking if they regret . . . '

'No,' Banda broke in, his voice relaxing. 'It's all right now. It's all right. Dr Bailey advised me correctly, for there wasn't a single doctor in the country at that time.' We returned to the Romans.

'The British were under Roman management,' said Banda. 'They definitely learned something from them.'

'And Caesar—he called the British the what?' asked Mama, mischievously. I sensed a private joke.

Banda rocked with laughter. 'You tell me!' he teased. Then he exploded with: *'Barbari!'*

'And also "the painted ones",' added Mama, who had not yet exhausted this theme.

'Caesar interested me very much because he was a politician and a soldier,' Banda volunteered. 'A politician—and tricky! Ho, ho, ho'—again he rocked with laughter. Did Mama's watchful eyes slide to mine with just a trace of unease? 'He knew his way about his politics!' Banda exclaimed admiringly. 'In those days, it was not easy!'

'Yes,' I said. 'He was a survivor.'

Soon after, I was told that His Excellency was tiring, and so we all stood up to take our leave. Having been divested of his headphones by Mama's capable hands, Banda took up his stout black cane carved with African motifs and waited with the same look of obliging compliance with which he had entered the room. Three steps led through a panelled door in the wall behind the long table. At the bottom, Banda stopped and turned to me.

95

'One more time,' he said holding out his hand.

After he had been safely escorted away, Mama returned to meet Kaliwo and me in the front reception room.

'He enjoyed himself,' she said to me. 'It is good that you laugh easily.'

Banda was at one time the longest-ruling dictator in Africa. Although I had mixed feelings about his regime, I had shaken his hand with real gratitude. He was unlikely ever to know it now, but it was because of a personal whim on his part that I had first come to Malawi thirteen years before.

In the spring of 1982, I'd decided that I wanted to live in Africa and had set about writing job applications to nearly every English-speaking institution in the continent. My letters implied, without fraudulently stating, that I was qualified to teach English as a foreign language (which I judged to be my best shot at employment) and played down my background in classics (which I judged to be beside the point). Half-hearted responses came from the universities of Kenya and Zambia—and a concrete offer from the University of Malawi. Improbably, the job was to establish a small department of classics.

I arrived in December 1982, at the beginning of the rainy season. Chancellor College, the arts and science campus, was in Zomba, a town in the south of the country, which had been the capital before Banda moved the government north to Lilongwe, and which was still characterized by comfortable, colonial architecture. Low, whitewashed buildings of mud-brick with verandas spread along the narrow roads winding into the foothills of the Zomba plateau, a massif three thousand feet high that overlooked the town.

The staff of the faculty were mostly Malawian and British, with a handful of other foreign nationals. Most of my students had come from Catholic secondary schools, where they had studied Latin for several years. I was twenty-six and had all the excitement and zeal of a missionary charged with bringing classical enlightenment to darkest Africa. I had ambitious plans for a small but bustling department which would integrate a traditional classics curriculum with what I thought might be Malawian interests: oral traditions (Homeric and African); the sociology of slavery; epic Roman and British imperialism; praise poetry (Pindaric and Zulu): these were some of the ideas that excited me and that I looked forward to presenting to my colleagues.

My assumption that my arrival would be greeted with reciprocal enthusiasm, however, was quickly shattered. 'So you're the one who's come to make us a real university,' said a fellow lecturer soon after I arrived. The sneer became typical. I was bewildered. At first I thought that, as a classicist, I was seen as representing the forces of cultural imperialism—though it was the British rather than the Malawians who seemed to resent me most.

The real cause was far less subtle and entirely more improbable. For years, no less a person than the president of Malawi himself, Dr Hastings Kamuzu Banda, had been haranguing the university, the national parliament, the press and the population at large about the need to study 'the classics'. Only two months before I arrived, he had told his audience at the university's graduation ceremony, speaking in his capacity as the university's chancellor, that first, no person was truly educated unless he knew Latin and Greek; and second, an institution could not claim to be a real university unless it had a department of classics.

That was how I came to Malawi, and that was why, thirteen years later, I was allowed to see Dr Banda in his home—not because I was a visiting writer interested in his trial, but because I was the founder of the classics department at Malawi University. Gustav Kaliwo, the lawyer who arranged our meeting, had been one of my students.

During the time I lived in Malawi, Banda was at the height of his power, the cult of his personality firmly established. The country had only one political party—his own, the Malawi Congress Party—and it controlled the only daily newspaper and only radio station. Any criticism of the regime, however implicit, could mean detention, or worse. But while his presence was felt everywhere, Banda himself remained largely invisible. One of his official houses was in Zomba, and I used to pass it on my evening walks and notice the feathery tops of bluegum trees peeping over its high brick walls, hinting at an intriguing, hidden garden. A friend of mine from the university lived close to this house, and on the mornings of official 'events', he would be woken early by the chatter and laughter of the President's *mbumba* dancers—droves of women identically dressed in clothes stamped with Banda's picture. They gathered there before being transported to the venue at, say, the stadium in Blantyre, a city fifty kilometres south. But Banda himself we never saw, and we could only assume that behind the smoked windows of the black limousine that would sometimes appear, travelling fast and silently on the main Blantyre–Lilongwe road, sat the Life President and saviour of the nation himself.

Banda's biography recorded a remarkable life. He was born, according to the best guess, in 1898, in a small village near Kasungu, in what was then central Nyasaland (as Malawi was known when it was a British colony). At the age of seven, he went to a missionary school, where he was baptized into the Church of Scotland and took the name of a Scottish missionary, John Hastings. Aged sixteen, he set out alone and barefoot on a journey to South Africa in search of higher education, which he found, eventually, in night schools run by the Methodist church in Johannesburg. He financed his ambition with hard work, as a miner and in other menial jobs, and lived cheaply in shanty towns. In 1922, he became a member of a black separatist church, the African Methodists, and two years later won a scholarship to the church's college in the United States, Wilberforce Academy in Ohio. Many years of study followed— with funds often provided by white Americans who were impressed by his devotion and ambition—and Banda gradually accumulated degrees: a BA in philosophy from the University of Chicago, a doctorate in medicine from Meharry Medical College, Tennessee, and, after he migrated to Britain in the 1930s, further medical qualifications from the Universities of Edinburgh and Glasgow. For seventeen years, he worked in Britain as a general practitioner, toting his doctor's bag and stethoscope round the poorer parts of Liverpool and Tyneside before settling down to a prosperous practice in London. During that time, he was involved in serious anti-colonial politics. He became the Nyasaland National Congress Party's man in London, a liaison between the party and the British Colonial Office, which was

planning to bring together its three central African colonies—
Nyasaland and Northern and Southern Rhodesia—in a
federation. The federation was created in 1953 and made the
British even more unpopular. The Nyasaland Congress invited
Banda to return home and serve the cause as party president. He
arrived on 6 July 1958, to a tumultuous welcome.

Banda was then sixty years old and had spent most of the
past thirty years of his life in Britain and the United States. From
the moment of his return, he made all his public speeches in
English, not Chichewa, with interpreters relaying his remarks to
the crowd. He wore a Homburg, a hat he'd taken to wearing as a
doctor, and his shirts and suits were made in London; Africa was
present in his person only in the fly whisk he invariably carried.

He was elected prime minister in 1963 and, after Nyasaland
became the independent republic of Malawi, he moved quickly to
consolidate his power. He appointed cronies to his cabinet.
Political rivals drifted, or were driven, into exile. In 1971, he was
made president for life.

L ife in Banda's Malawi, it seemed to me, was modelled on life
in the Ideal State outlined by Plato in *The Republic*. Banda,
naturally, was the Philosopher King. He made the decisions and
he was wise (two of his favourite pejoratives, often deployed in
speeches, were 'childish' and 'ignorant'). The role of Plato's
Guardians, the men who protected the state from internal and
external enemies, was fulfilled by the despised Young Pioneers, a
paramilitary group that roamed the villages and markets, sniffing
out any hint of disloyalty. Plato's lowly 'bronze class', the
working population, was represented by Malawi's subsistence
farmers whose labour accounted for more than ninety per cent of
the economy. Like Plato, Banda believed that this category
should not know more than they needed to; education in Banda's
Malawi never became free and universal, with the result that its
literacy rate was almost half that of neighbouring countries. And
then there was the matter of poetry. Plato said: 'We must compel
. . . our poets, on pain of expulsion, to make their poetry the
express image of noble character.' Banda followed his advice,
encouraging poets to adapt traditional songs to 'morally uplifting

99

themes', and expelling or imprisoning any poet who seemed truculent or disobedient.

Innovation was distrusted—another Platonic trait—and strict censorship reflected Banda's Victorian mores. Women were not allowed to show their knees or wear trousers, and censors screened imported publications for indecency. Plates in fashion magazines and photographs in the *National Geographic* were often inked over with crudely drawn blouses and frilly skirts. My mail was routinely opened, and I became accustomed to my letters arriving in clumsily re-glued envelopes. Once, a letter I received from abroad contained a page from a letter I'd posted to someone else the week before.

Banda's Republic divided opinion, privately in Malawi and publicly abroad. The extreme view said that his was the most oppressive regime in Africa, ignoring the spectacular excesses of Bokassa's Central African Empire, Mengistu's Ethiopia and Idi Amin's Uganda. A more sympathetic view held that he had to be given credit for running a stable and well-ordered country—a rarity in Africa. The most sympathetic view said that Banda himself was not responsible for his government's oppressive methods; that he was old (in his eighties even then) and not 'all there' (rumours of expensive monkey-gland remedies purchased in Switzerland), and that the power behind his throne was John Tembo, Mama Kadzimira's uncle and the most likely candidate to succeed Banda as president.

There is no doubt that the people around Banda, including Tembo, routinely conspired to give him a false picture of the country he ruled. For example, every year, Banda paid a visit to the Zomba General Hospital. Normally, the hospital was so ill-equipped and overcrowded that patients lay two to a cot, head-to-toe like sardines. I once visited a friend who was recovering from a motorcycle accident and found him sharing a pillow with the swollen, gangrenous legs of his cot-mate, who was adrift in a reverie of pain. Sticking my head around the corner of the maternity ward, I saw women lying on the floor beneath the beds, as well as in them. But when a visit from Banda was imminent, the hospital was newly whitewashed, and the wards half-emptied. What he saw was a neat line of cots, each tidily occupied by a single patient, while surplus patients lay heaped together in a central courtyard out of view.

My own life in Malawi was not oppressive. As a foreigner, the worst I could fear was deportation, and I had my work to occupy me. I taught Latin, tutored a theology student in Greek and lectured my Malawian students on 'classical civilization'. I had a four-year degree programme to develop, a library and slide collection to build, textbooks to buy. Malawi is one of the poorest countries in the world, and money that had been pledged did not often materialize. But where else in the world would I have been asked to establish a brand new classics department?

The house I lived in had a garden filled with frangipani, grapefruit and avocado trees. A graceful jacaranda grew at one end of the veranda, while the other end was screened with bougainvillaea. On my daily walk to Chancellor College, a mile down the road, I kept the long wall of the Zomba plateau to my left. On sunny days, it would stand out in hard, deep-blue relief. On rainy days, a thick mist seemed to billow from its base, rolling and steaming over the foothills. When darkness came, I could sit on my veranda and watch the Southern Cross rise above the tops of my pawpaw trees. Even while I was living there, I knew that the memory of these things would always haunt me—and I was right.

I returned to Malawi ten years almost to the week after I left. It was the dry season, and in Zomba the sky was dull with a *chiperoni* mist, but when it cleared, and the grave, blunt summit of the plateau appeared, I was almost disconcerted to find myself staring at a scene so exactly as I had remembered it. The town was, if anything, greener and lusher than before, and at Chancellor College, luxuriant trees and bushes of white poinsettia filled the campus which a dozen years previously was still being landscaped. Some of the female students and staff, I noticed, now wore trousers—Banda's anti-trouser legislation had been rescinded in 1993—but the greatest change had been wrought by Aids. Several old colleagues and droves of students had died.

I took my favourite walk across the golf-course of the Zomba Gymkhana Club, past the same towering grove of bamboo which still dipped over the lawn like a giant ostrich plume. Some distance beyond, women still bathed and washed their clothes in the river, unperturbed by the proximity of the golfers. Up the road, beyond the club grounds and tennis-courts, I eventually passed the Zomba State House, still a walled, secret garden in the heart of the town. Now the new president, Bakili Muluzi, lived there—or rather, one of his two wives did. Banda had been proud to be an Elder of the Church of Scotland; the new president was a Muslim. Under pressure from the western countries that gave Malawi aid—and especially from the United States—the Banda regime had agreed to hold a referendum in which people would vote for or against the holding of multi-party elections. In 1993, the people voted for them, and in 1994 the United Democratic Front, led by Muluzi, had taken power. A free press now flourished, and the Malawi Young Pioneers had been disbanded and disarmed. Banda was said to have taken his defeat, the end of his republic, philosophically.

At the High Court in Blantyre, the preliminary trial of Banda and his four co-defendants was winding down, and I was able to attend a session. Lawyers, bewigged and robed in the English fashion, bowed before the judge; indeed, the leader of the defence team, Clive Stanbrook, was English and a Queen's Counsel. Of the four prisoners in the dock—who did not, of course, include Banda himself—the most recognizable was John Tembo, a little waspish-looking man with a large head, who sat coiled and unblinking.

Their trial stemmed from a commission of inquiry, conducted in 1994, into the deaths of four members of parliament, including three cabinet ministers, whose bodies were found in a car that was lodged in a ravine at Mwanza near Blantyre on the morning of 19 May 1983. The government maintained that the men had been fleeing from Malawi to Zimbabwe, and that their deaths had been caused by a 'road accident', but few people ever believed that. On the Zomba campus in 1983, we knew, as did the rest of the country, that this was political murder. Rumours said that the car had been riddled with bullets or blow-torched, or that the bodies had been bludgeoned. It was this last that turned out, eleven years later, to be the truth.

One hundred and sixty-two witnesses testified before the commission of inquiry, and from their words a remarkably complete picture of the murders eventually emerged. The transcript of this inquiry runs to 1,066 pages, and of these none is more transfixing than those containing the testimony of Inspector Leonard Winesi Mpagaja, one of the nine surviving police witnesses who made the trip to Mwanza with the doomed men that night. The dialogue between the commission and the inspector is, in essence, the dialogue of Greek tragedy, the words of a Clytemnestra in answer to the ritual questions of the good citizens of the Chorus:

QUESTION: *They came out [of the car] and they were blindfolded. What followed next?*
ANSWER: What followed next was the killing.
Q: *Using what?*
A: They used hammers that are used when erecting tents.
Q: *What other weapons were there? No guns were there, no pistols?*
A: There were no guns there, but I remember that there was an axe. I cannot remember whether it was used.
Q: *No sharp instruments?*
A: No sharp instruments.
Q: *How many people were assigned to one person?*
A: Each group would pick one and take him aside . . .
Q: *As an example, what did you yourself do to Mr Sangala to make him die?*
A: My boys took Mr Sangala, blindfolded him and made him sit down. I was the one who had the hammer and I hit him at the back of the head where I knew, according to my police training, he would die immediately.
Q: *You hit him at the back of the head?*
A: Yes.
Q: *Using what?*
A: I used a hammer.
Q: *What else? Did he just collapse?*
A: He fell down.
Q: *He was already sitting down?*
A: He was already sitting down, so after hitting him he fell on the ground and died.

Q: *Did he not cry?*
A: No, he did not cry.
Q: *Because his mouth was gagged?*
A: He was not gagged. He was only blindfolded.
Q: *Would you say the rest of these people were treated in the same way, sat down, hit at the back and died?*
A: I believe the same method was used, but we were doing it at different places . . .
Q: *What conversation went on between you and them [the victims]?*
A: When we were in this vehicle, we did not talk to each other. There was no conversation.
Q: *They did not ask where you were taking them to?*
A: These people did not speak to us.
Q: *What about at the scene? Now you are taking Mr Sangala away. He did not say anything?*
A: As I said, the only thing he said was, 'How are you going to blindfold me with my glasses still on?' So we told him to remove the glasses, and he removed them and put them on the ground, and then we told him to sit down.
Q: *Were these people awake on this journey?*
A: Yes, they were awake.
Q: *Did they not talk to each other?*
A: No, they did not talk to each other.
Q: *Did they look to you to have been drugged with something? I find it strange that they travelled from here to that place without talking at all.*
A: I do not know, but the way I saw them, they were depressed.
Q: *Did they look to you that they knew they were going to be killed?*
A: It looked as if they already knew why they were there.

For all the haunting eloquence of the commission's report, in legal terms it was inconclusive, as the hard evidence to convict either Banda or Tembo as the instigators of this crime was lacking. The widow of the former inspector-general of police testified that her husband had told her that he had received his instructions directly from Tembo, and that these instructions were later ratified by Banda himself. Under Malawian law, only hearsay evidence 'against interest' of the source is admissible in court. From a legal point of view, the widow's testimony was ultimately unhelpful. (Banda's regime had cared less about legal niceties, despite their origins in English or Roman law. It was Banda's practice to throw his enemies to the mercy of the traditional courts, presided over by local chiefs, where hearsay evidence was admissible—a convenient recourse in those cases fuelled solely by rumour.)

The one hundred and sixty-second person to testify before the commission was Hastings Kamuzu Banda himself. One can only imagine what must have passed through the minds of the men and women of the commission—who had been listening now for nearly sixty days to memories of bloodshed, bereavement and anguish—when, in response to every question he was asked, the aged former Life President could only reply: 'I'm afraid, because it is such a long time ago, I have no information.'

How much did Banda know? How much had he ever known? 'I tell my friends that Banda was like Tiberius,' said the urbane Eric Ninganga, another former student of mine and now a prosperous tax official, over a drink at the Mount Soche Hotel in Blantyre. 'Really he is. He withdrew, like Tiberius did to Capri, and left the running of his empire to his minions.'

According to those close to him, Banda began to withdraw as long ago as 1974, paving the way for Tembo. Banda's critics, however, remain unmoved by this interpretation; a man who had declared himself Life President should, in their view, be held responsible for his government's actions right to the bitter end.

But was Banda even aware that the bitter end was drawing near? I watched a video of the Kamuzu Day ceremony of 1993—the last year in which the nation celebrated its founder's birthday with all the pomp that he had made traditional. There he was, an old man, indomitable in a top hat and tails, inspecting his army to the accompaniment of schoolchildren singing 'Kamuzu, you are number one.' By this date, the people had voted in favour of multi-party elections; the writing for Banda was on the wall. So what did he choose to tell this last great audience? Speaking as always in English through an interpreter, his subject was Malawi's army. Banda praised the army and then reminded the crowd that his army had learned from the British:

'And the British themselves . . . ' said Banda.

'*Ndi Ingelezi* . . . ' said the interpreter.

' . . . learned from the Romans,' and we were back on familiar territory.

Some people believed that if Banda had troubled to designate a successor—had, in the manner of the Roman emperors, adopted his Caesar—he might just have won the general election. In fact, Banda had indirectly addressed the issue of succession by founding the Kamuzu Academy—a much ridiculed élite secondary school, often dubbed 'the Eton of Africa'. From comments he made over the years, it is clear that Banda envisaged that his Academy would groom future leaders of the country—rather as Plato had founded his more famous academy for the education of statesmen.

Kamuzu Academy was so specifically the result of Banda's whim that I was curious to see how it had weathered the political change since he lost power. The school lies in the Central Region, the flattest and least attractive part of Malawi, close to where Banda was born. I drove across a sun-beaten plain past dispirited villages. When it grew dark, there was not a glimmer of light in any direction, no sign of habitation until at last I hit the silky belt of tarmac that led up to the school's wrought-iron gates.

My hosts were the de Kuypers, a couple of Belgian classicists whose contracts had just been terminated and who, together with twenty-four of the Academy's forty-three staff, were preparing to return to Europe. Their contracts stated that the Academy would pay for their return, but the Academy's funds had run out, and it looked as though they would have to ship out their possessions at their own expense. Dr de Kuyper pointed to a cabinet full of glassware. 'We were told to bring plenty of china and glass and linen,' he said. 'We were told to bring evening dress and formal clothing, because there would be so much entertaining. Well, it was difficult—you couldn't just ask people to dinner, because you never knew who was speaking to whom, which people would fight each other.' The Academy staff was predominantly British—

Banda had said that no Malawian was fit to teach there—and had exhibited their nation's penchant for recreational violence, something that it had perhaps inherited from the Romans. Since all social occasions ended in fights, the de Kuypers had ceased entertaining.

(Years before, I had ended my visit to the Academy with the conviction that there were only two sane motives for wanting to teach there: incorrigible idealism, or the furtive determination to write a book in the style of *White Mischief*. I had met three members of the school's classics department: a middle-aged man who implied that Africans were mentally unfit to study 'the classics'; an earnest young man who preached the benefits of Latin and Christianity with equal enthusiasm, and who had posters of leather-clad bikers on his walls; and a man whose posture of world weariness made it difficult to guess his age, but who later shocked his colleagues by taking the young male gardener as his lover.)

According to the de Kuypers, the Academy's future looked bleak. Their last pay cheques were only half what they should have been. The cafeteria, which had once made a point of serving classic British cooking such as sausages and mashed potato, was now serving rice and *nsmima*, or mealy-meal. Local markets and tradesmen would do business with the school only for cash.

I woke the next morning to the sound of bells chiming from the steeple of the school chapel. On the campus, the lawns and landscaped gardens were as immaculate as they had been ten years before, the houses for the staff still as smart; the place still looked like an American suburb. On my previous visit, the students had tended to behave with bewildered deference or smug arrogance when they came across a European sightseer. Now, they showed a sullen lack of interest. I sensed that few of them could these days be duped by the promised benefits of superior European culture.

From its inception, the Academy had been touted as Banda's personal gift to the nation. Other African leaders might crown themselves emperor or build the largest cathedral in the world, but Banda had—or so it was supposed—provided fifteen million US dollars from his own pocket to set up an institution of permanent social worth, with another large sum put in trust to cover the annual running costs of about two million dollars. But when the new government took over and did some basic auditing, it quickly discovered that the annual expenses had been lifted directly from the national educational budget, which could not even provide funds for a programme of universal literacy.

During the course of my interview with Banda, before we got round to Caesar, I had asked him about his school. He had said that he built it so that young people could receive the kind of education in Malawi that he had been forced to seek abroad. 'Some appreciate it, some don't. But that was my idea.'

According to the doctors called on by the court to assess Banda's mental capabilities, he has withdrawn in a way that is commonly observed in old people. I listened to a taped session conducted by the medical panel.

'Are you lonely?' Banda was asked by the psychiatrist. 'Oh I prefer to be alone most of the time,' Banda replied. 'Then I can relax, instead of talk, talk, talk, talk . . . I want to rest, be quiet.'

Years ago, Banda once lectured his parliament on the 'trouble with Africa', which he attributed to 'too many ignorant people who do not know anything about history, and if they do know anything about it they do not know how to interpret and apply it.'

That Banda himself offered a lesson for future rulers was a fact appreciated by the commission, whose report concluded:

> This Inquiry should also serve as a warning to all governments that however strong and unchallenged their authority may seem to be at a given moment in time, life is dynamic and things change, and that one day the meekest of the meek will be in a position to rise and question their deeds, and that the truth cannot be suppressed completely and forever.

Banda, I thought when I read that passage, would surely have loved its classical eloquence, its suggestion of white men in white robes declaiming from scrolls.

Blake Morrison
Bicycle Thieves

TOM PILSTON

L ate June, scorched grass and sprinklers, the sky as if scuffed
and beaten. Too hot to work, too lazy to think, I've knocked
off early to play tennis. I'm sitting on the edge of the bed, putting
on my trainers, when my son crashes in, a raspberry lolly
bleeding in his hands, huge breaths and distraught between them,
dragging the words from a well: 'My bike . . . they took . . . I left
. . . when I came out . . . my bike . . . '

'Don't cry, don't cry, we'll sort it out,' I say, pulling his wet
head to me. 'What is it, what's happened?'

'The bike. It was outside the shop. Two boys took it.'

'What about the chainlock? I've told you.'

'But I was only a minute.'

'Did you see them?'

'No, two little kids said. But I saw them outside before.'

'How old?'

'Bit bigger than me. Twelve or thirteen. The little kids
pointed where they'd gone.'

'OK. We'll go and have a look.'

We get in the car. It would have taken him ten minutes to
run back. Five minutes more have passed. They're quarter of an
hour away at least.

The shop is at the edge of a small estate. HAPPY SHOPPER it
says over the window, which is covered by a metal grille. This is
one of the better estates: one people try to move into, not out of.
You can tell because the shop has only a grille, not metal shutters
or wooden boards. Behind his sloping rack of sweets, the Asian
owner is upset.

'Sorry, no, I didn't see. I served the boy, yes. It's happened
before. You have to lock your bikes. I try to tell them.'

'I've tried to tell him too. But it was only a minute. You
didn't notice any boys outside?'

'No. Only two schoolchildren at a time in here. That's my
rule. It keeps down incidents. But outside . . . '

I duck out again, angry at these bullying great kids who've
taken my son's bike, and also excited. We pause by the shuttered
off-licence next door, CHEERS, long past its last closing time.

'Which way did they go?' I ask.

'The kids said here,' he says, pointing to a walkway between garages. We go down, glancing to left and right, in case the bike has been abandoned. At the end is a metal barrier, a pedestrian crossing over the road and, beyond, the Ferrier Estate. I've heard stories about the Ferrier—about murders, rapes and stabbings; about crack dealers ripping each other off; about the dangers of parking. You get the same stories about other estates. But I'm new to this bit of south-east London. I didn't realize the Ferrier was so close. I've not been paying attention.

We cross over and follow the dust-groove of a path across the grass. It runs by a high metal fence, like tennis-court mesh, but the concrete square beyond the wire has no markings—a compound of nothing. Where the high fence ends, a lower wood-slat fence begins, with a sign saying ANTI-CLIMB PAINT. A big-windowed building, some sort of institution, squats peeling beyond— a school, with spiked railings to keep the pupils in by day and out by night. We walk over the grass to where the first block of flats looms up on our left, like a docked cruise liner.

'I think those are the kids who saw,' says my son.

A boy and a girl, black, about six. They're holding a small plastic holey bat each, like a pair of waffles, the sort you're supposed to use with spongy-light balls. When they strike their yellow tennis ball, the bats flop limply, and the ball dies. Seeing us, they stop the game, curious, waiting.

'You saw his bike being stolen?'

'Yeh.'

'It was two boys?'

'Yeh.'

'Do you know them? Did you see where they went?'

'Up there. Past the yellow block, the next one, that begins with number twenty. One of them lives at number twelve.'

'So you know him?'

'No, but he lives there.'

'Do you know his name?'

'Andy, yeh, innit.'

The boy has done all the talking, but now the girl says: 'We're visiting. From Wandsworth. We don't live here.' She picks up the ball and whacks her bendy racket at it: 'Come on, Stephen.'

'Thanks,' I say, not knowing which of their answers is true—if any. A stolen bike: in my day, that would have been something, and if a boy and his father were out looking for it, you'd want to help, you'd join in the hunt, you'd . . . And yet they'd not been unhelpful. The spareness, the wariness: I recognized it from my own kids; it is how the young are taught to be with strangers. So we were looking for a bike; so they had seen the bike being stolen. It didn't mean they should trust us, cooperate, go out of their way. How they'd been was as unobstructive as anyone could be without running risks. To answer when strangers ask you questions—this is plenty, this is more than enough.

We press on, under the unfiltered sun, past the first block and into the square beyond—concrete slabs with weeds growing between them. The square is a giant courtyard, the four cruise liners (each with five decks) round the sides, a fenced-off adventure playground in the middle—slides, climbing frames, ravine bridges. Among the dozen or so boys here—shaven-headed, bare-chested, earringed—two are riding bikes. As we move towards the playground for a better look, I try to remember what the bike looked like—silver wheels, furry grey saddle, black foam bits (like the sort used to insulate copper pipes) over the handlebars. My son hangs against the wire like a prisoner. Then he says, 'Nah, not mine.'

'Are you sure?' I ask, wondering if—his father's son—he merely fears the confrontation. These bikes all look the same to me. High above, men in vests lean from balconies, watching, waiting. I'm glad, really, that I don't have to challenge these bikes' owners, or putative owners. And I'm glad I'm not black or Asian, not Jamaican or Pakistani or Tanzanian or Vietnamese or Somali, much riskier here—to judge from the stories I've heard—than being a middle-class white.

We pass on to the next square: no sign of a bike. Beyond, there's a light-blue map-board saying FERRIER ESTATE, and I try to get my bearings. Some of the names—faint and faintly foreign: Pinto, Gallus, Dando, Romero, Telemann—I can read, but most have been defaced, as if it's wartime and the signpost has been blanked out to confuse the enemy. The estate's much bigger than I thought. A railway runs through it, dividing east from west. A four-wheel drive nought-to-sixties in five seconds down the abbreviated street.

'Keep up,' I say to my son, noticing the kicked-in front gates, the flaky window frames, the front doors grinning broad and toothless where letterboxes must once have neatly gleamed. 'Keep up,' I say again, wondering how conspicuous we look, how much like strangers. We're in the second square now, and for a moment we lean against a wall, cupped by its shadow. Like all the other walls here, it's battleship grey and ribbed in texture. Searching for deeper shade, we sit in a gully of broken steps. Around us, pigeons purr and tick, scanning the concrete, something stuck in the back of their throats; the balconies above us are covered in chicken wire to stop them sitting and shitting there. A tyre-less old Escort sits on its arches. That fallout of glass must have been its windows once. Under the sun, the shards are like ice: I want to gather a handful and wipe them across our faces. Up ahead, the windows and vents are painted yellow, not blue. The next block on our left must be the one the little boy meant, if the first door is number twenty, which it is. We get up. We move on. 'Stay near me, pretend we're not looking,' I say, as if we're stalking a murderer, not a kid who may or may not have stolen a bike. The numbers run down to twelve: a front yard with a rusting washing-machine, a barbecue, a baby's car-seat, a toddler's scooter, a plastic patrol car, a box of empties. No bike. I hadn't expected it, out in the open. If I was bolder, I'd knock at the door. But I can't do that, not on the say-so of two six-year-olds. And what use would it be, even if I had the nerve? No answering kid would shop himself; no parent would shop him either.

We walk on, to the next square, painted red. Beyond there's a tall chimney, like a factory chimney, except that there's no factory. There's no sign of a bike. WHAT MUST I DO TO BE SAVED? asks an advertisement posted on what looks like a bus shelter but, windows intact, turns out to be a lift lobby. We search the brambled slope of a railway embankment. We search the next square and the squares beyond: green, purple, brown, pink, navy-blue. I'm getting the hang of the estate now, its fierce symmetries and sudden departures: the ground-floor yards and then, above, the decks of glass and metal, some with ensigns of washing, some with the foghorn of a satellite dish. It's like a gaudy chessboard, a square of squares, vertical squares of glass, horizontal squares of stone, different shades and different colours. But just when I think I've worked it out, I'm lost again, away from the thronging squares on a patch of broken concrete, the only sign of life a dog snarling from behind a wooden fence and then a second dog, snappish, running towards us.

'Fuck off,' I say, ready to kick it. Rather than harass us, it sniffs at the fence confining the bigger dog, driving it to new fits of frenzy. We move away.

'I don't think we're going to find it,' I say. 'I think we should go home and call the police.'

The sun presses down, unforgivingly hot, as if this were a foreign country we'd slipped into from some hole in the map. An ice-cream van ting-tangs an ancient pop song. On the path, disposed of, a disposable nappy. Did the child who was its wearer, toddling in these canyons, drop it here? No, some adult has tried to roll it up, to fold its odour in on itself, though not, in this heat, successfully. It seems an odd place for a nappy to have strayed, though I've known odder. One summer when my son was small, we parked in a rush at Stansted Airport and left the passenger window open half an inch. By the time we came back two weeks later, someone had posted a nappy through the gap. It sat there on the passenger seat, a welcome-home banner.

No sign of a bike. Disappointed and relieved, we soodle homewards back to square one, hoping to see the kids who'd seen the other kids, but finding only their tennis ball, the spoor of their limp game.

Back home, I phone the police, who take down details and promise to send an officer round, 'when one becomes available'.

'When will that be?'

'That I can't say, Sir.'

This is what being middle-aged means: not avoiding the police but needing them to come round and feeling pissed off when they don't. My son is pale still and bleared by his earlier weeping. But it isn't some ultimate, shaking grief: he knows how the world works, that possessions can't any longer (or not for long) be possessed. Boys steal bikes—and car radios and anything not nailed down in shops—as casually as they once stole apples. And those are the good boys. The bad ones take the cars as well as the radios. The worst ones take the cars, then crash them, or set fire to them, or both. Once, if something went, there was the belief, consoling to the liberal-minded, the guiltily affluent, that someone less well off must have needed it: that car, that bike, would be riding around somewhere, under different colours. Now the old motives—need, greed—can't be relied on: as often as not, stolen possessions pass into oblivion, wrecked or set alight. I remember seeing a piece of graffiti in the 1970s: I DON'T BELIEVE IN NOTHING. I'D LIKE TO SEE THEM BURN THE WHOLE WORLD DOWN, JUST LET IT BURN DOWN BABY. I'd imagined it to have been written by some druggy, disaffected twenty-eight-year-old, a nihilist philosopher of the streets. Now there are twelve-year-olds who think like that, kids for whom life holds out no promise except failure, kids who know for sure what most of us spend our lives not wanting to acknowledge as a possibility: that life is shit, and at the end of it we die.

Easy come, easy go, cheering himself up with Weetabix, my son seems resigned now—more resigned than I am, still angry at the world I've brought him into, which has now carried off his favourite thing. I tell him not to worry, that it wasn't his fault, that there are other bikes, that we'll buy him a new one which he'd have needed soon enough anyway. We're sitting in the kitchen, under the old fifties built-in cupboards we've never bothered to tear out, and I think of how the scene might have played itself out then: one of those epiphanies of childhood, bringing with it the end of innocence and a lesson in the epistemology of loss: the boy dries his tears and, harder, wiser, learns how to watch out for himself, how to mourn, how to stand up. But these are the nineties. It's only a bike, for Christ's sake. There are queues for them every day at Argos. Things get broken or go missing, and you replace them. What more is there to say?

Later, alone, I drive back through the hot night to number twelve and park. Small children pass in and out through the open door into the front yard. A teenager tinkers with his motorbike. The man of the house comes out with a can of Kestrel and leans against his wall. I duck down behind my newspaper till he goes back in to the flickering neon square beyond the net curtains. I sit on for an hour, until the ebb and flow of small children has ceased. But there is no twelve-year-old returning on his—or someone else's—bike. I drive back home, still scanning the estate, certain it's there. My car was stolen once, from outside a flat I had in Greenwich, and afterwards, convinced it was just kids taking a quick way home after the pub, I drove round the streets of south-east London, in a friend's car, madly exhilarated for hours, on the case like Holmes or Maigret, only belatedly getting out the *A-Z* and seeing what a small patch I'd covered. But a bike . . . it couldn't have gone far.

Later still, I lie awake in bed and hear sirens and more sirens. The estate seems close now, scarcely beyond the bottom of the garden. The late trains clattering down to Dartford, the sex screams of foxes, the whooshy tides of traffic on the A2: these, the usual night sounds, are drowned tonight by sirens. Infringements, impingements. I drift back to sleep and dream of a man entering the room, his knife bisecting my torso from neck to navel. I wake sweating and imagine blue lights surrounding the estate, police cars and fire engines and ambulances, and a solitary boy on a stolen bike at the centre of their arc light. But the sirens are speeding all over the city and suburbs, to diverse domestic incidents, the humdrum nightly toll, stabbings and smashed windows and stolen VCRs. It's up to me to solve this smaller crime. I lie awake, the same thoughts playing over, unable to exit from the file. I begin putting my clothes on. As I reach for my trainers, Kathy wakes.

'Where you going?'

'To look for the bike.'

'You're mad. It's three in the morning. It's only a bike. We can get it back on the insurance.'

'It's the principle. Plus I feel sorry for him.'

'He's OK about it. I've talked to him. It's you that's the problem. Anyway, they didn't hurt him, did they, they didn't beat him up? It could have been a lot worse.'

'He's my son. It was his bike. I should try my best to get it back. My father would have done.'

'Jesus, you have tried. He knows you've tried. Come back to bed. Leave it to the police. Didn't they say they'd be round?'

'When an officer becomes available,' I say, starting to undress. 'Meaning never.'

But an officer stands on the doorstep the following morning. I go through the incident again. I show him the 'owner's manual' for the bike, a four-page leaflet. I confirm that no, the bike hadn't been engraved or tagged with an ID number. I describe the conversation with the kids and mention the address they gave.

'Number twelve? Ah, yes, a family known to us, I think I'm right in saying: we'll pay them a little visit, though I don't hold out much hope.'

'Well, you never know . . .'

'There's a trade in stolen bikes, you see. The boys don't rob them for themselves: they sell them on. We think they're being shifted to second-hand shops up north. You really have to get your bike coded or make your boy use a lock.'

'He does, usually. But it was only a minute . . .'

The days pass, and the police don't ring back. Gradually, I stop scrutinizing every child's bike I pass: I'm not going to run into it; it's not going to run into me. But I acquire the habit of leaving work half an hour early and parking near number twelve on my way home. They're always about somewhere, in this hot weather: him with his chest hair spooling over the top of his vest; her with the black-sheen cycling shorts and the figure she's already getting back now the baby's eight months; and the older kids, Michael and Leah, and baby Charlene: yes, I've heard them shouted so often in reproach, I've learned their names. All of them small, though, no twelve- or thirteen-year-old bicycle thief. Where is he? It can't be Michael, who's nine at most. Nor the lurky biker, seventeen at least, who turns up on Tuesdays and Thursdays for a quick tea and fiddle with his Yamaha and who can only be a younger brother of one of the parents. Why did the police say they knew about number twelve? They seem a harmless lot; there'll be rent arrears and unpaid bills, but nothing big. They watch telly, sit in the yard when the sun comes round, take the kids off to school, drive off in the blue Transit to Safeway and that's about it. They don't look to have the energy for crime. Sometimes, as well as parking there, I get out and walk, not in search of the bike, not for exercise, just to get the feel of the estate. It seems less scary now. I notice things I didn't before: tenderly wired saplings; a woman cradling a cat leaning down to gossip from her sliding window, as if this were the old quarter of some distant city. 'He's a bastard, they all are,' says an eighteen-ish mother by her pushchair to two other mothers by their pushchairs, and they laugh together, happily conjoined in derision of the shittiness of men. Two boys are throwing something, their arms raised like stone-throwers in Belfast or the Gaza Strip; when I get nearer I see it's only a tennis ball. There are flats whose fronts are pretty with hollyhocks and hanging baskets, though round the back they've gone to hell. In the Wat Tyler pub, the rotor blades of huge fans sweep the ceiling. I buy myself a Guinness while Otis Redding, deep from the speakers, is just sitting on the dock of the bay. A man in shorts goes past, a rose tattooed on the back of his thigh. CHARLTON ATHLETIC and AC MILAN compete as graffiti opposite, as if Milan were as local as Charlton—and tonight, in this heat, it feels as though it is. When the sun eases off round eight and there's a pink glow over the roofs, the estate seems almost happy, relaxed, a good place to be, and for a moment I see it as the architect who designed it must have seen it, as if in miniature, in the glass case at the town hall, with green felt and fuzzy trees and someone's dreams invested in it. Light catching the westward panes, I'm back to the drawing-board of high intentions—wide spaces, protected acres, light-blessed windows, walkways like Venetian bridges, streets in the sky. There's glass under my feet, bottle glass, windscreen glass, bus-shelter glass, but at dusk, the lights coming on, it shines like scattered jewels. I know that the local papers say this is a sink estate, and sinking. I know that I have a score to settle. But for the moment, the sun goes down, and all this place was supposed to be is there in ghostly silhouette.

Another week passes. Now I stop off at the estate on my way to work as well as on the way back. I get my kids off to their schools, and there's still time to be round at number twelve to see

Leah and Michael trooping down to theirs—reception class in her case, middle school in his, or so I deduce, watching them go in at different times and by different entrances. Once, I keep an eye on Charlene, not trusting the pushchair to stay where her mother has left it just inside the playground, the compound of the peeling barracks. These mothers, don't they read the papers, haven't they learned there are some funny people about? I nearly say something as she comes out past the classroom window with its pasted cut-out dragons and Indian deities and smiling suns. She wears black leggings and a white embroidered blouse. She has a long nose and a no-crap manner. She could pass for pretty. She *is* pretty. The same this evening, in her cut-off denim shorts and yellow flop top, her bare legs slender and mulberried with varicose veins. It's hot still, even at eight, even with the engine running and the air-conditioner on. The dog days whine. Tonight it's a family barbecue: he's leaning over a rack of briquettes, turning sausages and chicken wings with his tongs. She hands him a Kestrel, and he stands there gripping it like a torch. All over London men are standing or walking with similar torches, tubes to light up with, to take the dark away. The kids pedal in and out of the yard. I should be at home with my own kids, having our own barbecue, but, for the moment, they've become anonymous: it's this surrogate family that obsesses me instead. I hang on at a safe distance, feeling conspicuous, a voyeur. This isn't Saab country, yet here I sit twice daily in my red 900i. It's as well that there are trees, and cars left by commuters at the station, and the indolence of a London estate in mid-July.

One night I come much later than usual, a bit drunk after a party. The estate is dark and silent. I park in the usual spot, between the rusting Bedford and the Escort with beaded seats. I step out on to the walkway, and light—from the moon or street lamps I can't tell—catches silver in the yard of number twelve. I hesitate in my stride, then adjust it like a hurdler, an extra step in it before I reach the gate. I stare in as I pass, and the bike's there, high above the plastic patrol car and the lowly scooter, black and gleaming like a timing device. I walk by, wondering if it's chained to something or if it's simply been forgotten. I turn after the last house, like a busby at the end of his beat, and cursor back along the line I've made, once more past the gate. No chain that I can see, no lock; it must be a mistake, the kind of mistake most kids have learned not to make, that their parents wouldn't make either, a mistake made tonight only through distraction or exhaustion. A bike for a ten-year-old shining brightly. I walk back to the car and sit there for a while and scan the line of flats for signs of life: not a bleep, not a chimmer. I wonder if I dare do what I want and feel a surge of elation, that once-in-a-decade certainty of being in the right. Tracy Chapman, on Jazz FM, dies with the ignition. I get out and listen. I ooze across the grass on my soft heels and I don't even need to open the gate, only reach over to where the bike is leaning against the low wall and tilt it away to upright. I pause and listen again, holding it there, my stomach muscles tensing as I raise it off the ground, one hand under the saddle, the other squeezing the mudguard and front wheel; no chain noise, no scraping against the wall, the thing hanging mid-air now as I draw it back and up towards my face like a giant pair of spectacles; one wheel revolving slowly as I lift it higher, raising it to my lips, over the summit of the wall, safely and in silence down this side on to the pavement, gently down, still not a noise. A last pause before I carry it up the walkway, not daring to put it down yet in case it squeaks. Then, ten yards on, I set it down at last, my wrist muscles tight and pinging, and I lift my leg over and clamber on, forcing the right pedal down as I do, wobbly for a second, far too big for it, my knees absurdly winging out each side. Inside, I'm a silent scream of triumph and reparation, the scales tipping back to middle, the world put to rights again. I'd do tricks if I could—no hands, see—but I spin over to the shadows by the railway embankment, look round to see all's clear, then leave the bike under the darkness of the fence while I go back for the car. All quiet at number twelve, no lynch-mob, no torchlights of outrage: I drive the Saab the hundred yards up to the sprawl of spokes, swing the big mouth of the boot open and lift the bike in, doubling back the front wheel to squeeze the whole frame in free of the catch. Boot locked, doors locked, I drive back through the spotlights and security glare of street after street, preparing my story should the police stop me and demand to see the contents of my boot: easy enough, 'my son's bike, officer', which is true. Then I'm home; I stow the bike in the garage and climb the stairs to Kathy under the duvet, saying nothing, saving my surprise for later.

I lie awake, listening for sirens, resisting the temptation to wake my son, thinking back to my own childhood and its deferred gratifications, the surprises my father once prepared for me. I remember the extravagant secrecy of his Christmas presents—the huge train set in the attic, which he must have worked at for weeks, joining the tracks, ensuring the points worked, painting fields and sticking down model bushes, and all the while me banned from the attic because, he said, he was redecorating, the ban lifted only on Christmas morning; and then the next Christmas, the pedal car in the garage, my old pedal car, which I'd nearly outgrown but into which he'd had the engine of a moped fitted so I could learn to steer and brake and accelerate, so I could bat around the outside of the house like Stirling Moss. For my father, the surprise had been more important than the giving. I grew up expecting surprises. Now I'd prepared one myself. I get up and scribble a note and leave it by my son's bed: A SURPRISE FOR YOU IN THE GARAGE.

In the event, though, I wake before him and have to rouse him to make him read the words on the note. He's confused and doesn't understand why I wrote the message and why I can't just tell him now what the surprise is, rather than making him trail downstairs. He dresses. We go below together. I turn the garage light on, waiting for triumph to light in his eyes as it has in mine.

'There,' I say. 'Your bike.'

He goes over to look, takes hold of the handlebars.

'It's second-hand, Dad.'

'Well, third-hand, I suppose. But at least you've got it back. Everything's OK.'

'But it's not my bike.'

'Well it may be a bit more scratched than it was but . . . '

'No, it's not mine. It's a different make. It's a Raleigh and it's got a fur saddle.'

He goes off to school, I drive to work, putting the bike in the boot while I try to work out what to do. I could go and knock at the door of number twelve and try to explain, but who'd believe me, or believe me before beating me up? I could go to the police, but they might charge me—'It's an offence, stealing: this was police business, Sir.' I could try to leave the bike in the night, just as I'd stolen it in the night, but won't they be looking out, extra vigilant? And if they aren't looking out, who can guarantee the bike won't be gone before they wake? I could hide the bike, and write a note telling where to find it, an anonymous tip-off, but how could I get the note delivered safely? The post takes too long, a courier would have my name and address, leaving the note myself means going to the door. I could do nothing, and keep the bike, but even if my son consented to ride it, would it be worth the shame and guilt?

I try to work, but can't. I feel stupid, criminal, a failure. Now, two bikes have been stolen instead of one. Seeking to cure my son's misery, I've made another child miserable. Setting the world to rights, I've added to its sum of little wrongs. God knows, the Ferrier is deprived enough without me depriving one of its children some more. I think of my father again, and of how pathetic a father I look beside him—he who gave, I who can't even repossess; he who seemed so certain of what was right, I who don't know what to do.

What I do is this: drive to the estate, get the bike out of the boot and wheel it over the quiet grass, in sight of Leah and Michael's school. It's three-twenty, coming out time, and I wait till I see them walking in my direction with their mother and Charlene. I turn and wheel the bike around the corner, ahead of me and them, then leave it in the middle of the path, sprawled there like an accident. It's risky, I know. They might choose a different route. They might not recognize this bike as the bike gone from their yard. It might be nicked in the two minutes before they reach it. But I remember the trap my father laid the night we lost the hamster: lumps of cheese placed across the wash-house floor, then up a ramp and abundant in the bottom of a deep cake-tin, tempting the hamster below. It couldn't work, we knew, and yet it did. And this will, too, if a man's to be allowed one small act of reparation: a bike returned as if from heaven.

'Fast-forward free-style mall mythology for the 21st century'

'The Quentin Tarantino of postcyberpunk science fiction'
VILLAGE VOICE

'The hottest science fiction writer in America'

'*The Diamond Age* envisions the next century as brilliantly as *Snow Crash* did the day after tomorrow ... when Stephenson talks, you get the feeling he's going to be right'
NEWSWEEK

THE DIAMOND AGE

NEAL STEPHENSON

Author of Snow Crash

£9.99  **VIKING**
paperback original

GRANTA

DOUGLAS BROOKER
LA WOMEN

I was bored. That was how it started. Anything I ever did that amounted to anything—or not—has always been the result of being sick of doing something else. Imagination by default. Mine is a history of avoiding responsibility, taking the easy way. I've never been susceptible to any vocation or calling; had no desire to sacrifice any appreciable period of time to study or work or exertion to fashion a means to any end. A slacker all the way. The tragedy was the absence of a sizeable trust fund to let me be my natural self. A recurring nightmare has me working in a Hot Dog on a Stick in a mall, enduring the humiliation of what few friends I ever made walking up and laughing hysterically at that neon-coloured, farcical uniform, with the two-foot high hat they make you wear.

My first camera was a cheap Kodak Instamatic that my parents gave me for Christmas sometime in the mid-sixties. Tearing open the gift-wrapping, I remember my dad saying, 'We looked at a lot of cameras, and this one seemed like a wheelbarrow full of value.' My mother weighed in with, 'Your father and I barely got anything for ourselves, I want you kids to know that.' This camera, this Instamatic, was a terrible piece of shit with all the character of a plastic can-opener.

My next camera was a Polaroid Land, the Automatic 100, that I bought with money from my paper-route and which I still have. Then came a drought of ten years, my roaring twenties: jobs I hated, abortive attempts to go to college, my final exit from higher education at San Francisco State, constant rejection from women, constant use of certain drugs. Towards my late twenties, I somehow managed to acquire a Nikon F2 and a few lenses, but everything about my life was such quicksand, it wasn't long before I had to sell everything. It was only when I reached my middle thirties, when I finally began to succeed in a business which had nothing to do with photography, more or less in spite of myself, that I got the money not only to start acquiring cameras, but also to build my own darkroom. And I stopped drinking and doing drugs. I was on a clear. I was alone, taking long, weird drives, by myself into the deserts surrounding LA, taking pictures just for the sake of taking them, so I could get back and develop the film—rocking the trays, watching the images emerge—and make

prints and see how they looked, then get in the car and do it all over again. Nothing ever got me out of bed like this; my bed, which in other periods of my life was like a kind of cushy jail from which I could not, did not want to, escape. Always a hard time going to sleep and a hard time getting up.

In spite of this new stimulation, my subjects—the desert, the dilapidated buildings downtown, the edgy sea—stopped pulling me as subjects. I was bored.

I am bored

I am too much alone. I look through some papers. *LA Reader* has some interesting ads. A little less FULL BODY MASSAGE-oriented than the *LA Weekly*, though not much. Mostly photographers looking for girls to pose nude with the promise of $$$. Girls! Girls! Girls! I think, Why not? Except I want to do it a little differently. I call the *Reader*, think up some copy and give them my credit-card number. The following week I see this:

> MODELS WANTED Photographer seeking unusual women for unusual project. Age unimportant. Looking for a certain walking surrealism, beyond punk, beyond fetishism, beyond faux retro, beyond standard-issue look in any category. If you consider yourself postmodern but have no idea what it means, call Doug

Lekili

Lekili calls first. She has a baby voice on the phone. The interview, I remember, is short, probably because I scarcely know how to conduct it. She seems unconcerned about her safety and offers to come over the next night to do the shoot. It occurs to me after hanging up that maybe I should have asked what she looked like. Whatever. I just want to get something different going. When I open the door the next evening, there she is. Something different is definitely going on. My first exposure to body piercing.

Name _____

Address _____

_____

_____ Postcode

95E5S51B

Every issue of Granta features fiction, travel writing, autobiography, reportage and more. So don't miss out — subscribe today and save up to 40% on the £7.99 cover price.

If I subscribe for 3 years, I save £38.38. (That's 40%.)

I want to take out a subscription (4 issues a year) to Granta.

❏ 1 yr £21.95 ❏ 2 yrs £41.00 ❏ 3 yrs £57.50.

Start my subscription with issue number _____.

Don't miss out on major issues. Subscribe now to Granta and save up to 40%.

Payment: ❏ Cheque, payable to 'Granta'
❏ Access/MasterCard/American Express/Visa

Expiry Date _____

❏❏❏❏❏❏❏❏❏❏❏❏❏❏❏❏❏❏

Signature _____

Overseas postage:
There is no additional postage for UK subscriptions. For Europe (including Eire), please add £8 a year. For overseas, please add £15 a year.

❏ Please tick this box if you do not wish to receive occasional mailings from other organizations and publications that may be of interest to you.

I want to give a one-year, £21.95 gift subscription.

My name:

Name _____

Address _____

_____

_____ Postcode

Payment: ❏ Cheque, payable to 'Granta'
❏ Access/MasterCard/American Express/Visa

Expiry Date _____

❏❏❏❏❏❏❏❏❏❏❏❏❏❏❏❏❏❏

Signature _____

£_____total for _____ gift subscriptions.

The gift(s) are for:

Name _____

Address _____

_____

_____ Postcode

95E5S51B

Overseas postage:
There is no additional postage for UK subscriptions. For Europe (including Eire), please add £8 a year. For overseas, please add £15 a year.

Don't let your friends miss out either. One year gifts (4 issues) are only £21.95.

Name _____

Address _____

_____

_____ Postcode

95E5S51B

GRANTA

FREEPOST
2-3 Hanover Yard
Noel Road
London
N1 8BR

GRANTA

FREEPOST
2-3 Hanover Yard
Noel Road
London
N1 8BR

Hope

Hope is the smartest person I've ever photographed. Her intelligence almost intimidates me. Her IQ precedes her a good ten feet when you meet her, but she is disarmingly open and friendly in spite of her intellect. People who know her say she is much more striking in my photographs than she is in real life. You seem to see her intelligence ahead of her femininity.

Hope lives in a bungalow court in the shadow of the Santa Monica Freeway right by the Robertson off-ramp. She is a fifties freak. Everything in her apartment, from furniture to books to kitchen utensils to clothes to small appliances, is from the fifties. She is like a museum. She is not a tenant; she is a curator.

In the same way that I make a bad boyfriend, I sense that Hope makes a bad girlfriend. She's too smart, sees through the sorry shit too quickly and, other than allowing someone through the door for short- or somewhat longer-term maintenance sex, she probably stays on a fairly self-contained plane. Other than smoking too much, she doesn't seem to have any real vices—did the standard half-dozen years of partying and then moved on. She had just graduated from UCLA when we met. She even invited me to her graduation party. I said I'd try to make it, but I ran into some cocaine instead and barricaded myself in my apartment till I ran out.

Hope may not seem to have any real vices, but the ones I started having more than twenty years ago seem to be re-emerging again. This thing with stimulants, then hammering down the raw nerves with drink or downers.

Douglas Brooker

Angela

Angela came to me through L., who had replied to the ad and done a shoot with me the week before. Angela and L. were in drama class together at the local community college. I always think that as an aspiring actress, Angela is on the wrong coast. It's always those binky-cute honey-bunnies who get cast in this town. Angela is like porcelain from the twenties. Everything about her, the set of her eyes, the short, tousled dark hair, the arched brows, the coy little mouth, the white, white skin—none of these features adds up to anywhere near this decade. And she is tall.

The thing I like about Angela is that we're both classy and trashy all mixed together. We both struggle with Style. She grew up in Seaside, Oregon, and has numerous brothers and sisters, pretty much each with a different father. Angela once said, 'I guess you might say my mother's a little bit of a wild woman.' All the girls in the family seem to succeed in life, while all the boys keep at least one foot in Loserville. From some of the stories, you get this picture in your head of all the girls living in nice little houses, and all the boys either in trailer parks, sleeping on the couch at Mom's or in jail.

I'm hopelessly in love with Angela. I don't say anything or show it in any way, other than by arranging more frequent shoots with her. But it's there. She's not even good for me. We bring out the misbehaviour in each other. I can't count how many times I've clocked a week or two of sobriety only to hook up with Angela and her usual loopy entourage and end up partying *in extremis*. But those rare times alone with her at three or four in the morning, a little *out there* of course: the back and forth of her wit and intelligence, the kindredness of emotional experience, the hazel-green of her eyes, the quality of her skin, the amazing dexterity of her fingers in the simple task of tapping the ash of her cigarette into an ashtray, the pure grace of her physical being.

I'm in love with Angela. Hopelessly.

Douglas Brooker

Trudy Truelove

Just check out the eyes. Louise Brooks on lots and lots of high-grade methamphetamine. That's just the impression you get. I remember when I shook her hand the first time, it was like it had just come out of the refrigerator—a little circulation problem there.

Her apartment building is located right next to the Hollywood Freeway, as close, probably, as building codes allow. As I climb the couple of exterior flights of stairs to the door, the noise of the traffic is so relentlessly ear-splitting you can close your eyes and swear they are all driving right over your head. Or into your mouth. I can hear guitar practice emanating pitifully from at least three other units. The breeze, apart from the gas combustion roar, is refreshing. A guy could like this place.

Trudy is quick to explain that this place she's in is temporary and belongs to a friend. 'He's like. A really good friend. Who is like. Out of town. At the moment. OK?'

We're in the little dinette area off the greasy kitchen, where even the ice cubes are grimy. Dust covers everything. Trudy is lighting another cigarette with the red end of a cigarette she's smoked down to almost nothing. A conservationist. No need needlessly to waste precious matches or gas from the range. She pops a cassette into a sun-warped ghetto blaster perched on a plank-and-brick system of shelves to the left.

Trudy sits at this dinette table the whole time, smoking, talking and stopping to stare into the lens of my big camera when I say 'Hold it' for a shot. More or less a long, weird conversation punctuated with the howitzer shutter sound of my Pentax 67. She is well read in science fiction. Her hair is impossibly retro. When I leave, she shakes my hand and it's still as if it's just come out of the refrigerator.

'I have like. Really bad. Circulation,' she tells me. 'Even Santa Ana winds. Like. Give me. You know. The chills.'

Tasha

'I don't know if you're interested,' Tasha said as I drove her to my place for our second shoot, negotiating the twists and turns of the Pasadena Freeway, 'but I happen to have a lot of Ecstasy right now.' She pulled a pharmaceutical-looking bottle containing a lot of pills from her purse.

'Ecstasy?'

'Yeah. It's really good, sweetie,' she giggled.

As I got to know her I found quirky contradictions in Tasha's pursuit of happiness. Her rule on taking dope: 'I never snort or inject or inhale anything; I only take what you can swallow.' As if that, in and of itself, guaranteed moderation and safety. She talked in a sometimes loopy, metaphysical, discarnate, LSD-inspired kind of run-on language, yet somehow she managed to make sense and was actually quite entertaining and fun to be around. She is by far the most conventionally beautiful 'model' I have shot so far. Her features are exquisite, her legs are long and sensuous, her skin is like buttermilk.

I'd never taken Ecstasy—probably the only psychotropic substance I hadn't 'test driven'— and so, fuckhead that I am, I bought some off her at twenty dollars a pill. Tasha told me she herself almost never took it, being a confirmed lover of acid, but the people she sold to—the rave set she hung with till dawn—said the batch was 'groovy'.

Tasha has since moved to San Francisco, where she has found work as a nanny. I'm still trying to process that. *Tasha, the nanny.* The mom telling her, 'Soon as you come down from your trip, Tasha, could you take Johnny and Suzy out for an ice-cream?'

Elizabeth

Elizabeth, though she called me via the ad and modelled for me, is actually more of a photographer. She's from Minnesota originally, went to UCLA as a philosophy major and now works in the art department of a major record company. She takes photography classes on the side at a nearby community college. When I found out she took philosophy, I asked her if she ever found occasion to use the word 'solipsism' in a sentence. She said no. We share an affection for speed. When she's had enough she does Prozac. Interestingly, she says, speed is a lot less expensive than Prozac. There is something weird going on: we've reached a point where legal drugs are now more expensive than illegal ones. I have one friend who used nicotine patches for a while, but finally went back to smoking simply because it was cheaper.

Elizabeth and I are discussing future photo projects. 'I was thinking I would change my ad,' I'm saying.

'To what?'

'I don't know. Something to attract the homeless, the disenfranchised. Like I get sick of these clichéd images of poverty and homelessness. Most of the homeless in LA seem, like, I don't know, just assholes, working the freeway ramps with their cardboard signs. So, like, I was thinking of going around and photographing homeless guys one at a time, dead on, you know, Avedon style, and asking them: "Why don't you have a job?"'

'That would be cool,' Elizabeth says.

'Yeah, then under that print their excuse for not having a job.' I'm feeling inspired. 'I'd do, say, fifty of them, right: fifty photographs; fifty questions; fifty excuses. I bet Republicans would go for a book like that.'

Elizabeth says: 'I've thought of photographing really, really ugly people, but how do you deal with that? How would someone feel about the fact that you're choosing them just because they're ugly. You know? I don't know if I could pull that off. It's just too weird.'

It's tough being an artist.

Shelly

One night, just as I'm about to leave a club where I'd been handing out business cards to women I thought I wanted to photograph, most of whom regard me with studied boredom, even mild contempt, I see a young woman moving around the club near the billiard table in a very animated fashion. She's far enough from the pool-area light that I can't quite make out what she looks like, except when the stroboscopes do their machine-gun bursts making everyone look like a rapid succession of still photos. All I can tell is that she doesn't look like she belongs here any more than I do. I'm very drunk, about to leave, but turn around anyway and lunge at her, arm outstretched, to give her my card. I'm trying to leave but she pursues me, yelling in my ear: 'I'm Shelly! What is this?'

'Just give me a call tomorrow. I'll explain.' I have to get out.

The ringing phone awakens me at nine on the dot the next morning. 'Hello . . . ? Oh, did I wake you? I'm so sorry.' The voice is almost surreally enthusiastic.

'Who is this?' I say.

'Shelly! You know, from last night? I woke you, didn't I?'

'No,' I say. 'I . . . I always get up about now after drinking a lot and turning in at three in the fucking morning . . . '

I have to pull the phone away the eruption of laughter at the other end is so volcanically loud. Who is this chick? Why am I not minding this?

We talk a bit. I tell her more or less what the deal is.

'So why do you want to photograph me?' she asks. 'I'm ugly.'

'No you're not.'

'How do you know? To tell you the honest truth, you didn't look like you could even recognize yourself in the fucking mirror.'

I meet her the following day and show her some prints. She loves half of them and hates the other half, no in between. She has the most expressive, elastic face I've ever seen.

Kim

Kim shows up at my place a little late. She looks fatigued, a greyish cast to her skin, hair a tad greasy, a make-up artist's nightmare, but that's not the sort of shoot I'm doing. I sense she's in some situation. She wants to know if I have anything to drink, and I pour us both some vodka, taking it easy for a few minutes before getting the shoot going in the makeshift studio set up in the dining area. I'm wondering what she's thinking, what's really going on under the surface. She is like some fragile psychological balancing act, sitting here quietly sipping vodka in my space. I feel I'd like to fuck her, but know I won't. I wonder why the trash of life has so much pull over me.

It's one of the most interesting shoots I do, and one of the most drunk. The two of us killed almost a litre of vodka. I knew at the time that what I got that night would not be flattering, but would have some other, ineffably sad quality that would move it into its own category. As she stumbled out the door, I told her I'd call in a couple of days, and we'd look over the contacts.

Three nights later, the phone is ringing. It is three a.m. It's Kim. She's calling from jail. She's sobbing uncontrollably, and I can't figure anything out. Apparently she got pulled over for something, and there was a bench warrant out for her parking tickets, so here she is. The other problem is, she's been on heroin and methadone for a while and she's terrified at the prospect of being in jail and waiting for the sickness that is already starting.

'You're the only nice, decent guy I've met in a long time,' she says. 'I didn't know who else to call. I don't know what to do. Nobody gives a shit about me. This guy, this fucking loser I've been staying with, he wouldn't give a fuck. I can't call him. If I could just get back into the methadone programme, but I don't have the four hundred dollars they always want, and they treat you like a dog, not like they want to fucking help you at all.'

All I say I can do is get the address of the jail and see what I can arrange tomorrow. The next day, though I kind of want to, I decide to do nothing.

I never saw or heard from Kim again.

Douglas Brooker

Less than wholesome

Should I vacuum? Pick things up a bit? The kitchen is scary, don't even want to get near it. I've come to, and it's five a.m. There's still about a half a gram of coke on the dresser. Sit up; it's an actual effort. Flop back and do a little reflecting. Money is not flowing like it used to. Haven't done a photo shoot in weeks and weeks. The last few months have been a see-saw of self-generated highs and lows.

I do a lot of printing at night in my bathroom-converted-to-darkroom, and during these sessions at some point reach the Vodka Threshold, call my dealer's beeper, hit the freeway to North Hollywood and do another parking-lot dope deal.

Back to my place, and several mega-lines of coke later, I'm printing and printing, rocking the trays, sipping Trader Joe's Vodka of the Gods to balance my head, washing the prints, toning the prints, washing the prints again, hanging the prints to dry, doing more coke, sipping more vodka.

Now I'm in my living-room; the table in the centre is piled high with hundreds of curling prints, the product of months of this sort of mania. I sit myself down and start sifting through the images, staring, admiring, discarding. I do more coke, sip more vodka, stare at the prints hanging by their corners on clothespins, staring, admiring, evaluating. Everything's OK. I'm together. No problem. I'm OK. Just have to get to the other side of this thing I'm going through. Week in and week out, this seems to be my lifestyle lately: voluntary solitary confinement, self-imposed house arrest. But there's the possibility it's all worth it: that twenty minutes of pure unmitigated ecstasy and joy, even if it's followed and punctuated by hours and hours of horrible tedium, depression and this utterly paradoxical feeling of driven indifference.

144

LINDSEY HILSUM
WHERE IS KIGALI?

The Tutsi king Mwami Mutara and the chief of the Twa, 1950

Evariste was the nightwatchman. He and I were alone in the house in Kigali, the capital of Rwanda, when the killing started. It was on the night of 6 April 1994. A plane carrying the presidents of Rwanda and its neighbouring state Burundi had been shot down, and everybody on board had died. In Kigali, there was confusion. Bands of men armed with machetes, rocks and clubs were roaming the town. Beyond the foliage that enclosed our garden, Kigali shook with rocket-fire and grenade explosions.

I listened to the strokes of Evariste's broom as he swept the terrace at the back of the house. He filled his hours cleaning, making tea and listening to the radio. I was usually on the phone, talking to people elsewhere in Kigali to find out what was going on, and calling London to report.

Every hour or so, I would go out on the terrace, and we would listen to the gunfire and exchange anxious platitudes.

'It's terrible, isn't it?'

'Yes, it's terrible.'

'It sounds as if it's getting worse.'

I tried to open the front gate and look outside. Two soldiers patrolling the dirt road waved their rifles to tell me to get back into the house.

During the day, I was too busy to feel scared. At night, I lay in bed and wondered if I would ever get out of Kigali. Evariste slept outside. Each day started with the crack and sputter of shooting. He showed no fear.

At first—isolated in the house with the taciturn Evariste—I didn't understand that terror lay in the quiet times, when the killers moved undisturbed around the suburbs.

How many men, women and children were killed in Rwanda that year? Half a million? A million? Various organizations give various estimates, but nobody can be certain; for certainty you would require teams of reliable body-counters and grave-excavators, neutral statisticians free of the political need to exaggerate or diminish the number. And the total dead would take no account of the mutilated: men minus arms, children without legs. All I know is that the killing began in earnest during the time I spent trapped in the house with Evariste. My notebook doesn't reveal much about those days; a few phrases, a few 'facts' which I relayed to the BBC and which later turned out (as is sometimes the way with facts reported from places of terror and confusion) to be not quite true. I still dream about that time—the dreams usually involve pits and writhing bodies. When I first got back to London, my friends were concerned. Had I had counselling? Surely I should talk to someone? I didn't see how this would help—a therapeutic conversation with a well-meaning person in a consulting-room in London—because the only proper reaction of the therapist would be horror; there would be no way of learning to 'deal' with it. What I witnessed in Rwanda was genocide—a word that needs to be used carefully, but which I use as Primo Levi defined it: as the 'monstrous modern goal of erasing entire peoples and cultures from the world'.

In Rwanda, I couldn't stop the smallest part of it. I am only slowly beginning to understand it. At the time, I could only watch and survive.

Why was I there? Because freelance journalism can be an unreliable and therefore varied trade. For the past ten years, I'd worked mainly out of Africa as a reporter. Occasionally, I work for aid agencies in what they call 'emergency countries', where war has brought destitution, hunger and disease. I'd never visited Rwanda. During the 1980s, when I was based in Nairobi, the journalists I met said it was boring—a place where farmers farmed and the government governed. It was the most densely populated country in Africa, more than seven million people trying to live off the land in a country no bigger than Wales. Coffee was its main export. Rwandans were obedient—only the Jehovah's Witnesses refused to perform *umuganda*, the obligatory unpaid communal labour that enabled the government to build a national network of roads, plant forests and construct terraces to contain soil erosion on the hillsides. Aid agencies were well-disposed to Rwanda in those days. President Juvenal Habyarimana's regime was seen as authoritarian, but efficient. Society was so constrained that there was little corruption—if money was provided for clinics, then clinics were built. The Swiss, seeing a society in Africa as disciplined as their own, gave more

MAP BY SUE WORTH/LYVENNET

money to Rwanda than to any other country on the continent.

Last year, I was offered a two-month contract in Rwanda with Unicef, the United Nations Children's Fund. I was to produce a newsletter which was supposed to help the dozens of aid agencies in Rwanda and Burundi work together more effectively, and to help them understand the politics of both countries.

149

There had, of course, been four years of war. But that had ended in a peace accord, and when I arrived in Kigali in February 1994, two months before the president's plane came down, the country was peaceful except for sporadic grenade attacks and the occasional political assassination. Outside Rwanda, those hardly counted as news. Inside Rwanda, everyone was waiting for something to happen: for political accords to be implemented, for the war to restart, for something to give.

Kigali is scattered across a series of hills and, when I arrived, the country around it was covered in crops and flowers, and everything was a lush green. The city, however, was ugly. Paint peeled off the walls of the concrete blocks, and in the afternoons, the torrential rains that came each day would wash mud down the steep roads. When I walked in town, children followed me, calling *'Mzungu, mzungu'*—'white person', signalling a lack of sophistication that you wouldn't find in Nairobi or Kampala or even in Bujumbura, the capital of Burundi. Food purloined from aid consignments was on sale in the market—square cans of cooking oil marked with the Canadian maple leaf or the stars of the European Union. If you knew whom to ask, you could get a hand grenade for three US dollars.

'Political power,' an African diplomat told me one evening, 'is the only way to wealth in Rwanda. Most of the politicians here don't even have farms to go back to. If they lose power, they'll have nothing.'

The diplomat took me to dinner at a restaurant owned by a Maronite Lebanese called Afif, whose chief business was construction. We were the only diners. A handful of musicians, in robes intended to represent traditional Rwandan dress, played mood music. The mood was glum. The Ministry of Public Works owed Afif money, and he couldn't get his hands on it. 'Since democracy, you can't even drink the water,' he said. He and the diplomat spent much of the evening on the phone, calling politicians to discover what deals had been brokered to shore up the government. I asked Afif about his contacts. He said he had bribed most government ministers, and they were afraid of him.

My daytime conversations were different. Western aid

workers preferred to take another view of Rwanda, a humanitarian attitude expressed in terms of how many bags of food had been delivered the previous week and how many children had been immunized. Politics, how Rwandans thought and felt about their present and future, hardly existed in this world. The map on the office wall showed clusters of camps, inhabited by two sorts of refugee: in the north, those displaced by Rwanda's war; in the south, those who had fled a coup attempt in Burundi a few months before. There was a drought in some places, incipient famine, and malaria was on the rise. Nearly half the pregnant women in towns were HIV positive. The population was growing; land was scarce. Talk of food sacks and immunization programmes was a way of avoiding the what-is-to-be-done conversation, the indulgence of despair.

Most of the Rwandans who worked at Unicef simply refused to talk about politics at all. The secretaries showed me how the computers worked and promised to introduce me to their dressmakers. They shrugged off my questions. 'Rwandans are terrible,' said one. 'They will just lie to you.'

And then one day, I made a mistake. Compiling my first Unicef newsletter, I quoted an internal report by the Catholic Relief Services in south-western Rwanda on the problems faced by the country's tiny population of forest or pygmy people, the Twa. 'The Twa cannot find work as farm labourers because of the drought, so they have taken to stealing. When they are caught, they are killed.'

My draft came back from Unicef with a line through the offending quotation. I was told to expunge the reference and never to mention the Twa. Or Hutus. Or Tutsis. Referring to people's ethnic group—their *ethnie*—was too sensitive, too dangerous. If one or other group was attacked, or suffered disproportionately, I shouldn't draw attention to it. All the people of Rwanda were Rwandans.

This denied a truth that was obvious to the most ignorant outsider, though it was a well-meaning denial. When a foreigner comes to Africa and sees something cruel and ugly, perpetrated between citizens of the same country, then the easiest explanation is contained by the phrase 'ancient tribal hatred' and the idea that the neat colonial boundaries of Africa, drawn up by Europeans, are no more than a result of cartography; that they have disguised, but never resolved, long-standing struggles for territory or power between different peoples—tribes if you like—who happened to find themselves under the same flag of a new nation state. Then the foreigner meets Africans who point out that white people don't talk about 'tribalism' when they analyse their own conflicts; that the European colonists have exploited tribal distinctions to retain power; and that 'tribalism' obscures the complexities of African politics and history. And so the well-meaning foreigner stops using the word: we are embarrassed by it, become frightened to ask about ethnicity in Africa in case it causes offence. Afraid of the words, we gloss over what the words are trying to describe.

In Rwanda, the idea of tribalism is particularly inappropriate. Most of the distinctions—language, customs, territory—that mark one tribe from another elsewhere in Africa do not apply. The people who live in Rwanda speak the same language, Kinyarwanda; share the same culture; and farm together on the same hills. And yet there is a division. There are the Hutus, who form the great majority (perhaps as much as ninety per cent of the population, though the census is unreliable). There are the Tutsis. And there are the Twa. A child's guide to Rwanda would say that Tutsis are tall compared with Hutus, generally speaking, and then be stuck to find other obvious signs of difference.

Rwandans know better. They can tell each other's *ethnie* through conversations about family and lineage. Foreigners are not so artful, so don't know how to ask. Yet *ethnie*—a complex sense of self shaped by history and ideology—is the defining point of identity for Rwandans. It is something at once more subtle and more consuming than tribalism. Foreigners might believe that ignoring the politics of ethnic division is the safest course of action, but we didn't understand it, and if we had understood it, we wouldn't have believed its consequences. For *ethnie* was to determine who was to live and who to die.

2

I suppose I'd known for some years what this business of *ethnie* could do because I'd met Rwandan refugees in Uganda. They were the evidence that Rwanda, where the sole and ruling party described itself as a movement for development, had known violence and political strife. The refugees were Tutsis, the minority that had ruled Rwanda in the pre-colonial age and continued to dominate it during its time as a colony. They had been driven out after the Hutus, the majority, seized power when the Belgians left in 1962. The Tutsis lived in camps close to Uganda's border with Rwanda, but they were a successful community; some sent their children to universities in Europe and North America. Then, in 1990, an army of these Tutsi exiles, calling themselves the Rwandan Patriotic Front (RPF), invaded Rwanda. They were almost immediately beaten back, but they regrouped, and war began. By 1994, the RPF had become a sophisticated guerrilla army that had advanced and retreated and advanced again.

War had forced up to a million Hutu peasants to leave their homes. Several hundred thousand were camped uncomfortably on hillsides outside Kigali, but the plan was that soon they—and the Tutsi refugees from previous decades—would be able to return to their homes. A peace treaty had been signed at Arusha, in northern Tanzania, in August 1993—a power-sharing arrangement between government and rebels and United Nations troops brought in to oversee it. Rebel leaders would become ministers in a transition government. Diplomats began to talk of the Arusha Accords as a model for the resolution of conflict in Africa. (And there was certainly a lot to resolve. Rwanda had another displaced population of about four hundred thousand people who had crossed its southern border from Burundi after an attempted military coup in that country in October, in which Burundi's Hutu president had been killed. The Burundi army was dominated by Tutsis; the refugees in Rwanda were Hutus. They lived in miserable camps, which were marked on the map on our office wall. The international community had failed to provide enough food; many of their children were dying.)

In March, I went to an RPF rally on the Ugandan border. Busloads of RPF supporters, all Tutsi, drove up from Kigali, talking of the good times to come. Thérèse, a secretary with the UN, was excited at the prospect of finding a husband among the RPF. 'These boys are handsome—when the RPF comes to town, we'll even find one for you, if you want.'

She had spent four months in prison in 1990 on suspicion of supporting the RPF. She was in her mid-thirties and had never married. Her explanation was *ethnie*. 'Hutu men who have good jobs like civil servants aren't allowed to marry Tutsis,' she said. That wasn't strictly true. Only soldiers were banned from marrying Tutsi women—among powerful men, Tutsi wives were a status symbol. The real issue, I thought, is that well-educated, middle-class Tutsi women like Thérèse don't want to marry Hutus.

I tried to settle into my rented house. With the foreigner's tact, I had never asked Evariste his *ethnie*, but he was quite tall and slim, with a narrow nose, a typical Tutsi physique, and the owner of the house told me that she believed he was a Tutsi.

Anyway, I scarcely knew him, and his *ethnie* was none of my business. He was simply the nightwatchman. Expatriates and the native rich in Kigali employ watchmen, known as *zammu*, for their houses, as they do all over urban Africa. The wealthy live besieged and guarded by the poor. In Kigali, as crime and shooting increased, the *zammu* learned to open the gate only to whites or to black people who came in cars marked with the symbols of aid agencies.

Our exchanges were the routine greetings of employer and employed: *'Bonjour Madame.' 'Bonjour Evariste, ça va?'* His French was hesitant, and he didn't invite conversation. He helped us install the generator. In the tense weeks before the president was killed, electricity in our part of town was restricted to two evenings a week. The growl of the generator masked occasional grenade explosions and gunshots; the light it powered enabled us to work or read. I didn't go out much at night.

During my first weeks in Kigali, I had stayed at a hotel. I would sit at one of the rough wooden tables under the thatched roof of the bar and watch people. One evening, a young man in a leather jacket came over and started talking. He told me that he had a university place in Belgium but had been refused a visa.

I wanted to find out about *ethnie*—it was easier to talk to a stranger—so I asked to see his identity card. He pulled it out of his wallet. Name, father's name, place of birth, place of residence, *ethnie*. The choices were Hutu, Tutsi, Twa, *naturalisé*. The last category was for foreigners who had taken Rwandan citizenship.

'It's the fault of the Belgians,' he said. 'The Belgians made us carry this card.'

'But the Belgians left thirty years ago! Why didn't you ditch the cards then? That's what the Kenyans did,' I said.

'You don't understand what the Belgians were like,' he said. 'They colonized us and gave us these identity cards. Now they won't even let me have a visa. It's racism.'

One Saturday night, a group of men threw grenades into the hotel bar. Eight people were killed and thirty injured. The hotel was owned by the only prominent Tutsi politician in the country. A few days later, fragmentation grenades were thrown into some Tutsi homes. The hospitals were filled with people slashed with machetes and injured by shrapnel. Soon after, I moved from the hotel to the house. I stayed at home in the evenings and read *Middlemarch*. And then, the president's plane was shot down.

3

Evariste and I developed a routine in those few days after the president was killed. I would sleep a few hours at night, after the shooting had died down; at dawn, as the gunfire started up again, I would start work by the telephone. Foreigners were scrambling to leave the country, but I reverted to my role as reporter and stayed.

The killers were murdering people at roadblocks and in their homes. Once a day, Evariste would call a neighbour to try and find out if his wife and two children were still alive.

I thought: their targets are Tutsis. At any moment, they could come for Evariste.

I tried to persuade him to sleep in my absent landlady's

bedroom, where I believed he would be safe from the mob, but he refused, saying first that it was not his place to sleep in the bed of *la patronne*; and then that the patrolling soldiers had told all the *zammu* in the neighbourhood to stay outside and keep to their duties, protecting the rich people's houses. The soldiers' authority was greater than mine.

Fragments of news came in by phone for me to piece together and relay to London. A group of men had been to one aid worker's house and demanded that he hand over his Tutsi cook. He refused, but they found the cook and killed him anyway. The prime minister, Agathe Uwilingiyimana, a Hutu, and the Tutsi hotel-owner were dead. Ten Belgian UN soldiers had been killed, because Belgium was regarded as pro-RPF; the killers were saying that Belgium was behind the shooting down of the president's plane. The RPF had left their bases in the north and were heading for Kigali.

The Rwandans I knew from Unicef called me from the suburbs. They had abandoned their reserve, the opacity that I'd found so impenetrable in the office, and were desperate for help. One Rwandan colleague, François, was a Hutu, but his son, who was tall like a Tutsi, had lost his ID. 'They said they would kill him, so I gave them the radio, and they spared him. What shall I do when they come again?'

'Give them money bit by bit, don't give them everything at once,' I suggested.

'But there's another problem. They killed my next-door neighbour, Monsieur Albert. They say I was his friend, but it's not true, I didn't really know him. He was Belgian, but I've called the Embassy, and they won't come and get the body. Now the body is beginning to smell.'

'Bury it,' I said. 'It's a health risk.'

'But he's a white man; he should have a proper burial.'

'It doesn't matter what colour he is; he's dead. Just bury him and say a prayer.'

'But what if the soldiers say I buried him because he was my friend?'

'Tell them you didn't know him, but you had to bury him because of the smell.'

François rang back the next day. 'Thank you,' he said. 'I did what you said. You were right. We dug a grave at the front and buried him. Maybe the Belgians will come for him after the war.'

'Maybe they will,' I said, thinking: is this it, is this all I can do? Tell someone to bury a body?

The phone kept ringing. Another colleague, Françoise, rang. She was a classic Tutsi—tall, light-skinned and lithe—one of the women I'd travelled with on the bus to the RPF rally the previous month. Now, she was sobbing hysterically and hiding in a cupboard. Her cousin had been killed on the road outside her house, she knew that her family was next on the list. 'They don't kill you if you give them money and jewellery, but we have given them everything.' She wanted the UN to rescue her, but the UN was evacuating only foreigners.

An RPF contingent had broken out of the old parliament building and had taken on the Presidential Guard; fighting blocked the road to the airport. All the politicians who supported the Arusha Accords were dead or in hiding. A new government had appointed itself.

I tried to plan how to rescue the people I knew. I was fooling myself—I couldn't do it. Tutsis trying to escape were being pulled from vehicles and slaughtered on the road. I had scarcely any petrol in my car. I didn't know the suburbs where the people lived.

One afternoon, a delegate from the International Red Cross rang. He had seen hundreds, maybe thousands of bodies, evidence of a slaughter far worse than we had imagined. I knew that I had to see for myself if I was to report first hand. The next morning, I drove through the streets, past soldiers swigging beer, and abandoned bodies, to the Red Cross headquarters, and from there, with a medical team, to a Red Cross depot in the suburbs. Two women lay inside, moaning from the pain of bullet wounds. Five bodies lay round the back. Up a hill, two soldiers shifted uneasily outside a house and watched us go in. The bodies of five women lay piled in the flower-bed. Their faces were fixed in terror; flies crawled over the blood of their machete wounds. A woman who had watched from the other side of the valley said that some Tutsis had gathered at the Red Cross depot for safety. In the morning, twenty soldiers had come. Those they did not slaughter on the spot, they marched to the house up the hill and murdered there.

In the house, we walked through shards of glass, torn paper, wrecked furniture and broken crockery. The mess spoke of a frenzy of killing, of anger and madness.

We took the wounded to the central hospital. The dying lay two or three to a bed and on the floor, blocking the entrance to the ward. Nurses stepped over them. Blood ran down the steps and along the gutters. Trucks kept arriving, loaded high with more bodies. A woman came into the ward carrying a baby whose leg was partially severed, the tendons and muscles exposed. Relatives patiently told their stories, always the same—Hutu neighbours and soldiers had thrown grenades in their house because they were Tutsis.

That night, after we left, the soldiers went into the wards and finished off most of the patients.

I went back to the house. Evariste was still there. The next morning, after a sleepless night, I went into the living-room, sat down and started to cry.

Evariste sat silently opposite me. Eventually, he said, in French, 'Why are you crying, Madame?'

'Because I'm scared,' I replied. He waited.

'Don't be scared,' he said, at last.

I told him I would have to leave; I couldn't stay much longer in the house because the telephone would soon be cut off and, without the telephone, I couldn't work. I needed to go to the hotel where other journalists were. But I didn't want to abandon him. To Evariste, the answer was simple.

'You are a European; you should be with other Europeans,' he said.

The UN security officer, a flamboyant French former policeman known by his radio call-sign, 'Moustache', was driving around town with a single armed guard rescuing foreigners. When he asked his headquarters in New York if he could help Rwandan UN staff, he was told no. He had no support from the UN troops because they had retreated to barracks. Two months earlier, when all UN staff had been asked to mark their house on a map in case of emergency, I had decided not to bother. In case of emergency, I might want to stay. Now I rang Moustache.

'At last you ring me!' he said. 'Tell me where you are and I am coming for you.'

He took me to a house where, as Evariste had predicted, I found other Europeans. Other journalists began to arrive, and I moved into a hotel. After a few more days, I left Kigali for Nairobi, and then Nairobi for Burundi, where I would go to the border to meet the first refugees heading south, away from the charnel house Rwanda had become.

4

The Rwandan president, Juvenal Habyarimana, who died in the plane crash on 6 April, had been hated by the RPF Tutsis, but extremists close to his own Hutu family and political party had come to hate him even more.

Habyarimana had done everything he could to avoid implementing the Arusha Accords. Under the agreement, the presidency would have lost most of its power, and his party, the National Republican Movement for Development and Democracy (MRNDD), would have had to govern not only with opposition Hutu parties, but with the Tutsi-dominated RPF. His negotiators had let him down, and the rebels had struck a hard bargain. After twenty-one years of unfettered rule, he was committed to a policy which would destabilize his power. His wife was not pleased.

In Rwandan politics, every institution had its unofficial counterpart. The president ruled, but then there was the *akazu*— the 'little house', a clique named after the court that surrounded the Tutsi kings during the nineteenth century. The president's wife, Agnès, and her brothers controlled the *akazu*, and with it access to wealth and power. And while the president's party supported the Arusha Accords, the Committee for the Defence of Democracy (CDR), secretly funded by Habyarimana, propounded a Hutu extremist ideology, against all compromise with the rebels.

The parties had militias masquerading as youth wings: the MRNDD militia was the *inherahamwe*—'those who attack together'; while the CDR militia was called the *impuzamugambi*—'those with the same goal'. The militias carried out politicians' orders by bombing, shooting and stabbing, while the party leaders talked peace. Even the army and the government radio station had their shadows. A cease-fire in 1993 had, in theory, confined the army to barracks, but members of it, the death squads known as the Zero Network, went on operating under the command of an army colonel. And while the state-owned Radio Rwanda supported the official line—brotherhood and amity—the commercial station, Radio Mille Collines, broadcast Hutu extremist propaganda, folk songs and chants—'*I hate the Hutus who eat with the Tutsis*'—as well as lists of Tutsis who were to be killed.

Habyarimana manipulated and schemed and split the opposition parties with a mixture of bribery and threats. The Arusha Accords had specified which portfolios would go to which parties. By March, the parties were in disarray. Twice, the diplomats and dignitaries were in their seats waiting for the president to swear in the new assembly. Twice, he failed to turn up. He consulted his friends, Presidents Mobutu of Zaire and Eyadema of Togo, past masters at staying in power without popular support. The UN peacekeeping force, there to oversee the transition, began to mutter about withdrawal.

In the end, at a summit in Tanzania, Habyarimana bowed to pressure from other regional leaders and agreed to stop prevaricating and to implement the Accords. It was on his way back to Rwanda that his plane was shot down. It is not known who was responsible, but the evidence points to Hutu extremists who had once been close to Habyarimana.

5

Genocide in a small country with little access to sophisticated technology relies on bombs, guns, sticks and knives; people to wield them; and a plan—whom to kill and when. Then there is the question of motive. Ideology supplies that. Thus, you could argue, genocide requires three kinds of people: killers, strategists and ideologues. Rwanda's shadow armies and political parties and radio broadcasts provided all three: the CDR, the *inherahamwe* and Radio Mille Collines. But they were all recent institutions; none could have existed without history and myth.

All societies are sustained by myth, and in Rwanda the myths are especially potent. Stories of the past blend history with legend, and are reworked and retold to justify the power of rulers or the protest of the ruled. The past—who are we? where did we come from?—resonates in the present: who has the right to land or a country, who is condemned to exile? One well-known Rwandan myth is this:

> At the beginning of time, Kigwa, the first king of Rwanda, descended from heaven and sired three sons: Ga-twa, Ga-hutu and Ga-tutsi. He asked each of them to take care of a gourd of milk overnight.
>
> Ga-twa became thirsty and drank the milk.
>
> Ga-hutu fell asleep and knocked the gourd over.
>
> Ga-tutsi guarded the milk carefully and was guarding it still when Kigwa returned in the morning.
>
> Kigwa decreed everyone's social status—Ga-tutsi would be his successor, own cattle and be excused manual labour. Ga-hutu and his people would only be allowed cattle if they worked for Ga-tutsi. Ga-twa would have no cattle and would be an outcast.

The idea of Tutsi superiority is in the subconscious of all Rwandans; denying the attitudes it engenders requires conscious self-defiance. Ideology rather than knowledge is the tool; you choose your interpretation of history to back up political propaganda, or to justify murder.

European explorers searching for the source of the Nile first came across Rwanda in the second half of the nineteenth century. They found three groups of people in this part of Africa, each playing a distinct social role. The state was embodied by the king—the *mwami*—who had a sacred drum or *kalinga*. The Tutsis gave the Hutus the right to rear and tend cattle and to cultivate land in exchange for labour. Social divisions were permeable—a

161

A Tutsi chief and, opposite, a Hutu peasant during the 1950s

Hutu could become a Tutsi by acquiring cattle, and then marrying a Tutsi woman—though they were becoming more rigid under the last of the pre-colonial kings. Many questions could have been asked of this society: were the Hutus merely serfs who were repressed by the Tutsi aristocracy, or was the relationship of benefit to both? But the question that obsessed the Europeans was much simpler: why were the Tutsis so tall? In a Darwinian age which was beginning to develop racial theory and was equipped with a set of sub or pseudo sciences—anthropometry, craniology, phrenology—there was no shortage of answers. The Tutsis had captured the European imagination. John Hanning Speke, the British explorer who discovered the source of the Nile in 1862, decided that they had descended from the Oromos of southern Ethiopia—that they were a superior race which had conquered the inferior Bantu people, the Hutus. Colonial rule, first by Germany from 1890 to 1916 and thereafter by Belgium, brought further theories: the Tutsis were the lost tribe of Christendom, they were survivors of Atlantis, they were descended from ancient Egyptians,

163

they were refugees from Asia Minor. Eventually, a consensus emerged that was close to Speke's original idea: the Tutsis were 'Nilo-Hamites'—Nilo from the river Nile, Hamites because they had descended from Noah's son Ham—who had migrated south from Ethiopia in the sixteenth century.

The Duke of Mecklenburg, an early German explorer, wrote lyrically: 'Unmistakable evidence of a foreign strain is betrayed in their high foreheads, the curve of their nostrils and the fine oval shape of their faces.' The Hutu, by contrast, 'are medium-sized people whose ungainly figures betoken hard toil, and who patiently bow themselves in abject bondage to the later-arrived yet ruling race, the Tutsi.'

Belgian anthropologists instituted a programme of measurement. The average Tutsi nose, one study noted, was 55.8mm long and 38.7mm wide; an average Hutu nose was 52.4mm long and 43.6mm wide. Stature, weight, 'nasal index', face height and 'facial index' were also measured, the results tabulated and sent back to Brussels. From the perspective of the late twentieth century, this obsession with the human physique may sound risible, but in Rwanda, a month after the president's plane was shot down, I watched doctors bandaging the hands of children whose fingers had been sliced off by Hutus because long fingers were thought to be a Tutsi characteristic. Hutus also cut off Tutsis' legs at the knee, to make them 'as short as us'.

Size was too crude a mark of identity for the Belgian administration, and in the 1930s, such categorization was refined with the introduction of identity cards. Anyone with more than ten cattle was defined as Tutsi, those with fewer were Hutu. By the 1950s, the few Hutus who had been educated in mission schools were agitating for change, for government jobs, for access to power. Elsewhere in Africa, anti-colonial movements were encouraging Africans to burn identity cards that specified 'tribe'. In Rwanda, however, Hutu political leaders wanted to keep the cards so that the Tutsis could be identified, and their social, economic and political dominance ended.

The Tutsis were, in any case, becoming unfashionable. Social democracy was gaining currency in post-war Europe, and many of the missionary priests who came to Rwanda found the Tutsi monarchy, with its assumption of superiority and its monopoly on power, distasteful. Moreover, as independence approached, the Tutsis adopted the rhetoric of pan-Africanism and anti-colonialism; the Belgians began to worry that they would take Rwanda into the Chinese or Soviet camp. The Belgians decided to save Rwanda from feudalism and communism in one smart move. After forty years of shoring up Tutsi power, they changed sides and backed the Hutus. The violence began in 1959, two years before independence, and Belgium did little to stop it. Tutsi political activists assassinated Hutu leaders, and in retaliation Hutu peasants swept through the countryside in bands of ten, each led by a 'president' with a whistle, burning Tutsi homes. The peasants called it the *muyaga*, the wind that blows itself into a hurricane. By 1963, it had forced 135,000 Tutsis to flee Rwanda, and the fact that many children of these refugees later formed the core of the RPF was never forgotten by Hutu leaders. Léon Mugesera, a Hutu extremist ideologue, told a gathering of Hutu peasants in 1992: 'Our fatal error back in 1959 was to let them flee.' By 1994, Hutu leaders were advocating mass slaughter: 'This time, we will kill them all.' Those who murdered children used a Rwandan proverb: 'If you want to exterminate rats, you mustn't spare the little ones.'

And so, after independence, a new Rwanda was established which turned the old hierarchy on its head. Quotas were introduced; as always, *ethnie* determined whether you got a job or went to school or could hold political office, only now the powerful *ethnie* was Hutu. The *kalinga* or drum that had been the symbol of Rwanda at the time of the *mwami* was rejected as an emblem of Tutsi domination. Instead of a symbol, post-independence Rwanda had an ideology: Hutu power, rooted in a culture of obedience and control. From birth all Rwandans were members of President Habyarimana's Republican Movement for National Development, the only political organization. A group of households comprised a *cellule*; every *cellule* had a spokesman who reported to the *conseiller* who was in charge of the next administrative unit up the ladder, the *secteur*. He, in turn, reported to the *bourgmestre*, who was in charge of the *commune*. And the *bourgmestre* reported to the *préfet* in charge of the *préfecture* . . . and so on, to the highest reaches of the government. If a Rwandan wanted to leave his hill, he first asked the authorities for permission. Unlike most African capitals, Kigali remained small and largely immune to urban drift; Rwanda had pass laws stricter than those of South Africa.

What outsiders saw, or chose to see, was an ideology of discipline, development and conservative Christianity which made a pleasant contrast to countries such as Zaire or Sudan, where political breakdown and apparent chaos rendered western ideas of development meaningless. What outsiders did not hear, or chose not to hear, was the idea of *ethnie* that fuelled the ideology; the fear that history in the shape of the old Tutsi hierarchy would return. After all, to the south, in Burundi, where the Tutsi army continued to slaughter Hutu peasants, it had never gone away.

Hutus, therefore, were taught the lessons of history as it was interpreted by the new Hutu élite. Ferdinand Nahimana, professor of history at Rwanda's National University and the founder of Radio Mille Collines, tried to demystify the Tutsis by explaining that while European scholars studied subjugated Hutus in Tutsi kingdoms, few had examined the Hutu principalities that had resisted Tutsi expansion until the 1920s. This demonstrated that Tutsi rule was not inevitable, so long as the Tutsis were kept in check. Tutsis were to be denied not only citizenship, but life itself, because they were *inyangarwanda*—'haters of Rwanda'.

Léon Mugesera, who was vice-president of Habyarimana's party in the President's home *préfecture*, adapted history in a different way. He subscribed to the European belief that the Tutsis were relative newcomers who had arrived in Rwanda from Ethiopia four centuries before. In a speech in 1992—by which time Hutu ideology was well-developed—Mugesera said the Tutsis should be returned to their original home via the expedient route of the River Nyawarungu. Two years later, the bodies of murdered Tutsis were floating down the Nyawarungu and into the Kagera river, in which they could be seen passing under a road bridge on the Tanzanian border at the rate of one per minute. Ethiopia, given the river-flows of Africa, was an unreachable destination. The bodies came to rest on the shores of Lake Victoria, where they rotted in the sun.

6

Two months after I left Kigali, I returned to Rwanda, to Butare, a city in the south of the country that had once been well-known for its tolerance and spirit of liberalism. The Hutu *inherahamwe* were now in charge of the roadblocks (though they would not be for long: the RPF, having dislodged the 'interim government' that had appointed itself in Kigali after Habyarimana's death, was now advancing south), and thousands of Tutsis had been slaughtered there, as well as Hutu students and lecturers at the university, who were seen as the RPF's fellow-travellers.

I went to Gikongoro, a town in the hills a few miles to the west of Butare. French troops on a 'humanitarian mission' had occupied the area, which was filling up with Hutu refugees. Two young men, a teacher and a Red Cross volunteer, were among them. They tried to explain to me what had happened in Butare during the previous ten weeks of murder.

'The Tutsis formed an association,' the teacher said. 'They were planning to kill all the Hutus, and there were documents to prove it in their houses. When the people found these papers, they grew angry, and that's why they killed the Tutsis.'

I asked about the Hutus at the university who had been killed by other Hutus.

'They were plotting, too.'

'So who was responsible?'

'The victims were responsible.'

I persisted with my questions. 'The children who were killed, were they responsible for their own deaths?'

'That was a question of hatred between families,' the Red Cross worker said. 'Many Tutsis sent their children to join the RPF, so people said: "I don't want the child of a person who does such bad things."'

These were educated men, fluent in French. They spoke without irony; I believe they were convinced of their own story. They faltered just a little when I asked if they had taken part in killings themselves.

'No, I didn't personally take part,' the teacher said, and the other concurred. 'But we understand why people did it. This is war. It's sad that people die.'

'Are you sad the Tutsis died?' I asked.

The teacher quoted a proverb: 'If there's a trap ahead of you, and someone removes that trap before you fall in, then you're happy. So we're happy.'

7

By the time I reached Kibuye, in the west of the country, in August, the bodies of the four thousand Tutsis who had been killed in a church there were long buried. The church stands among trees on a promontory above the calm blue of Lake Kivu. The Tutsis had been sheltering inside when a mob, drunk on banana beer, had thrown grenades through the doors and windows and then run in to club and stab to death the people who remained alive. It had taken about three hours. A few days later, another organized mob did much the same at the local sports stadium where the *préfet*, Clement Kayishema, had told Tutsis to assemble. Eleven thousand people were gathered there. They couldn't kill them all on the first day, so they came back the following morning. Once, there had been sixty thousand Tutsis in Kibuye *préfecture*, about twenty per cent of the population—an unusually high proportion. French troops now estimated that about nine in every ten Tutsis had been killed, and that half the male Hutu population, and a smaller proportion of the female, had taken part in the killings.

A Lutheran pastor, Bernard Ndutiye, was—as he put it—a 'passive participant' in the slaughter. When I met him in Kibuye, he had turned a local primary school into a home for orphaned and abandoned children. He was thin and anxious; he said he couldn't find enough food for his charges. There was also the matter of his conscience. During the months of killing, he said, the *inherahamwe*, their faces and genitals covered with banana fronds, had moved through Kibuye at dawn every day, blowing whistles and beating drums. 'They went from house to house, saying: "Come on, attack. The RPF are killing people. We must kill all accomplices of the RPF."' At Ndutiye's house, they found three Tutsi children, schoolfriends of his own children, whom he was hiding. They took the two girls away; the seven-year-old boy they clubbed to death then and there. 'They said I had hidden the children of the RPF, so I was an RPF supporter. Afterwards, they forced me to follow them. They wanted everyone to participate,' he said. 'The people who put up resistance were forced. To prove you weren't RPF, you had to walk around with a club or stick. We followed behind and buried the bodies.'

'Did you try to resist?' I asked.

'I bandaged my leg as an excuse. Being a priest was no answer because they told me there are priests who are RPF. They said: "You can have religion afterwards."'

I asked how it was possible that so many had taken part in the slaughter, and that men like him hadn't refused.

Ndutiye searched his vocabulary for words a foreigner might understand.

'There are times when you lose faith, when a man loses control and is under the influence of the devil.'

Some people did resist. When I went back to Kigali later that year, I met an elderly Hutu who risked his life to hide seventeen Tutsis. He was a hero in his neighbourhood. He wasn't the only one, but he was unusual. People struck bargains—their own Tutsi relatives would be spared if they took up a machete to kill Tutsis on another hill. Some Hutu women married to Tutsis were forced to kill their own children, while others saved their own children by agreeing to kill those of their neighbours.

During the genocide, one academic handed me a sheaf of papers marked 'Ministry of Defence' and ostentatiously stamped SECRET. It was entitled 'Definition and Identification of the Enemy', and I was told that it had been widely circulated in Rwanda from late 1992 onwards. The primary enemy was defined as 'Tutsis inside and outside the country, extremists nostalgic for power.' Other enemies included Tutsi refugees, Hutus discontented with the current regime, Nilo-Hamitic people of the region, criminals on the run and foreigners married to Tutsi women.

Despite what the Tutsi women had told me on the bus to the RPF rally, intermarriage between Hutus and Tutsis had increased during Habyarimana's regime in the 1970s, especially between Hutu men and Tutsi women. Foreign men preferred Tutsis too, especially the archetypal long-legged, light-skinned young women. Foreign aid agencies tended to employ Tutsis because many came from successful families and had studied abroad. The Hutu magazine *Kangura* published the 'Hutu Ten Commandments' which began:

> 1. Every Hutu should know that a Tutsi woman, wherever she is, works for the interest of her Tutsi ethnic group. As a result, we shall consider a traitor any Hutu who marries a Tutsi woman, befriends a Tutsi woman or employs a Tutsi woman as a secretary or concubine.

> 2. Every Hutu should know that our Hutu daughters are more suitable and conscientious in their role as woman, wife and mother of the family. Are they not beautiful, good secretaries and more honest?'

The fourth commandment condemned as a traitor any Hutu who did business with a Tutsi. The tenth stated that:

> The Hutu ideology must be taught to every Hutu at every level. Every Hutu must spread this ideology widely. Any Hutu who persecutes his brother Hutu for having read, spread and taught this ideology is a traitor.

The efficiency of the Rwandan state made sure that this message was spread to every corner of the country. The same efficiency—the discipline and order so admired by foreign aid workers—meant that when the orders came on 7 April for the killing to begin, they were usually obeyed. Numerous witnesses have told how the *bourgmestres* in conjunction with local military or police instructed people to kill. Fear drove the killers on—fear of the invading enemy, fear of their neighbours, fear of execution if they refused to obey orders. If everyone breaks the rules which govern society, the rules no longer apply; group solidarity is strengthened, guilt becomes collective.

8

From April into June, the rest of the world did nothing. The UN peacekeepers withdrew. Diplomacy was at best misguided and at worst damaging—the UN kept calling for a cease-fire, when an RPF victory was the only hope of ending the genocide. Eventually, late in June, the West sent its envoys: aid workers, representing individual altruism, a belief in the power of good; and soldiers.

By the time the French troops arrived, the genocide had continued unchecked for ten weeks. A few thousand gaunt and terrified Tutsis emerged from their hiding places in roofs and banana plantations and gathered in camps to be guarded by French Legionnaires. The *inherahamwe* still controlled the surrounding hills.

The motives for French intervention were complex. The French were playing on a larger stage, pointing up the incompetence of the UN and the autonomy of France as a world power. But France did have an attachment to Rwanda. For many years, the head of President Mitterrand's Africa Unit at the Elysée Palace was his son, Jean-Christophe, who formed a friendship with President Habyarimana. When his plane—a gift from the French—was shot down, his widow and her family were flown straight to Paris. The French regarded the Rwandan government as a protector of *francophonie* in Africa, a bulwark against encroaching Anglo-Saxon influence. Here was Europe's ancient tribal rivalry played out in the heart of Africa in a clash of culture and language: the RPF, schooled in Uganda, spoke English, while the Hutu government spoke French. France empathized with the Hutus: the French too had overthrown a monarchy and staged a revolution.

The French troops on the ground, however, were none too sure which side they were on. President Mitterrand had sent them on a 'humanitarian mission', and they were saving the Tutsis, who had been attacked by murderous bands of Hutus. But the Hutus thought the French were there to save them from the advance of the RPF. Roadblocks where Tutsis had been killed were decorated with *Tricouleur* flags and signs saying VIVE LA FRANCE; the Hutu

171

militia drove around in pick-ups brandishing machetes and singing songs of welcome. The French army knew about Africa and its wars; they had played an important part in French colonial history, and French troops still did regular tours of duty in the Central African Republic and Djibouti. But nothing had prepared them for Rwanda. One day, I was talking to the commander of a marine unit, Lieutenant-Colonel Erik de Stabenrath, about his experience. He was a career soldier, from an old-established army family, and he had served in Bosnia and Beirut, but the intensity of the killing in Rwanda had shocked him. 'It was the most terrible massacre in world history,' he said, 'not in terms of numbers, but in the manner in which it was carried out.'

He had come upon thousands of bodies buried in shallow graves, churches where hasty scrubbing had failed to remove the blood from the walls. The stories told by survivors were often worse than the evidence: Tutsis hunted down and slashed with machetes, beaten with nail-studded clubs, shot with small arms, gang-raped and blown up by fragmentation grenades. His own estimate was that half a million had been killed, a rate of seven thousand deaths a day.

Another French officer, Colonel Patrice Sartre, the commander in Kibuye, was more cynical: 'Elsewhere in Africa people don't like to work. They beg,' he said. 'People here are more educated and hard-working. They don't beg, but they kill.'

I asked if, given the atrocities perpetrated by the Hutu government, France would now support the RPF. 'No,' he said. 'France will always be on the side of the slaves.'

9

The RPF never forgave the French for their support of Habyarimana's government, nor for occupying part of Rwanda and preventing a complete RPF victory, nor for allowing the key leaders of the genocide to escape across Rwanda's borders. None the less, the government army, the Forces Armées Rwandaises, knew by June that it had lost the war. In mid-July, its commander-in-chief, General Augustin Bizimungu, fled with his army to Goma, just inside Zaire. They had been defeated, but their forces had survived largely intact.

Much of the civilian population went with them. This was the awful, spectacular exodus, witnessed by hundreds of reporters and dozens of television crews, who never tired of repeating that it was the largest recorded exodus in history, meaning that a million people had come through one point in an international boundary within the space of three days.

It is difficult to forget: dust, children lost and weeping, the weak trampled underfoot in the crush. Fear drove them on—the terror that, if they stayed in Rwanda, the RPF would exact revenge from the Hutu population for what they had done to the Tutsis (and their fear, as I and others discovered later, was not misplaced).

The flight to Goma was chaotic, but it was also stage-managed. Entire communities moved together. They were still following the same leaders and obeying their instructions: Radio Mille Collines and the *bourgmestres* told them to flee to Zaire, just as some weeks earlier they had told them to kill their Tutsi neighbours. Many of them, however, did not escape death by fleeing Rwanda, because Goma became for them an act of collective suicide. Human excrement piled up in the gutters, while the bodies of those who collapsed of exhaustion lay unburied along the road. Cholera set in. Thousands died on a great black plain of volcanic rock, where graves could not be dug. Instead, bodies wrapped in rush matting lay two and three deep along the road to the airport, some with children whimpering beside them. Eventually, French soldiers in masks used a mechanical digger to carve out a large trench, into which they bulldozed the dead.

Goma was a trap for the refugees, but also an escape route for the guilty among them. International agencies talked about separating the *inherahamwe* from the innocent, but the threads of guilt and responsibility were too deeply woven into Hutu society for outsiders to tease them out. The Hutu leaders, meanwhile, rented large houses in Goma and Bukavu, another town in Zaire, at the other end of Lake Kivu, and set about recreating their structures of control. The aid agencies needed these structures as the only efficient way to distribute their aid. Compassion worked

173

against justice: if the aid workers wanted to save lives, including those of the thousands of dying children, they would have to shore up the system which had produced the *inherahamwe* and turned peasants into murderers.

Here, in the middle of this pitiful chaos, while I waited to interview an aid worker in his office in a Goma backstreet, I heard a familiar voice: *'Bonjour Madame.'* It was Evariste, the nightwatchman. Three months had passed since I had last seen him. We had spoken once by phone at the end of April, but then the line had been cut. I couldn't believe he was still alive. He had stayed in the house, he said, until the RPF entered Kigali. No one had touched it, or him. His wife and children were safe.

What was he doing here, among the Hutus and their leaders? At last, I asked: 'What *ethnie* does it give on your identity card?'

'Hutu,' he replied.

I had been stupid. Why had I assumed he was a Tutsi and a potential victim? Perhaps because he was employed by an aid agency, or because I had needed to trust him when I was afraid. Perhaps because even when the killing was at its height, one of my main emotions was embarrassment—I assumed he was Tutsi so I could avoid talking about *ethnie*.

Evariste handed me the keys to the house which he had carried with him after he had locked up. I gave him money. He disappeared into the crowd, one refugee among a million, facing the possibility of death more acutely now than ever before.

10

In December, I visited the Oxfam office in Kigali to see one of its staff, Esther Mujawayo. During the first week of killing, she had hidden, together with her husband and their three children, in the school where her husband taught French; in April, I had tried and failed to get messages to her from friends in England. In early May, soldiers took away her husband and shot him. Esther and the children spent another two months in hiding.

Esther has an intense, energetic way of talking, leaning forward in her effort to make her listener understand. If you ask her, she will show you photographs of her wedding. She will point to her father, mother and aunt—all of whom were killed in the village where she was born. Then she will point to the people who killed them—neighbours, people she grew up with.

Thirty-one members of Esther's family were killed. Her seventy-eight-year-old invalid mother and an eighty-year-old aunt were dragged from their bed and thrown live on to a pile of corpses. It took nearly a week for them to die as they lay exposed to the sun and rain while village boys threw stones at them. Her cousin died in a pit latrine; when she reached up to struggle out, a Hutu cut off her hands.

'What is very sad is that I don't think my family tried to hide,' Esther said. 'I can understand that people have been manipulated—politicians and the radio can change people—but how could they use such horrible ways of killing?'

Esther told me that she had forced herself to return to the village to try to discover what had happened.

'I thought it would be safe to go to my parents' place to be clear with myself that it's finished, and to see the hole where they are. It's very impressive. They wanted to erase everything. They killed people, they completely destroyed the house, they cut down all the trees and they started to cultivate everywhere. They even ploughed up the road leading to our home to show us that we were finished.

'I have no roots in Rwanda now. I can go anywhere as long as I am with my three children.'

The survivors of genocide, unable to bear the prospect of remaining where their families were slaughtered, have drifted to Kigali. Many of them feel guilty because they are still alive. They feel as though they are ghosts—strangers without a home. Monica Uwimana, one of those who had called me for help during the first week of killing, survived, though her five children were killed. When I met her again, she had no sense of future. She said: 'There's a saying these days, when you meet somebody: you say, Oh! you're still alive! As if it's a miracle. As if you were supposed to die.'

But Kigali, in December, was flourishing. Tutsi refugees who fled the violence in 1959—'Fifty-niners'—had returned from Belgium, Canada, Burundi and Uganda to reclaim the homeland. The disco had reopened; my old hotel had been repaired. There was a wave of weddings among former guerrilla fighters celebrating their new life. In the countryside, the newcomers had begun to cultivate their fields left by the dead or by those who fled to Zaire or Tanzania. The Arusha Accords stated that those who left in 1959 had no right to reclaim their lands, but who was to stop them?

11

And now, in the summer of 1995, Rwanda has become the new draw for the emergency aid industry. One hundred and fifty non-governmental organizations are there, along with myriad branches of the UN. Eager young Europeans and North Americans drive white Toyotas with logos on the doors and radio aerials thick as whips waving on the bonnet. They talk in acronyms, walkie-talkies strapped to the belts on their jeans.

Each new foreigner is issued with a white laminated card produced by the UN peacekeeping force, which failed to stop the genocide and now fails to prevent continued killing. The card shows a map of Rwanda and an explanation of the UN Security system—Green Alert, Yellow Alert, Red Alert. There is a list of useful phrases, the words in Kinyarwanda for: 'Yes', 'No', 'Stop,' 'Hello,' 'My name is Bob,' 'Where is Kigali?' and 'Do not shoot.'

Until the end of May 1995, aid was concentrated in the former French zone in the south-west of the country, where a quarter of a million Hutus were still living in camps. It was easier to feed refugees than to start rebuilding the country, and it felt more urgent.

But the new RPF government saw the camps as cover for the *inherahamwe* and weapons that had been smuggled from Zaire. In May, it ordered troops to break them up. According to government figures, 338 people died, mostly trampled in a stampede. Foreign doctors said that they saw four thousand dead and thousands more injured, mainly shot in the back by RPF soldiers. The government's message to the foreigners was clear: national security is more important than humanitarianism. Its message to the Hutus was unequivocal: we are in charge.

Foreigners, struggling to think of a solution, often come up with the word reconciliation. Esther Mujawayo told me that was a concept she found difficult. 'It's a word I hate because I don't know what it means,' she said. 'Even if I were ready to reconcile—with whom? I've never met anybody who felt guilty, who said sorry. Who is asking me for pardon?'

No one is likely to ask Esther or any other survivor for pardon as long as the authors of the genocide—the old members of the *akazu*, the organizers of the Zero Network, the ministers of the government that appointed itself in April—remain at liberty. They fly between Zaire, Kenya, Tanzania, West Africa and Europe drumming up support, doing arms deals, planning their comeback and promulgating their own version of what happened in Rwanda. They include General Augustin Bizimungu and Jean Kambanda, the prime minister of the April government. Kambanda now calls himself 'prime minister of the government in exile' and lives in a lakeside house at Bukavu in Zaire, from where, across Lake Kivu, he can see Rwanda.

The Hutus in exile like to present the killings in the context of an ethnic war between the Hutus and the Tutsis, the result of an uncontrollable hatred between two peoples. The RPF, on the other hand, says that the killings were prompted by a government that tried to wipe out the Tutsis and all opposing Hutus in a brutal attempt to ensure that they would hold power forever. The RPF, which likes to see itself as a non-sectarian force, says that its quarrel is not with Hutus, but with the former regime (to the RPF, the history of injustice in Rwanda begins and ends with the past thirty years of Hutu power; the centuries of Tutsi dominance—and the repression of the Hutus—are seen as a benign old order). The RPF has filled Rwanda's jails with people 'arrested on suspicion of participating in genocide', but locking up or even executing hundreds or thousands of peasants will not exorcize the collective crime.

The organizers of the genocide are well-known, and the evidence against them is well-documented. But only a handful have been arrested. A faltering and poorly funded International Tribunal is gathering more evidence. If arrest warrants are ever issued, the accused will no doubt get adequate warning and retreat into the more chaotic reaches of Africa to evade capture.

Those who led the genocide still have authority over the mass of Hutu peasants in Zaire and Tanzania. There is no pressure on them to acknowledge what they did, let alone atone for it.

The wealthy world's fault in all this is not that it does not care—many millions of dollars have been spent to keep the refugees alive—but that it does not understand. Rwanda lurched into view only when Habyarimana's plane exploded, and because we denied its history, the genocide had no meaning. We knew nothing, so we could do nothing. We could not comprehend that ideology and culture can subsume individuals into the mass, that collective identity can come to matter more than personal feeling and character.

Foreign governments say the RPF must share power with 'moderate Hutus', but the 'moderate Hutus' were the first to be killed; certainly, the RPF government contains Hutus, but its centre of power is the top rank of the Tutsi army which won the war.

Across Lake Kivu, just inside Zaire, the *inherahamwe* and Hutu soldiers look east to their homeland. They dream of return and train with new weapons, even as the sons and daughters of Tutsi exiles from thirty years ago stream in from Uganda with great herds of long-horned cattle, their dream of returning fulfilled.

12

The last time I went to Kigali, I looked for people who had known Evariste. By the time Esther Mujawayo took me to meet a driver who had news of him, I had guessed what the news would be. The driver told me he had crossed a roadblock near the house where I had stayed about a week after the killing started and had seen Evariste on one of the barricades.

'What was he doing?' I asked.

'He was carrying a gun.'

'Could he have been forced to do it?'

'They only gave guns to certain people, those they trusted. He was with them—he was one of them. We know that.'

The driver, who was a Tutsi, faced death as he approached the roadblock. He pretended that he was employed by the Belgian Red Cross. 'Evariste didn't look at me, and I didn't look at him. I pretended not to know him, but I saw him.'

I wondered whether Evariste had waited until I left before beginning his work, or whether he had already started, those nights when he refused to sleep inside the house. I wondered what deals he had done with the soldiers outside. What had he been thinking, why did he do it, what did it mean to him? Had he been a member of the *inherahamwe* before, or did it start then? Was he forced or did he believe in what he was doing? I wondered at how I could not have known, at my foolishness, at my painful ignorance, at my inability to understand or just to see. The days we had spent together in the house in Kigali had been the most terrifying of my life. I had been through all that with Evariste, yet I had known nothing of him, nor his people, nor where he came from, nor how he felt and thought.

Subscribe to the 'leading intellectual journal in the US'

—Esquire magazine

GRANTA

EDWARD BLISHEN
TROUBLE AT THE WATERWORKS

Edward Blishen

'I don't know if you have any idea,' he said, 'how your bladder works?' He didn't pause for a reply; he was already sketching eagerly on a sheet of paper in his hand. 'This sort of thing,' he said. It was the Aswan Dam, I thought: a prodigious reservoir, prodigiously contained. And *that*—a quick scribbling—was what he was declaring to be an average amount of urine, though it seemed to me as much as would turn any of us into a walking rain butt. And here were the taps and sluices and the general system of hydraulics by means of which this flood could be voided. 'You are having to wait for it to begin?' he asked. Well, I understood now why I had to wait—even in my prime I'd have been hard put to it to pump up, and eject to a suitable distance, even half of the accumulation the doctor's artwork suggested.

Having to wait for it to begin was certainly one of the embarrassments that had brought me to the surgery. You'd be in a public convenience, a creature from a world of slow motion marooned in a world of the speeded-up. You would wait and wait, and younger men would arrive, disadjust their clothing, noisily discharge themselves (sometimes insolently humming), zip themselves respectable again, and vanish, to be succeeded by others, and others, while you continued to wait and wait. You were ready to be officially questioned about this dilatoriness. DO NOT LOITER IN THESE TOILETS, said a notice I'd seen on Paddington Station. For me, now, doing what between roughly 1922 and 1929 I was encouraged to call 'number one' was synonymous with loitering.

'How would you do against a wall?' the doctor asked. For a moment I was surprised by the question. It had a schoolboyish sound about it. Then I thought that this old playground measure of one's vigour must be a perfectly good criterion to appeal to.

As it happened, not a hundred yards from this surgery, at numerous moments in the 1920s, I might have been seen making boastful use of a wall with three or four others from Barley Road School. The wall was still extant. In those days, it marked the limit of the territory owned by the PSA, a gentle religious body offering Pleasant Sunday Afternoons. I don't think we took the competition seriously, or even bothered much to note the result. We'd reach the wall together and obey a common impulse and, having effected our swift splashes, would shout our claims and clatter onwards. We had these built-in water-pistols, and they must be brandished.

'Badly,' I told the doctor.

He was boyish, now I thought of it, young Dr Rowe. He had this admirable intention that a patient should understand what was going on, and set out to ensure understanding with his diagrams. Sometimes, I wished that he'd taken a crash course in drawing. Amateur illustrations of one's innards, meant to pacify, could appal. Last year, I'd come to him with a cough that wouldn't go away and that was always preceded by a curious helpless upward bubbling and gasping of breath, as if you were seized by laughter: the laughter didn't come, but the cough did. Delighted always by an account of a problem—it was as if you had asked his help with a crossword clue—he cried, helplessly beaming: 'That's bronchial asthma!' And he snatched up a sheet of paper. At the top, he wrote: MR BLISHEN'S LUNGS, and below this, he drew what he declared were my bronchial tubes, dripping uncontrollable fluid.

I was condemned to twice-daily use of an inhaler, with another for emergencies. Pollution, Dr Rowe said, was the culprit. I'd been in the presence of cars too long: had been unwisely, if unconsciously, dining on carbon monoxide.

So there I was, doomed to gasp for the rest of my days. The question: How many of those days will there be? had been thrust upon my attention on the very morning of this raffishly illustrated lecture on the bladder. It had come through the letter-box—one of those messages from corporate strangers who address you, courtesy of their computer, by your name. WHO, MR BLISHEN, enquired the headline, WILL CARRY THE FINANCIAL BURDEN OF YOUR FUNERAL?

I took it that those behind this document must have glanced at the idea that I'd be reading this at the sink, in my over-large dressing-gown, at the frail hinge of awareness between night, aswamp with dreams, and day, to which (the task made more difficult by those dreams) one had to reconnect oneself. The most naïve understanding of human nature would suggest that such a question at such a moment would amount to a macabre slap in the half-asleep face. Making half a turn, the recipient, groaning, would thrust the document into the piggy bin.

But there was this huge new trade, a fruit of the frightful years since Mrs Thatcher came to power in 1979, springing from the view that life was all a shuffling and shifting of money: the trade in financial advice. And one of the effects of pursuing it was severance from the most simple grasp of the ordinary human scene. In this case, my advisers chorused:

> Not many of us, Mr Blishen, like to spend too much time thinking about our own funeral. Nevertheless, funerals are expensive affairs which can sometimes impose a heavy burden on those left behind.
>
> Today, even the simplest arrangements can cost between £1,500 and £2,000, and should your spouse or family want to be able to give you a more memorable tribute, then £5,000 is not unusual . . .

How heavily each delicate step these fellows took landed on the early-morning toes of their personalized victims! Having been obliged to think of a funeral groaningly assessed as costing £x, you found yourself face to face with the insinuation that a halfway decent spouse or family would aim at a less perfunctory tribute, and that you should strain to provide for this ambition of theirs by setting aside for it something of the order of £3x. Such a tumult of miserable thoughts, there in the night-haunted kitchen! That your nearest and dearest might be among those not near or dear enough to want to see you disposed of in any but the most frugal fashion! Then, the curious difficulty of knowing for whom this superior act of riddance was meant to be memorable. Somehow the prose, the whole address, suggested that your financial advisers had *you* in mind, and that made you aware that the occasion in question would be the first major event at which you would demonstrate your inability to find anything, whatever, memorable.

What did they have in mind as a mark of that increased memorableness? I could think, waiting for the kettle to boil, only of trumpets. Did they mean trumpets?

No, bugger them, they meant a better class of coffin. They meant some morbid form of keeping up with the Joneses.

Healingly then (as I warmed the pot), I seemed to see the face of my friend Harry Frost, on a recent Saturday-morning encounter in our local, the Friar's Holt. In his early seventies, Harry was part of a confederacy I'd lately become aware of: a loose union of the ageing, astonished, indignant, rueful—some, as in Harry's case, actually becoming, as they grew older, unmistakably younger. Harry had spent most of his life as a lecturer in carpentry. For a long time, it had been a plain matter of woodwork, he said, until with the approach of retirement came a growing curiosity about the edges of his craft that took him into design, and design took him into a hundred other things that now were in serious and energizing danger of becoming a thousand other things. He was always pouncing on ideas, if they were not pouncing on him, and reading had become a form of chain reaction, any one book making it necessary to read two or three others, so that he was involved in a widening explosion of borrowings from the library and purchases from our incoherent local bookshop. He had always with him, in a carrier bag, an astonishing mixture of books. With all this, he was a perfectly unpretentious man, amused by his own seriousness; and on that occasion in the Friar's Holt, when he'd been talking about his recent package trip to Russia—which had caused him to be interested in lacquered miniatures, and to begin reading Gogol, and to feel restless because he knew barely anything (yet) about the history of underground railways (and how to find time to satisfy his curiosity about Peter the Great?)—he'd said with a grinning twitch of the shoulders: 'I find being old very interesting . . . I wish I had tried it before.'

D r Rowe was communing with his computer. He smiled at me absently as the screen offered, as I guessed, news of the latest state of play with respect to bladders. I recalled the coarse laughter Harry Frost and I had surrendered to, again in the Friar's Holt, when I'd happened to mention Samuel Pepys's friend Captain Cocke. We'd laughed because of the shared thought that it was unusual for a Cocke to be promoted above the lowest rank. I'd been talking of Covent Garden, knowing it in a twice-weekly way when I'd worked for the BBC at Bush House. Pepys was among its astounding ghosts. He had strolled with the Captain in the Great

Square of Venus, as they'd called it, 'among all the bawdy houses'. And it was on a visit to Cocke that (perhaps because the Captain on his arrival was still in bed) Pepys had recalled his last night's dream: that he had had my Lady Castlemaine in his arms and was admitted to use all the dalliance he desired with her. And he'd reflected that since it was a dream and he'd taken so much pleasure in it, what a happy thing it would be if when we were in our graves we could dream, and dream but such dreams as this, for then we need not be so fearful of death.

Somehow, my concern with Covent Garden had impregnated Harry (so easily fertilized) with a delight in the Thames Embankment and then in its statuary, his favourite example at the moment being the memorial to Sir Arthur Sullivan in the Embankment Gardens. Here was the profile of this substantially moustached Englishman, staring severely towards Fleet Street, and against the plinth a naked young woman in black marble had dashed herself, in the worst extremes of grief. In her anguish, she had snatched up a stray sheet, but it was ill-chosen, could never have seemed large enough to cover her. Among other aspects of this disarray, Harry was struck by the fact that it involved a detail of nakedness more often associated, nowadays, with plumbers. He was impressed altogether by the distance between the sobriety of the hero of this monument, in his tweed, collar and cravat, and the quite other convention in which the distraught young woman was cast: that of a confusion of sorrow with sly nudity.

It expressed, surely, though in a decadent form, Pepys's thought that death, against all probability, might turn out to represent yet another erotic opportunity.

Dr Rowe turned from the computer with a murmur of impatience. There was a blood test now, he said, that addressed itself entirely to the prostate and the associated bits and pieces. But he couldn't remember how it was identified. He turned back to his spread of gadgets, pressed a button and spoke to a colleague. The colleague couldn't remember, either. He tried two more, drawing rueful blanks. A last call was successful. 'Just one among my partners knew the code,' said Dr Rowe. I'd no right to feel superior, I said. I was engaged nowadays in forgetting on a massive scale. 'No doubt about it,' I said. 'After seventy, it gets worse . . . '

'Varies . . . varies . . . ' said Dr Rowe, beginning to scribble his way furiously through a sequence of forms. I and my deranged bladder were becoming part of the archives.

Well, it didn't vary all that much, I thought. That confederacy of those who'd turned a corner and found themselves ancient were united in their nervous desire at once to monitor and not to monitor the frequency of their forgettings. Even my oldest friend, Ben, had recently confessed that he was torn between anxiously noting, and anxiously ignoring, the moments when, for example, a word wouldn't come to him.

Since our schooldays, Ben had been against the whole idea of our not lasting for ever. Four or five years ago, he'd have said nothing about the words slipping out of his memory. We'd met once, about that time, by arrangement, in a pub. 'You'll have a drink?' he'd demanded on my appearance. I thought: he can't have imagined that I'd have agreed to this meeting place if I'd wished to avoid drinking. Then it struck me that, of course, by getting this question in first, he'd hoped to rule out that usual opening enquiry: how one was. But now Ben too seemed to need such comfort as the confederacy had to offer.

'How long do you think we've got? Ten years?' he'd asked at our last meeting, with the jauntiness that had always marked those moments when, with a great show of not doing so, he was admitting to a weakness. I told him of my prostate trouble, conjoined with recent constipation. I couldn't stop one thing, and couldn't start the other. And we laughed into our glasses. The drift of our talk had demanded whisky. Ben said he had these cancers that periodically had to be burnt off his head. That was a consequence of combining baldness with sunbathing. We remembered the lawn at a house we'd shared when we were young men with young families, and how we'd lain on it on glorious summer afternoons in the fifties, incurring cancers. He had, he said, abandoning himself to the swell of laughter this discussion was causing, a massive irritation on his belly that he was convinced was malignant. By now he had begun to weep: extremes of laughter, often caused by some accountancy of this sort, piling up the odds against ourselves, had always brought him to helpless tears. He'd wept in such a manner in 1939, when we were talking of the unlikelihood that we would outlive 1940. My own laughter made me cough. I mentioned my bronchial asthma. Then, of course, there'd been the blotting out of my eyes, in turn, by rapid cataracts . . .

Having wiped his own eyes, Ben refilled our glasses. It was for this sort of thing that whisky was distilled.

'Well,' said Dr Rowe, glancing through the forms he had filled in and signed with the frown of someone who couldn't believe what he saw, 'the blood test is what must come first. And we'll go from there.' I took from him the now-familiar form to be presented at the hospital. Lately, I seemed to have done little but have blood tests. There were times when I suspected commercial use was being made of me: lorries were waiting outside pathology labs to thunder this way and that through the night with my blood. It was like the requirement to give one's date of birth. Everywhere, medical computers were choked with mine. Mysteriously, it seemed even more powerful an identifier than one's name. I was rapidly slipping into being 29.4.20. There'd been the young woman, one in the chain of inquisitors, all asking the same questions (beginning with the date of birth), who'd supervised my admission to hospital for my first cataract operation.

'You're *not*,' she said busily.

'I'm sorry?'

'You're not seventy-one.'

It sounded like a compliment (or, of course, the reverse), but it was impossible to smile (or, of course, to scowl) because there was on her face no expression to indicate that she intended to give pleasure (or offence). Fleetingly and flatly, she was stating a view of her own, and she went straight on to this other vital matter of my postcode. For a few days, I'd allowed myself to feel that perhaps I looked as I felt, about twenty-three; but such cautious, half-ashamed exhilarations never last. Though it was odd how little perception of age there was from within. It was rather as if you were baffled to find yourself on a train you'd

189

obviously been unwise to travel by. The rolling stock was old, there were problems arising from rust and lack of oil: this was a line where stops occurred at every station, and at an increasing number of points in between. You, the passenger, were as moved to be buoyant as you'd ever been, but the suddenly ponderous and mechanically doubtful vehicle you were travelling in was no setting for the bright, light activity you had in mind. And all the carriage doors were locked.

Dr Rowe said: 'Writing anything?' A question always difficult to answer. When it was part of the politely busy final exchange in a surgery, there was really no way of answering it at all. I had this absurd uneasiness about being superficial which would lead me naturally to reply in depth, trying to convey the untidy truth as to my work—how much of it consisted of broadcasting, and how that couldn't usually be counted as writing, though a little writing did come into it. Then I would fear that I was being solemn, and would make a number of statements about the unimportance of what I was describing. I would then say that as far as I could make out, I was being prevented by the loss of energy that came with ageing from writing a book that would be about being prevented from writing a book by the loss of energy that came with ageing. I could probably contrive to say all that in a decently short space of time, by a modest prodigy of précis, but being aware of all the others waiting for Dr Rowe's attention would make me stammer, aim at a phrase and miss it, perhaps tie myself into knots that resulted from the entanglement of the attempt to be exact with the attempt to be brief.

But in the end, it was a matter of being nervous of doctors. They were of the order of people I'd never been wholly at ease with: among the attitudes I'd acquired when young, awe of doctors remained powerful. They were gentlemen (not a lady among them then); they were copiously, swaggeringly educated; and they had what I'd taken to be a scornful and capricious power over one's physical well-being. Their knowing how to make you well seemed close to an ability to leave you as you were—unwell. And there was a depth of unease below that, arising, for example, from the fact that, uncertain of access to medicine, my mother had put her faith in a gasometer.

That was in New Barton, down the road from Barton, where I'd moved when I was six, and where I've lived ever since. Barton was very much Older Barton, but was too proud to say so. Nowadays, my wife, Kate, and I walk on some Sundays though Barley Woods to the Carpenter's Arms in New Barton. We cross the railway by a bridge that continues above the gas company's main depot. The bridge has become a gallery of sprayed graffiti, immense scrolls in thick, fierce colour, a sort of sweating sullenness of paint. Every three or four years, the council paints them out; within days, they are back. Lesser artists add plain messages of mostly generalized derision. And so you step into Albert Recreation Ground. As long as I've known it, and that is seventy years, it has had a desultory spirit. Typically, a slow cyclist, perhaps two, make sad circles, trying for that moment when a bicycle will topple and fall sideways. Cycling is against the by-laws that rule the Rec, but the Rec has never had a particular air of being ruled.

And beyond the wire fence bloomed the gasometer. I'd walk with my mother alongside that fence, she pushing a pram that would have had my brother in it (who died on his first birthday though a misdiagnosis of his condition). The year would have been 1923, and we were there to sniff the air with our noses as close to the gasometer as we could get. There was gas in the air; I thought of it as smelling grey, the colour of the gasometer; and my mother held that gas sniffed out of doors, close to its origin, was a cure for several conditions. I'd been marked out as a particular plaything of those conditions, from colds through mumps to measles and beyond. I can't think this therapy of exposure to a gasometer made me any less liable to be stricken down by one or other of these distresses, but that wouldn't have deterred my mother, who needed to believe in the odd kindly freak of magic. Once born, we were steered away from the perilous starting line and through the shaky early laps by various of her fetishes: in respect of cotton being good for this and disastrous for that, and wool having certain efficacies, and it being a good or bad thing to do this or that at such and such a time. It was a world, after all, in which access to rational medicine was something to be had by way of a *letter*. 'She's been given a *letter*,' they'd say: it was a letter to a hospital, and being given it was like being granted a visa to a country difficult to enter.

I smiled at Dr Rowe, whose parents might well not have been born when I'd gone sniffing alongside that fence in awe of the immense grey barrel beyond, and said, oh I was writing this and that—when I wasn't sleeping. 'Too much sleeping,' I said, as if he might call me back from where I stood at the door to his room.

'Too much sleeping? Take this prescription. I guarantee it will protect you from being withdrawn from circulation after lunch.'

'And after nine o'clock in the evening?' The time for reading, writing, walking, gazing, thinking was becoming so appallingly pinched.

K ate asked now: 'What did he say?' I told her of Dr Rowe's sketch of my bladder, wanting to make her laugh; but she remained anxious. It is what happens between you, on this last lap. One or the other, unbearable thought, is to be left alone: the leaving and the being left equally gross and unthinkable acts. So you watch over each other, aren't quite able to be relaxed about each other's misfortunes, no matter what amounts of comedy accompany them. In any case, I guessed Kate would welcome any procedure that would limit the number of occasions that I got up in the night. She is a deep sleeper, and I had perfected a silent exit and return, had made myself an absolute master of door handles and floorboards. But from time to time, this very creeping about must have woken her, for another effect of ageing would appear: a failure of balance, so that I'd find myself falling against a cupboard door, or an insubordinate knee would crumple and throw me against the bed. She'd be glad for that to stop. The difficulty of smiling at my jokes about Dr Rowe's draughtsmanship now lay rather in the general difficulty of believing that a manageable threat might not develop into an unmanageable one. It might be an overgrown prostate, but it might also be a cancerous one.

Old age is a sustained process of injury. You are being very distinctly shot at. Kate's arm in mine said: Please duck! Please let it turn out that you kept your head below the parapet!

CLAIRE MESSUD
THE PROFESSOR'S HISTORY

The professor wiped his forehead with his handkerchief, and then took off his glasses and wiped them too, fussing over their wire arms and squinting in the vast light. The train spat clouds of grit and steam as it hauled itself back into motion and off, towards the naked mountains.

Around him, there was no station to speak of, just an empty shack with no door, and a jarring French railroad sign pinned to the wall, its fancy blue letters neatly, but dustily, announcing CASSAIGNE.

The professor—a slight, weathered man in his mid-forties, with a small forehead and a Gallic profile, carefully attired in a cream linen suit with a crisp straw hat—was not a man to look absurd: even alone, at the side of the endless ladder of the track, in the middle of the scrubby foothills, he managed to retain some of his composure. When he saw, in the distance, a man swaddled in a burnous, he did not call out. As befit a Frenchman, and especially a Frenchman so long in Algeria, he waited. The Arab made his way, unhurried, towards him.

Their exchange was terse, conducted in a pidgin that allowed each the room of his own language—for the words that mattered most. The professor was headed to Necmaria, a village in the foothills of the Dahra, midway between Algiers and Oran. He needed food, a couple of mules and a guide. It would be possible, said the local man, but would involve waiting, and leaving at dawn, aiming to traverse the fifty or so kilometres in a single, exhausting day. The man would not go himself, but his brother, who possessed two mules, could perhaps lead the expedition. They would take the man's son, a boy of about fifteen: there was strength in numbers. Tomorrow was possible. Tomorrow it would be. The professor could sleep the night with the brother's family—theirs was a larger house, the provision more adequate for a foreigner.

The Arab did not ask, then, by the train tracks, why the professor wanted to go to Necmaria. He thought he knew. It was an uncomfortable history between them, Arab and Frenchman, better not made explicit. Both were aware that the only reason for a Frenchman to travel to Necmaria was to see the caves of Dahra. A history better left buried.

In fact, the professor was working on a book. A strange thing to do, in the mountains of North Africa, in the middle of a war, when metropolitan France teetered (the line was so close to Paris that the troops were sent to the front in taxis), and all Europe was confusion and fear. The professor should not, for so many reasons, have been pursuing these stories, ugly and old as they were. If anything, he knew it was a time to be looking forward, beyond the war. He was driven, though, by something he had read, a sentence in the letters of a colonel. Bent over yellowing pages in the city library, intent upon his research, he had unearthed the letters of St Arnaud, and with them the promise, or threat, of historical discovery: an act, an immense act, had passed unrecorded. A glimmer in a dusty corner, it drew him back, and back, and then, eventually, out of the city library and out of the city itself. Silently, the professor had grown convinced that this history was relevant—or even, when the glimmer was at its most insistent, crucial—to the current conflict. He carried the leather-bound volume of letters with him at all times, like a prayer-book. But he knew enough not to discuss his work with anyone.

Mustafa, the local man's brother, was not as restrained as his sibling. That evening, as they sat down to supper by the quivering fire, beneath a candy-coloured mackerel dusk, Mustafa asked why. He was entitled: they were his mules, and he was to lead them. But the question brought, nonetheless, a silence in which only the bleating of goats and the sharp reports of the burning kindling gave answer.

'I have business with the *caid*,' answered the professor at last. He mopped at his stew with grave concentration and chewed on his bread. The firelight was reflected in his glasses, and the other men could not see his eyes.

'What business would that be?' asked Mustafa, playing his fingers in his beard. 'He is not—may Allah forgive me if I am mistaken—not a man of any importance to your government.'

'I am not a government official,' said the professor, suddenly weary. 'I am a historian. I record history.'

'The caves,' said Ibrahim, Mustafa's nephew, only now understanding. 'You wish to visit the caves of Dahra.'

The professor would neither confirm nor deny it, and

Mustafa and Ibrahim knew it was so.

'Will you want us to stay, while you do your business?' asked Mustafa. 'Or will you not be coming back to Cassaigne?'

The professor looked up, seemingly surprised that the wash of night had closed in around them, carried on the waves of chill air. 'I don't know,' he said. 'I will decide tomorrow.'

The professor did not sleep well. He felt oppressed by the secret music of other people's slumber—these exhalations and whisperings somehow more alien for being Muslim—and the earthen floor of the house poked bony and cold into his spine. Although very tired, or perhaps because of it, he found his mind restless, his imagination conjuring scenarios he could not wish to contemplate. It occurred to him that he did not know what tribe his hosts belonged to; nor did he know how long they had been settled in Cassaigne or, indeed, been settled at all. He did not know what to expect of Necmaria; nor could he gauge the relationship between Mustafa's people and those of that village. And where might the allegiances of the people of Rabelais fall?

The professor, in following the account in the colonel's letter, proposed to move onwards from Necmaria to Rabelais, a distance of a further hundred kilometres. There were caves near Rabelais also, and although their name—the caves of Sbéhas— did not carry the same weight of dread as did that of Necmaria, it soon would, if the colonel had written truthfully, and if the professor was to convey that truth to the world. In both cases, Necmaria and Rabelais, the story of the caves was not only a tale of Europeans and the natives: there were tribal tales, too, of betrayal and unsavoury rewards. The professor did not know enough. As he sought to align his limbs to the ungenerous curve of the ground, as he drew his coarse blanket closer around him and inhaled its greasy stink, he recognized that he did not know the full meaning or consequences of his work, that he was a learned man who knew nothing outside the walls of the city library. For a long time he lay, cold and sweating in his papoose, eyes open to the blackness, watching without seeing and measuring the darkness.

The journey was long. Wakened before dawn by the call of the village *muezzin*, the professor performed his ablutions separately from the Muslims and busied himself with his notebooks while they prayed. In the city, despite the subjects of his research, he was conscious of these rituals only as a charming Oriental flavour to his adopted land. He found it at once embarrassing and miraculous to be at their centre, among the men and their families and their prayers in a guttural language, as if he had stumbled upon a naked woman for the first time and could not define his response to her shimmering flesh.

The mules were loaded as the sun rose. The professor was to sit upon one, while the other bore his case and the supplies. He was surprised at the pace set by Mustafa and Ibrahim, who walked behind and flicked, intermittently, at the baggage mule with a switch. There was no sound but this, their steps and the ticking of insects. None of them spoke. The route they followed was along the foothills, the mountains rising always alongside them. The terrain, although unsteady and, for the professor—whose back ached already from the night before—uncomfortable, was not difficult. The mules were dogged and unfaltering in their progress, but Mustafa and Ibrahim seemed to find them too slow. They yelled at the blinking beasts, who merely flicked their ears and did not change their pace. In the course of the day, the troupe paused only for prayers and a hasty *casse-croute*, consumed in the paltry shade of a wild-limbed shrub.

Twilight hovered as they glimpsed the cluster of houses that was Necmaria. In the gloom, the red dirt walls of the habitation glowed like embers. The professor's eyes were heavy-lidded, his glasses, unwiped, so smeared with dust that he could barely see. But the proximity of rest, of the long-imagined destination, revived him, and he straightened his frame as best he could. He made an unspoken effort to reassert his European authority, remembering that he commanded the two Arabs and not they him, a fact which their progress had served to deny. But it was Mustafa who approached the first fire they came upon and asked for the *caid*'s house; and Ibrahim who helped the professor, bent to the shape of his mule, to dismount.

In so small a village, the *caid*'s house was not difficult to

197

find. Two storeys high, it loomed over the others, its heavy wooden doors studded and bolted to the street, and the high slivers in the walls that were its windows unlit.

Mustafa and Ibrahim had called four times before they heard the bolts shifting angrily on the far side of the door. It opened just a little, revealing a boy younger than Ibrahim, unbearded, bearing a torch. Alarmed, he proceeded anyway with the formal greetings in a tremulous tone.

'We wish to see the *caid*,' explained Mustafa. 'This man has business with the *caid*.'

The professor stepped forward, into the pool of light. He spoke in French, and the boy did not understand. He tried again, his Arabic slow and careful. 'I am a historian. I am here to discuss history with the *caid*.'

'The *caid* is not here,' said the boy. 'He is from home on a journey of some weeks. His steward, my father, is with him. You are welcome, but I can offer you little.' He opened the door wide to the gloomy passage, at the end of which spread the courtyard, where a small fire was visible. 'Come in.'

Ibrahim handed the professor his case, and the two men from Cassaigne made as if to withdraw. The professor was suddenly uneasy: he had not expected to be in the hands of a child, and he feared both that the expedition would prove fruitless, and that he would not find a way back from Necmaria. The city seemed very far away, and his worth in this bare world slight. Elsewhere, he remembered, there was war.

Mustafa sensed his confusion, and for a moment drew close enough to touch him. 'We will sleep by the first fire, on the edge of the village. If you need me, send the boy.' Then they were gone.

'Who remains, in the absence of the *caid*?' asked the professor, as the youth slid the iron bolts between them and the street.

'I do.' The boy coughed. 'My name is Menouira.' The cough was an ellipsis that the professor understood: now within the walls, he could hear the sounds of living, the muffled ring of voices and occasional laughter. The women—the *caid*'s wife, perhaps, and daughters; the boy's mother; the servant girls—were in residence, but the professor would not see them.

The courtyard was encircled by arcades, and a dead fountain

squatted at its centre, a mosaic trough that shone dry beneath the stars. There were doorways in the cloistered corridors, but all were shut. The boy stoked the fire and crouched down beside it.

'This is a house with many rooms,' he said, 'but I fear you will have to sleep by the fire with me. The *caid*, in his wisdom, does not leave me the keys. I cannot open any of the doors.'

Even Menouira's food, it transpired, came not from the house stores but from his cousins in the village. The women were locked in their quarters like penned sheep, with food and water and lamplight enough for the duration of the *caid*'s absence.

'But what if something should delay his return?' asked the professor, amazed, picking at his meagre half of Menouira's supper and thinking of Mustafa and Ibrahim, warm and plentifully fed, on the edge of the village. 'Surely this is a dangerous way for the *caid* to leave his affairs?'

The boy's face registered nothing. 'The *caid*, in his wisdom . . . ' he began again. There was a circle of laughter in the walls, as if the women had heard and made mock.

'What sort of man is the *caid*?' the professor asked.

'He is a very learned man. A wealthy man. A just man.'

'Of what age?'

'His beard is white, but he is not so old.'

'And did he build this house?'

'His grandfather built this house.'

'And his grandfather also owned the land?'

'He was given the land,' said the boy, 'by your government. By the government of France. It is a line of *caid*s, always on good terms with the French. The land belongs to him on all sides, as far as you can see on a bright day.'

'And can you see to the cave—the cave of the Ouled Riah, in the Dahra?' asked the professor.

Menouira was suddenly wary. 'You can see to the cave, although you cannot distinguish it from here,' he said, and was quiet.

'Were the *caid*'s people in the cave?' persisted the Frenchman, knowing the answer was everything.

'No,' said the boy, sullen now. 'The Ouled Riah are not the *caid*'s people.'

'And the people of Necmaria?' continued the professor.
'They are of the Ouled Riah, perhaps half of them.'
'And yourself?'
'My mother's family, yes. But not my father. Nor I.' The boy
poked angrily at the flames with a stick, and turned his body
sideways.

This was the story of the caves of Dahra, as the professor
knew it: on 19 June 1845, around a thousand people—men,
women and children—concealed themselves from the French
troops in the cave, along with their animals and belongings. It
was a cave the Ouled Riah had used for generations, father to
son: a resting place, a hiding place.

The times, a mere fifteen years since the end of the nation's
occupation by the Turks, were uncertain; and the French were as
jumpy as the tribes were hostile. The Maréchal Pelissier—a
brutal, straightforward, awkward man—found that his men, on
approaching the refuge, were fired upon by the Ouled Riah. And
in his anger, Pelissier ordered that the entrance to their hideout
be blocked by fire, and burning torches thrown inside.

The troops stood by in the moonlight, while the screams of
the families and animals echoed in the caverns like the laughter
of the *caid*'s womenfolk in the house walls, and the rocks burst in
the heat. For a long time, they did nothing. At dawn, as the
anguish abated, Pelissier deemed his military goal accomplished.
The soldiers—not hastily—doused the conflagration and removed
the debris from the mouth of the cave. Under Pelissier's orders,
the men then helped the choking survivors to safety, a mere
hundred or so, those who had lain closest to the ground and
hoarded the air from the dying. Their skin was blackened with
smoke, and their eyes were streaming, their wails of mourning
trapped in their lungs for lack of oxygen. Battered and humbled,
these survivors stayed in Necmaria, making their lives in the
shadow of their deaths, bearing their children before the
monument of their holocaust.

The caves harboured another story too: Pelissier and his men
had been seeking the tribe of the Ouled Riah, to conquer and
adopt them in the name of France. But they could not discover
their encampment. Nor would they have, not knowing about the

existence of the cave, which was as well hidden as that of the Forty Thieves. But Pelissier unearthed, in the form of the *khalifa* of another tribe, his open Sesame. Feuding with the Ouled Riah, this *khalifa* cleaved to the French. He clearly explained the location of the hiding place (this knowledge had been passed on, father to son, for generations); and when the troops still could not find it, the *khalifa* dispatched his attendants. These loyal men revealed the cave to Pelissier and his battalion, leading them to it from above so that they could approach undisclosed.

The *khalifa* was well rewarded for his pains: he was named *caid* of Necmaria, and given the land around the village as far as the eye could see, for his own benefit and that of his descendants. A stone's throw from the site of his treachery, the *caid* raised his family in prosperity and ease, in the warmth of the French embrace; he ruled, and his offspring ruled, over the tattered remnants of his enemies.

'Will you take me to the cave tomorrow?' asked the professor.

'If you wish.' Menouira did not look at him: he was pacing the arcades in search of an extra blanket for the professor. As he handed it to him, he said: 'You are the first Frenchman in my lifetime to want to visit the cave. You shouldn't have come. It is better left buried.'

The women's laughter carilloned in the walls.

In the morning, Menouira and the professor breakfasted with Menouira's relatives in the village. Under the clear sky, the professor could see the land dropping away on the far side of the *caid*'s house, an immense, roseate plain dotted with trees, and sheep and goats, and the hillside nubbed by the early shoots of crops, patterns of green in the red earth. The glistening mirror of Oued Zerifa zigzagged its way across the land. The *caid*'s triumph was glorious.

Mustafa and Ibrahim found him there.

'What of your business?' asked Mustafa in a voice that seemed to the Frenchman no longer friendly, but sneering. 'Will you go to the cave without the *caid*?'

'I intend to.'

'It is perhaps better that the *caid* is absent,' Mustafa continued. 'These, my brothers, are the people to whom the tragedy belongs. It is their place.' He smiled, and Menouira and the others smiled also, as if this were a happy fact. 'And will you return to Cassaigne? We shall wait.'

The professor hesitated. 'I would like to go on tomorrow,' he said. 'I hoped to go on to Rabelais.' He paused. 'Will you take me there?'

The group fell silent.

'I have important business in Rabelais,' he insisted. 'If you will not take me, perhaps someone else?'

'It is two days' journey. Why did you not tell me before?' asked Mustafa. 'We would need another mule. We would need food.'

'This could be arranged,' said another man. 'If you so wish it.'

'In Europe, there is a war,' said the professor, as if this were an explanation. 'I must get to Rabelais. It is important.'

'We will take you,' said Mustafa.

'I will rent you a mule,' said Menouira's cousin.

'I can provide food,' said another. And the deal was struck.

Menouira and the professor set off to the cave near noon. The entrance itself was invisible from Necmaria, hidden among a cluster of coppery boulders. The path Menouira took, along the ridge of the slight escarpment, snaked outwards in an 's' from the village, dipped only to the *oued*, which they crossed on stepping stones, and rose again to bring the pair to their destination from above, just as Pelissier had been brought. The descent to the mouth was awkward: twice the professor slid, the second time scraping his hands as he fell, knocking his glasses from his nose. Menouira retrieved them and attempted to brush the red earth from the professor's sullied suit, to no avail. The dirt clung in the creases of the fabric like streaks of dried blood.

The professor, in his research, had not been able to picture the cave. He had not realized that a small stream would trickle so carelessly into its mouth; nor that the overhanging rocks would reach so ominously downwards, their tentacles like pointing fingers; nor that the breadth of the coloured plain would lie, like an invitation and a promise, at his feet.

When they entered it, the cave was not what the professor had, till now, understood by the word: strictly speaking a riverbed, it was comprised of a single gallery through the rock, without branches or smaller tributaries, wavering only slightly in its downward course. The *oued*, once underground, became a floor of muck rather than a river. The walls sweated, dripped their moisture like irregular footfalls into the mud. As Menouira led the way, the professor realized that the cave did not open out into any chamber, and at times, his elbows, outstretched, measured its width. There were moments when the torch-smoke wavered upwards into the darkness without illuminating any ceiling, so high was the gallery; at other points, Menouira's arm would reach backwards to him, urging his body into a stoop, as the passage dwindled to less than a metre tall. Throughout, their little light cast fantastic shadows, as of contorted figures beckoning along the wet walls, made surprisingly pale and uneven by accretions of guano. Hollow recesses offered the only variation: some high, others at the level of the men's knees; some rounded, as if sanded by craftsmen, others jagged enough to cut.

The professor stopped, after a time, and watched Menouira's torch diminish in front of him. He turned a full circle, breathing deeply. He fought the pressure of his heart in the cave of his ribs, the force of history like a life around him. A thousand men, women and children, with their animals and belongings, peopled the space: hunched in crevices, pressed against the moist walls, their cheeks to the cold stone, their buttocks and arms and feet meeting in the subterranean night. The animals lowed, the young women nursed their infants, soothing them with rhythmic words, clucking at the children who clung to their legs, up to their ankles in mud. There was no place to lie, no square metre any of these ghosts could claim for their own, huddled against one another and their beasts, cramped and stinking, giving off a sour heat. He heard the still waiting; sensed the cramping of muscles, the wriggling, weary children; shuddered at the dim whine of the sick and injured. And then the smoke, filtering slowly, then more rapidly along the gallery, cloudy whorls spiralling up to the invisible ceiling and drifting slowly back downwards, great bowls of smoke wafting into the minute spaces between the living beings.

'Menouira,' the professor called sharply, focusing again on the now-distant button of light, '*Ça suffit.* Enough.'

On the walk back, too, Menouira led the way. The distance which had seemed so great was now a matter of a hundred metres, the surprised O of the sky widening with each step.

Not far from the exit, the professor stumbled over something. He reached down and pulled up a long, narrow object, slimed with mud. Menouira held the torch beside him, and he did his best to wipe the thing clean, but he knew before he had exposed its ivory cast, before even it saw the light, that he held a bone.

'I believe,' he said, handing it to Menouira for inspection, 'that this is a human femur.'

Menouira took the bone and turned it in his hand. Without a word, he raised his arm and hurled it back into the darkness, where they heard its dull clatter against the wall of the cave, and the sucking thud as it settled back into the *oued.*

Only when the afternoon breeze swept upon his face and dried his tears did the professor realize that he had been crying.

Progress with three mules proved slower than with two, and the professor's crossing to Rabelais came to seem interminable. Hour after hour, the animal beneath him jangled his limbs and assaulted his spine, kicking up dust until his suit was wholly pink.

Ibrahim no longer waved his switch at the mules: he kept his eyes to the ground which, as they climbed higher, grew more unyielding. Mustafa strode several paces ahead, eyeing the landscape warily, scanning the horizon and the hills for movement. When they stopped, the two men from Cassaigne did not smile and made no attempt to converse with the professor. They spoke quietly to each other, almost furtively, and they ate their meals with their bodies hunched over upon themselves.

The professor was made nervous, but did not show it. Self-control was, he knew, the source of authority. But sometimes, as they jolted forwards, his stomach would leap. He wondered if uncle and nephew planned to murder him in the mountain pass, to abandon his corpse to the hyenas, and to return, in haste and with their extra mule, to Cassaigne. The Oriental character, he knew from his research—and from his experience with Menouira in the cave—was alien to his own. The compassion, the civilized impulse, was not there. Menouira had walked the length of the sepulchre where his ancestors had been massacred, and felt nothing. The Ouled Riah could live without revulsion under the rule of the *caid*. What, to such people, was the life of the professor? They did not see the necessity of his work: history, too, meant nothing to them.

When they stopped to camp for the night, by the edge of an *oued* between two crests, the professor withdrew from the fire, and unbuckled his case. He took from it, surreptitiously, the wallet that held his money, and stuffed it against his belly, beneath his shirt, tucked into the waistband of his trousers. In this way he felt protected, somewhat, from the danger he imagined he now saw in Mustafa's gaze, in the way his delicate fingers plucked at his beard.

In the night, the professor woke to see Mustafa still seated by the fire, watching him and smoking. Conjuring a flicker of menace in the Arab's eye, he felt for the wallet, his wealth resting, like his name, against him.

'Do you not sleep?' he asked, in Arabic.

'I will sleep tomorrow night,' said Mustafa. 'When we reach Rabelais.'

The professor closed his eyes again, and dreamt of his own murder.

R abelais was a larger town, and merited a French administrator, who welcomed his bedraggled compatriot with enthusiasm. He was a tall, square man with a round, lined face, and he clapped the professor on the back, causing small puffs of coloured dust to whisk about them. Ushering him into the tiled domain, he offered him a bed and a hot bath, and hospitality for as long as the professor cared to stay. He also offered a cigar, which the professor smoked luxuriantly, seated, filthy as he was, in a soft chair in the administrator's office.

Through the window, he could see Mustafa and Ibrahim watering their animals at the fountain in the cobbled square, waiting for his instructions. The professor was overcome by annoyance at the two men from Cassaigne whom he believed had

205

cast such doubt on his mission. Their busied forms were reproachful, and he wanted them gone.

He excused himself from the administrator's office and, cigar in hand, called to Mustafa from the steps of the government building. The French flag snapped and billowed above his head. Pulling the wallet at last from his belt, he counted out half again as much as they had agreed, a thick wad of notes, and pronounced them free to go. He was not a man to feel absurd, and it did not occur to him that he looked odd, beneath the flag, his clothes grimy, his glasses slightly askew; nor that it was strange to grant freedom to two free men.

'I wish you a safe journey,' he offered, magnanimous.

'*Inch'allah,*' murmured uncle and nephew in unison.

'We wish you luck with your history,' called Mustafa, as the two men turned towards the narrow Arab streets at the edge of the square. The professor could have sworn he caught a smile quivering, insolent, in the Arab's beard.

The administrator, although he had been a decade in Rabelais, had no knowledge of the caves of the Sbéhas. He had not visited them, and showed only a bemused interest.

'I think you are mistaken,' he repeated several times. 'The *enfumade*—a great tragedy—befell the Ouled Riah, near Necmaria. That is the cave you should visit. Not that there could be anything particular to see.'

'I have been to Necmaria. I've just come from there. I want to see the caves of the Sbéhas. Was the then Colonel Saint-Arnaud not stationed near here in forty-five?'

'Perhaps,' said the administrator. He offered his guest another glass of local wine, holding his ruby glass to the light. 'You might think it was from home, no? The viticulture is improving so rapidly.'

He, too, to the professor's irritation, saw little point in the expedition. 'Even if there was such an incident, it is best forgotten, surely?' he asked with a smile, his lips disappearing among the lines of his face. 'Who wants to remember? In France, there is a war on: morale is of the essence. Who could wish to know about such a disgrace? These things are accidents of war; and our attention must be on the accidents at hand. I hear they are sending our boys to the front in taxis. May God save Paris from the Boche! Persistent buggers. Uncivilized.'

Washed and changed, the professor became again his unflappable, urbane self. He sat in the comfort of the administrator's drawing-room, his head against an antimacassar crocheted by Monsieur's charming wife. He opened the Colonel's letters, a leatherbound volume that he had carried with him from the city, all that way, and in which he had marked the relevant pages. He read again the correspondence from Saint-Arnaud to his brother, dated 15 August, 1845:

> The same day, the 8th, I sent a reconnaissance to the grottos, or rather, caverns. We were met by gunfire, and I was so surprised that I respectfully saluted several shots, which is not my habit. The same evening, the 53rd came under enemy fire, one man wounded, measures well taken. The 9th, the beginnings of the work of siege: *blocus*, mines, grenades, summations, instances, entreaties that they should emerge and surrender. Answer: insults, blasphemies, shots fired. 10th, 11th, more of the same. So, on the 12th, I had all the exits hermetically sealed, and I made of the cave a vast cemetery. The earth will cover forever the corpses of these fanatics. Nobody went into the caves—no one . . . only I know that interred therein are 500 brigands who will no longer slit French throats. A confidential report told the commander-in-chief everything, simply, without terrible poetry and without descriptions.
>
> Brother, nobody is good by taste and nature as I am. From the 8th to the 12th I was sickened, but I have a clear conscience. I did my duty as a leader, and tomorrow I will begin again. But I have taken Africa in disgust—and am taken with disgust for Africa.

The professor closed the book and wiped his glasses. He had found no record anywhere of the confidential report, and no mention was made of the event in histories of the campaign. But the professor believed. He closed his eyes and smelt again the cave at Necmaria, the air of death, and he was certain that Saint-

207

Arnaud had not lied to his brother. The secrecy had been his military triumph: the deaths, expedient, had furthered the battle, and the dead could not speak.

'Perhaps I could speak to the locals?' he suggested over supper, served at the administrator's oval dining table, brought by boat and train from France and carrying with it the heavy smell of French polish.

'Perhaps,' said the administrator's wife, who spoke little and, when she did, waved her plump, pale hands like mittens in the air. 'Perhaps the professor should consult our hermit.'

The administrator emitted a jolly snort and slapped the professor's forearm on the table. 'Naim will take you to the hermit. If you find nothing else, he, at least, will provide a subject for study.'

'What sort of hermit is he?' asked the professor, gingerly retrieving his arm from the administrator's grasp.

'Up in the hills,' said the wife, 'we have a hermit. A count, no less, and a very extraordinary man. He has wandered the desert for—how long, *mon cher?*'

'Decades.' The administrator gulped his wine. 'He is, indeed, a man of God, ordained by . . . I forget by whom. But our church doesn't seem to be a priority. He doesn't preach, or even venture very often into Rabelais. He seems to prefer the company of natives, although I don't believe he has any intention of converting them. He has been known to deliver the Muslim prayers for the dying when the need arises. A sideline as an *imam*, if you like.'

'I like him,' said the wife. 'He's a gentle man, and has taken the time to listen to these miserable people. They trust him. Whereas with us'—she fluttered her hands, a glinting implement in each this time—'Who can say? I don't like to be here when my husband goes away, because their faces . . . their eyes . . . you do not know.'

'They carry the history we have forgotten,' said the professor. 'Our beginnings here were brutal.'

'They have no interest in history,' said the administrator. 'The past to them is like their soil in summer, scattered on the wind. At Necmaria, you know, the *caid* is descended not from the

Ouled Riah, over whom he rules, but from their enemies. And
they don't know it, or care. Like dust, it's gone.'

'They know,' countered the professor, with new
understanding born simply of dislike of the administrator. 'And
they won't ever forget. They live in front of their defeat, and it is
always with them. But they're different from us. They know what
is necessary for survival.'

'And they will use it when they can,' said the wife, sombre
now. 'Don't think, *mon cher*, that they won't. They harbour it
like a seed, and nurture it in secret. One day, we will all pay.'

'This is why the stories must be told,' said the professor, eager
yet again to convey his vital purpose. 'There is a war in Europe
now. We must learn from the past before mistakes are made. Do
you see? For the progress of France, here and at home, the truth
must be known. Knowledge . . . ' he stammered, flushed from the
wine and conviction, 'knowledge is the only salvation. For the
past and the future both.'

'Noble sentiments indeed,' said the administrator. 'But I
suspect you have only the experience of your library. Forgive me,
but I speak as a former military man, and I can assure you, the
maps of old battles are of very little use in the field. Wits and
courage are what's called for: the rest is a waste and a distraction.'

The professor did not respond.

'Tell me, what good is it? What difference will it make, to tell
your story, even if it is true?'

This time, the professor did not bother to try.

Naim, the administrator's steward, took the professor up into
the hills. They walked for two hours, Rabelais reduced
behind them to a silent hive, its French quarter invisible in the
lacy comb of native houses.

The hermit's encampment, though remote, had a clear view
of the town. The clay of the one-room building was weathered
and covered, in places, by creepers, and in front stretched an area
of ground trampled flat and even as a floor. Outside the doorway
waited a neat pile of firewood. There did not, at first, appear to
be anyone at home, and Naim beat his staff against the ground
and called out in Arabic.

Two figures emerged from along a path that ran behind the building: a surprising sight. In front walked the hermit, a towering, skeletally thin man with attenuated limbs that stretched, puppet-like, from the cuffs and hem of his gown. His skin was so browned by the sun and his coarse garments were so ragged that initially only his shock of silvered hair confirmed his European breeding. A closer inspection revealed his patrician profile and his pale blue eyes, and the rich timbre of his French voice when he spoke left no room for doubt.

Behind him loomed an immense black African, powerfully muscled and clad in equally ill-fitting clothes. He was introduced as Kofeh, the hermit's assistant of long standing. He did not stay to talk with them, but returned to his work, skinning the sheep a local tribe had donated for their food.

Naim and the hermit spoke for some time in Arabic, about Naim's relatives and the birth of his third child. The hermit conversed in Naim's language as readily as in French, and the two spoke to each other as friends, without any lingering reserve. The hermit asked after other families in Rabelais, but he did not mention the administrator until he turned and spoke in French to the professor.

'How is our good friend, the standard-bearer of French glory?' he asked. 'Do you know, he does not allow Kofeh into his drawing-room, and so I can't visit him often. I am partial, however, to his wife; and when he is called to the city, I try to stop in on her. They have no children. She is very alone in that house.'

'I can imagine,' said the professor. 'She appears to have a nervous disposition. But I found her most sympathetic—it was she who suggested I consult you. You've lived a long time among these people, and I thought you would know of their history.'

'I know a little.'

'I wish to write a book. In seventy years, no one has told the truth about our campaigns in this region.'

'That may be.'

'The cave at Necmaria, from which I have recently travelled . . . I believe it is not the only cross we have to bear. Here, too . . . '

'Yes, here, too.'

'You know, then, about the *enfumade* of the Sbéhas?'

'It is spoken of. Those French who acknowledge it speak only of a handful of brigands. You won't find any Frenchman who can tell you the story. Saint-Arnaud covered his tracks well, and who would wish to expose them? The lesson they leave, next to Necmaria, is that of a job well done. Not an agreeable lesson, but a useful one: if you want to succeed, kill them all. Leave nobody alive who can speak. It is a lesson I fear that mankind—even European men—should not learn too well. Because none of us is civilized enough. Even, and perhaps especially, to the enlightened, extermination is not a lesson to be taught.'

'There were no survivors then?'

'Maybe that is what is to be gleaned. There are always survivors.'

'Where can I hear more?'

The hermit looked to Naim, who frowned.

'Will you not?' the hermit asked, his face coaxing, his eyebrows slightly raised.

Naim spoke without looking at the professor. 'My grandfather was one of those in the cave who survived. He was only a small boy. You walked on the corpses as on piles of hay,' he said. 'The cave is an underground *oued*, on two levels. Only those in the upper chamber had any hope of survival. At both ends, the cave is entered through waterfalls: the French did not only smoke them in, they cemented the exits, and camped, two weeks almost, outside, so no rescue could be attempted. The dead gave off gases, purulent rot, poison. And the water which kept the few alive ran beneath their decomposing bodies. My grandfather thought that he, too, had died: his mind was deranged. When at last he saw the light again, he believed he was in heaven, and that the men who helped him through the curtain of water to the air were his brothers and cousins, the very ones who had lain, homes to feasting maggots, in the mud beneath his feet.'

'How did they get to safety?' asked the professor, the memory of Necmaria vivid in his mind. 'Did the troops relent?'

'It is said,' said Naim, 'that a *caid* from a neighbouring region prevailed, finally, upon the commander. That he was desperate to see again the most beautiful woman in the mountains, whom he had planned to marry. And that he was determined to have her, alive or dead. The commander, it seems, who showed no mercy to a thousand of his fellows, understood the love of a woman and permitted the opening of the cave.'

'And the dead?'

'She was among them, but the *caid* did not take her away after all. Her face had pulled back upon itself, the skin and the eyes were gone. He knew her only by the length of her hair and the gold around her neck and fingers. He left her there, and all the others. The cave was their tomb.'

Kofeh, at this point, returned from behind the house, bringing tea. The story was at an end.

'My heart is confused,' said the hermit to the professor, 'when I hear of our legacy. What is the purpose of such violence? And yet, how else would I be here?' He paused to drink. 'Must we believe that this is the will of God? Or does our life's struggle pass unheeded in heaven? I have no answer.'

'Do you see that I must tell this story?' asked the professor, believing that he had found at last a man of vision and justice.

'I see that this is your struggle,' said the hermit. 'It is with you, and with God.'

Back in the city, the professor compiled his notes. Weeks, and then months passed. The days in the mountains of Dahra stood out from his life like the plain in front of the mountains, hazed in the light, an unreachable promise. The library where he worked was still and dark, its high windows and thick walls a silent, stifling enclosure against the contradictions of the country. The call of the *muezzin* reached his ears only as a muffled wail, the keeper of ritual and the passage of time.

For the first time in his many years of study, the professor was uneasy about his work. Even were he to finish his book, who would read it? It was not clear that this was a time for truth: extermination was not a lesson that the people needed to learn. But what might be the consequences of silence?

Eventually, he forsook the library for the clamour of the port, where the men worked bare-chested, heaving and shouting as the ships were docked and unloaded. He wandered, too, in the maze of the kasbah, among the hot perfumes of spice and dung. Even the bustling, bourgeois arcades of his compatriots were preferable to the silence of the library. He neglected his students as well as his work: he sought in the city the truth of the mountains, the air of the caves catching him, here and there, in gusts.

He learned that his nephew—only a boy when he had seen him last—had been killed at the front, in a battle over a patch of wet ground north of Paris. He learned, too, not long after, that the hermit of Rabelais and his hulking disciple had been slain in their sleep, their throats slit in crimson grins that neither Kofeh's strength nor the hermit's gentle patience could close up again. The newspaper made much of the hermit's noble birth, and the end of his lineage, of the fact that an ancient castle in south-western France would now pass into the hands of strangers. The professor could see only the small building, alone on the plateau in the Dahra, crumbling again to dust, its firewood standing unused in a neat pile; and the town of Rabelais far below, living on, oblivious.

Long before he had even planned his excursion, before these stories had begun to consume him, the professor had discovered, within the safety of the library itself, mementoes of his ancestors' conquest. Unable to confront this horror, he had chosen to ignore it: it had been as easy as shutting a drawer. But now, troubled, he returned to the library. There, carefully stored in a cupboard in the corner, was a large jar of tinted liquid, in which swam a swarm of pinkish shrimp-like creatures. These perfect curls, some still trailing strands of hair, no two quite alike, were the preserved ears of native rebels, claimed by the French as a warning and a marker in the early days of the colony. For seventy or more years they had floated in their brine, waiting, listening for something unheard. For them, the professor decided at last, if only to them, he would tell his story.

The details of events at the caves of Dahra and Sbéhas are to be found in L'Algerie et la Metropole *by E. F. Gautier, Payot & Co., Paris, 1920.*

CLIVE SINCLAIR
THE LADY WITH THE LAPTOP

It is Friday, and I am at the airport waving a little flag, a one-man welcoming committee. There is a name on the flag. I survey the arrivals, trying to put a face to the name. I do not have much to go on, just one telephone conversation.

'How will I recognize you?' I asked. 'Do you have any distinguishing features?'

'I'll be the lady with the laptop,' the voice replied, chuckling.

'What is so funny?' I asked. Of course I like to hear women laugh, but only when I have made the joke.

'Nothing,' it said.

'In that case,' I replied indifferently, 'I'll take my leave until next Friday.'

'Not so fast,' it said. 'I want you to check that I have a nice room and to make sure that it overlooks the Nile.'

'Madam, you are mistaking me for a travel agent,' I replied. 'Your creature comforts are not my business.'

'Do it anyway,' it said, still giggling, 'and remember that I'll be the lady with the little Toshiba.'

I refused to bid a polite farewell to the minx. On the contrary, I slammed down the receiver. Everyone looked at me with respect, save our oleaginous supervisor, who rose from his chair and began to move in my direction. Let him come! *Je ne regrette rien.*

The arrogant madam obviously assumed that I was an oh-so-ignorant gippy who had never heard of Anton Chekhov. As it happens, I am well acquainted with 'The Lady with the Lap-dog' and, being a man of the theatre, have witnessed countless productions of Chekhov's melancholy dramas too. Enough! Why should I care what a strange woman thinks of me? Who is she anyway? Who is Chekhov, for that matter? Did he ever win the Nobel Prize, like our own Naguib Mahfouz? It is not in my nature to boast, but I have to tell you that I am personally acquainted with Mahfouz, or am at least the friend of a friend.

Shafik Sherif and I went to the same school. In our younger days, it was fashionable for wealthy families to send their sons to ersatz Etons. So Shafik and I were both packed off to St George's, near the British Embassy in Cairo's Garden City, where we were tutored and tortured by ruddy-faced buggers with old English surnames and Spartan vices. Shafik shone, but I was more like the stars at midday, ever-present but invisible. Thus it has continued ever since. Shafik prospers, while I labour. Shafik edits the literary pages of *Al-Ahram*, while I perform menial tasks for the Institute of Translation. As such, it is Shafik's privilege to serialize the novels of Mahfouz, even before they have appeared in hard covers. Not only does Mahfouz publish his fiction in *Al-Ahram*, he literally invents it in an office at the newspaper. According to Shafik, he turns up every day at about nine o'clock, having already scanned the early editions and taken morning coffee at the Café Ali Baba *en route*, and writes solidly until noon, whereupon he makes a modest exit, returning home to take a nap.

For years, Shafik had been saying, 'My dear chap, you simply must meet Mahfouz—the man is a national treasure,' without ever progressing to an introduction. So the summons to the Café de l'Opéra came as a complete surprise. When I arrived, Shafik was reading the old man a letter. Since Mahfouz is hard of hearing, the recitation was slow and clear, enabling all within earshot to grasp that the sender was none other than François Mitterrand, the President of France. *'Je vous adresse mes félicitations les plus chaleureuses,'* concluded Shafik sonorously, *'et vous prie de croire à mes sentiments très cordiaux.'*

'Thank you,' said Mahfouz, patting Shafik on the hand, 'your voice is like a bell.'

'Allow me to present my dear friend Yonnan Wassef,' said Shafik, turning to me.

'Your name is strangely familiar,' commented Mahfouz. 'Are you not the young man who wrote *Mourning Becomes Electrolux?*' I blushed and sat down, tongue-tied.

'He is indeed,' said Shafik, 'the very man who was hailed by wise critics as the author of the season's *chef d'oeuvre*, the saviour of Egyptian theatre.'

'They were wrong,' I snapped bitterly. 'It turned out that the theatre of the absurd was redundant in a country where bureaucracy is an art form.'

As I spoke, a coffee-pot alighted upon our low table like a copper toucan. Three cups followed in formation, as well as bowls of pralines, pistachios and a platter of Turkish delight.

'I am no theatre-goer, being deaf and half-blind,' said Mahfouz, 'but I do recall being intrigued by your play. Tell me, Mr Wassef, what possessed you to make a tragic hero of the humble vacuum-cleaner?'

How could I resist?

'Mr Mahfouz,' I replied, 'I understand that you do not like to travel. Had you done so, you would surely have observed that whereas most airports are overflowing with luxury items such as camcorders and music centres, the duty-free shops at Cairo proudly display an infinite variety of vacuum-cleaners.'

Shafik poured the coffee and offered the bon-bons; sweet-toothed Mahfouz took a handful of pralines. He chewed them thoughtfully and, as he did so, inclined his head towards me.

'Why is this?' I continued. 'The obvious answer is that Cairo is a dusty city, famously so. But I pondered the subject more deeply, trying to tease out the esoteric meaning. I began with the user. Modern woman, whatever she may say, remains dedicated to provocation and procreation; her sworn enemies are ugliness and decay. See how she stands before the looking-glass with her lipstick and her rouge, aiming to disguise time's depredations; see how she dusts every cranny of her chamber, determined to eliminate the physical evidence of erosion. But in a city like ours, where the past is ever-present, smothering us like desert sand, her struggle seems hopeless. Enter the hero! A brand-new Electrolux from Sweden. Efficient, phallic, built like a flame-thrower. It is love at first sight. Modernity woos and weds tradition. Woman may falter, but the machine is inexhaustible. Night and day, day and night, her brave Viking sucks up the dirt, the dross, the debris and the decay. He is the answer to her prayers! But, alas, our Nordic *Übermensch* has bitten off more than he can chew. Lungs clogged with the residue of desiccated hopes, the salty dust of lost lives, he begins to shed tears from his ducts.'

'But what are you saying about Cairo that we don't already know?' said Mahfouz.

'That it is a place where the phallus has been feminized,' I replied, 'transformed into a womb on wheels.'

'Yonnan is something of an El Sayed,' explained Shafik, referring to the infamous Don Juan dreamed up by Mahfouz. 'He

219

is a dear man, but he is notorious for his bad behaviour towards women.'

Goodness knows what impression Mahfouz formed of me during that first encounter, but it couldn't have been too bad, because we continue to meet from time to time. To be frank, these encounters are the highlights of my life, unlike the all-too-frequent confrontations with my immediate superior; one of which occurred—you'll remember—immediately after my introduction to the woman I now await.

The hierarch paused before delivering his chastisement, merely to prolong his pleasure. He removed a silver box from his waistcoat pocket, opened it gingerly and extracted a pinch of maccabaw, which he placed in his snout and inhaled with a porcine snort. Raising his head, he inspected his domain with a dolorous eye. I was just another of his minions, condemned to toil in a vast office with a dozen other trapped souls. Our task? To translate the jewels of modern Egyptian letters into infidel tongues. It is painstaking and soul-destroying work, this casting of pearls before swine. That is why my colleagues were so excited by the heated exchange with the virago. 'Ditch the bitch,' was their unanimous advice. Only the slave-driver dissented. He leaned over me and sneezed, spraying my desk with attar of roses. 'What do you think you are playing at?' he cried. 'Where are your manners?'

'She thinks she is Cleopatra,' I replied, 'but I am no lackey. It is not my style to take orders from a woman.'

'The world is changing,' said my supervisor, 'and we must all alter our habits accordingly.'

'A woman is bad enough,' I protested, 'but a Jewess from Tel Aviv is beyond the pale. I have my pride.'

'Swallow it,' he advised.

If bile were a convertible currency, I would long since have become a billionaire. As it isn't, I spat the filthy stuff into the gutter as I pushed my way through the reeking Khan El-Khalili until, God be praised, I reached the café where Shafik awaited me. At last, I closed the door upon the hubbub of *hoi polloi* and entered an oasis where hubble-bubbles gargled like hot springs.

The horrible day was done. Sweet aromas of tobacco, coffee and sweat combined to form a meaty brew that engulfed me in a masculine embrace. 'My dear fellow,' exclaimed Shafik, as soon as he caught sight of me, 'whatever is the matter? You look like you have lost a pound and found a penny.'

'That is exactly how I felt until this very moment,' I said, 'but the prospect of your company as well as that of your esteemed colleague fills me with relief.'

Naguib Mahfouz, looking very dapper in a Chairman Mao jacket, nodded in acknowledgement of my compliment. 'What an excitable fellow you are,' he pointed out. 'One minute you are soaring, borne aloft by wild fancies; the next you are in the very deepest of the dumps.'

'Mr Mahfouz,' I said, 'since my days as a dramaturge came to a premature end, I have earned my wages at the Institute of Translation. It is my punishment for failure.'

'Forgive me, Mr Wassef,' said Mahfouz, interrupting my flow, 'but you are forgetting that I was a civil servant for thirty-seven years.'

'That was different; you are a genius, you had your self-respect,' I explained. 'Besides, I doubt that you were ever subjected to the humiliations that are my daily bread. For instance, were you ever plucked from your desk and sub-contracted to another ministry? Turned from an academic drone into something even worse . . . a dogsbody?'

'What has occasioned this alarming metamorphosis?' asked Shafik.

'Don't you read your own paper?' I cried. 'Don't you know that next week our city will be hosting the UN conference on population? Fifteen thousand delegates are expected from all over the world. Meanwhile, our compatriots in the *Gema'a Islamiya* have threatened to slaughter the lot. If any actually turn up, they will require assistance. And I have been conscripted. Officially I am listed as an interpreter, but unofficially I am expected to be a guide and escort as required.' I sipped my bitter coffee. 'No overtime will be paid, of that you can be sure.'

'Now I remember!' exclaimed Shafik, banging the table. 'This is the conference that has attracted the attention of a world-

221

famous beauty, a *belle dame sans pareil.*' He plucked a piece of Turkish delight from a blue-and-white bowl and popped it in his mouth, dusting his lips with white sugar. 'My beloved Barbarella, better known as Jane Fonda of Hollywood,' he said, smacking his chops. 'What are you bellyaching about, you miserable fellow? There is not a man in Cairo who would not gladly swap places with you, myself included.'

'You inhabit a fantasy world,' I replied. 'I have as much chance of meeting her as I have of being the first man on Mars.'

'*Carpe diem,*' advised Shafik, already calculating his own prospects.

Instead of Jane Fonda, I am awaiting a woman who thinks I am a fool. At 11.45, the passengers on the Air Sinai flight from Tel Aviv begin to appear at passport control. I recognize her at once. She is of medium height, sports a beret, a white T-shirt, tight blue jeans and has—this is conclusive—a little Toshiba swaying from a shoulder-strap. She sees my pennant with her name upon it and nods. I approach her, bowing and smiling like a carpet-seller. 'The lady with the laptop, I presume.'

She doesn't know how to react; is this mockery, or typical Egyptian hospitality? Later, I compound the confusion by requesting permission to park the minibus outside the airport mosque in order to recite the midday mantra. She looks at me in surprise. I am wearing a suit and tie. Is this a disguise? Has she fallen into the hands of a Muslim fundamentalist in mufti? She knows the mosque is swarming with fanatics who would drive her people into the sea, but she has a liberal heart and believes in religious freedom. 'Please,' she says, 'I have no wish to stand between you and your god.' To tell you the truth, I have not prayed for years. I am doing so today only in order to embarrass the Jewess.

Actually, it is far worse than she imagines. Even I am taken aback by the imam's smouldering ire. He prefaces his remarks with a pun: not *population*, but *copulation*. It is a pun, but it is not a joke. He consigns the conference and all its participants to the pit. 'A terrible punishment awaits us if the conference proceeds,' he wails. 'A plague will fall upon the land; there will be tempests, torrents and thunderbolts. Cars will be washed into the sea, planes will fall from the sky, trains will topple from their tracks. The fuel will spill and ignite, and our rivers will flow with fire. I see villages engulfed. I see the charred bodies of donkeys, goats and dogs. I hear the screams of the doomed as they are boiled alive in the steaming mud. I hear the survivors cry, "There is only one God!" as they seek refuge in the mosque. It will truly be a Day of Judgement.'

'Stirring stuff,' comments my wife's cousin Samir, who sports a white robe that shines as if it were laundered in paradise. I regard my fellow worshippers bobbing up and down like dabbling ducks as they conclude their prayers and wonder if I don't have more in common with my enemy in the Toyota.

'It's like Fort Apache,' says the lady with the laptop as we enter the heavily guarded atrium of the Rameses Hilton. Yes and no. There are certainly scores of policemen in evidence, but they are mostly unarmed. This is probably a sensible precaution. Many are illiterate boys from the country who more likely than not support *Gema'a Islamiya* and wouldn't know whether to shoot the delegates or save them. The deputies themselves are a motley assembly. Looking around, it seems that all of them are trying to register simultaneously. Fortunately, I recognize the receptionist. It is my cousin Walid. We greet one another. 'This lady is my responsibility,' I say, handing him a few pounds. 'Please find her a nice room at once.' As it happens, the room does overlook the river. However, it is not yet ready. I have no alternative; I must invite the Israeli into the lounge for a coffee.

The place is full of fat cats from Saudi who fly north every August to enjoy the illicit pleasures of a laxer society. They drink, they gamble, they fornicate and they examine my companion from head to toe as she crosses the room. We find a quiet table in a corner, beneath a vainglorious relief chipped from an obscure tomb in the Valley of the Kings. A waitress brings our order on a large tray. My companion raises the steaming cup to her lips.

'What do you think of Cairo?' I enquire.

'It gives me a buzz,' she replies. 'Its arteries may be European, but its heart is Arab.' She means it as a compliment, of course, but I decide to take it otherwise, to punish her for her patronizing manner.

'You mean we're picturesque,' I snap. 'An exotic novelty to pep up the jaded appetites of the pan-Americans?'

'I'm not an American,' she says, 'I'm an Israeli.'

'Is there a difference?' I say.

'Why do you keep up the pretence that we don't exist?' she asks. 'After the peace treaty was signed, we flocked across the border like Joseph and his brothers. We wanted to find out all we could about our once and future neighbours. That was fifteen years ago. It's still one-way traffic. Why? Aren't you the least bit curious about us?'

'To be honest, we are not,' I reply. 'I know you find this lack of curiosity incomprehensible, thinking yourselves so fascinating, but to us, you are upstarts, not really worth our attention.'

'In that case, Mr Wassef,' she says, smiling, 'you probably don't want to hear what one of our finest playwrights thought of *Mourning Becomes Electrolux.*'

Despite my better judgement, my undernourished ego lurches for the bait like a starving salmon. 'You mean you've heard of my play,' I gasp, 'in Israel?'

'Sure,' she says, beginning to reel me in. 'Our home-grown Ionesco came here a few years ago. He's an eccentric fellow. Some even call him perverse. In my opinion, they have a point. Did he visit the pyramids or King Tut's treasure? Not him! All he wanted to go to was an abattoir—don't ask me why—and the theatre. He saw half a dozen plays and hated them all. Save one.'

'Mine?' I ask.

'Yours,' she replies. 'In his judgement, it has the potential to be a great movie. He called you the new Buñuel.'

The movies! The Jews know how to do two things well: they know how to complain, and they know how to make films. Perhaps there is hope for me, after all. I imagine coming home, a million-dollar contract in my hands, able to impress my wife at last. My wife is a dreadful snob. We married while still at the university, when it seemed that I had unlimited prospects. We had two boys in rapid succession, who now attend a German-run boarding-school. It costs a fortune to keep them there, but they show me no gratitude. Nor does my wife. She constantly belittles me. I tell her we would have more money if we sent our kids to an ordinary school. She won't hear of it. 'We are poor because you are a failure,' she says, 'not because our children are receiving a good education.' Is it any wonder that I spend most of my time out of the house: at work, or in the cafés with Shafik and his cronies, discussing the three els—literature, life and love.

Once, during my fifteen minutes of glory, I was invited to the United States, to the famous Writers' Workshop at the University of Iowa. It was there that I met my first Israeli, the celebrated Palestinian writer Anton Shammas. But that is not why I mention my trip. No, I want to tell you about my excursion to Yellowstone, where I went with my wife and our two babies. Driving through the park in a rented limo, we suddenly came across a crowd of people, all reverently staring in the same direction. Naturally, we were curious. We stopped the car, and the host of good people, seeing the babes in our arms, parted to let us through. And then we saw the object of their adoration: not the Virgin Mary, but a moose. The great beast continued to drink obliviously from the silver stream.

Well, the same atmosphere of profound wonderment suddenly falls upon the vast lounge of the Rameses Hilton. All eyes—Saudi eyes, Egyptian eyes, Yankee eyes, French eyes, sub-Saharan eyes, Chinese eyes—are turned towards a figure that has just emerged from the undergrowth of extras. It is a celebrity. It is Jane Fonda.

She walks through the room as if unaware of the stares that are accompanying her. What panache! And then, as she passes me, our eyes meet. She registers my existence. It is not exactly a miracle, more a reward—my reward for attending midday prayers. I smile at the future star of *Mourning Becomes Electrolux*, but she is gone.

While we are still transfixed by this spectacle, another beautiful woman enters our field of vision. She is an Egyptian, dressed from top to toe in black. Her tight chador is spun from black silk, and her headpiece is a black turban. Only her eyes are visible. The lids are darkened with kohl, which emphasizes the supernatural translucence of her irises. She moves with the grace of a cheetah and is—sacrilege—sexier than Jane Fonda herself.

She is escorted by a handsome young fellow, exquisitely dressed
in the sort of clothes that you ask for by name. I recognize them
as such, even if the names themselves are unknown to a poor
Egyptian scribe. He is obviously wealthy but also, I am glad to
note, beginning to grow fat. In the years to come, he will surely
lose the ability to contain her wildness.

'She's a real beauty,' whispers the Israeli.

'You are not unattractive yourself,' I reply, obviously
inebriated by the moment.

'Tell me, Mr Wassef,' says the Israeli, ignoring my remark,
'do you think she is circumcised?'

'There are three types of female circumcision,' asserts Aziza
Hussein, the notorious president of the Cairo Family
Planning Association. 'First, there is the slight cut; second, the
cut that removes part of the girl's clitoris; and third, the worst of
them all, the pharaonic cuts in which all the girl's genital organs
are excised. The operation is usually performed by the village
barber without the benefit of anaesthetic. His tools are the tools
of his trade: scissors and razor. This assumes that the girl is
lucky; most have the misfortune to be worked upon with broken
glass or a slice of tin.' The assorted harpies—black harpies,
yellow harpies, red harpies, white harpies, but all harpies—shake
their heads in horror. Oh, the pity of it! Their collective self-
righteousness fills the room like a bad odour.

'It is estimated that thirty per cent of the girls who suffer
complications are left to die of so-called heart attacks,' continues
Dr Aziza. 'When I ask mothers why they do this to their
daughters, they tell me: "It is tradition." And it is. A shameful
tradition that predates Islam. It survives because parents still
believe that circumcision will protect a girl's virginity, dampen
her libido, stop her running after men. Deep down, they are
convinced that no decent Egyptian will marry a girl who is not
circumcised. The tragedy is that the effects do not wear off after
she is wed; she cannot enjoy sex before marriage, nor does she
take any pleasure in it after.'

How does she know? Has she been speaking to my wife?
Monday has dawned, and I am a reluctant participant in a

seminar sponsored by the Society for the Prevention of Traditional Practices Harmful to Woman and Child. The Israeli woman sits tapping at the keyboard of her little Toshiba, occasionally looking to me for enlightenment when our native tongue is used. What am I to her? Nothing more than a useful adjunct to her machine. As I translate yet another phrase into the lingua franca, I remind myself why it is necessary to go on hating the Israelis. It has little to do with their Jewishness (though that is hardly to their advantage), but everything to do with their espousal—nay, their creation—of the modern world. They are like a bacillus in the body politic, and more and more of our people are being infected, especially the women. Do you really believe that Dr Aziza dreamt up her campaign against female circumcision all on her own? No, it does not smell Egyptian. You can be sure that the poison was first poured into her ear by her liberated sisters from over the border.

'Mr Wassef,' complains the lady with the laptop, 'you are losing concentration. I am missing too many of the contributions from the floor.' Oh, if I had the power I should drive her back across the Suez Canal. In 1973, the Third Army made a glorious assault upon the Israeli bunkers and restored our national pride. Would that I could do the same for our manhood. Instead, I am compelled to listen to this alien propaganda in the heart of our capital. Tell me, how would the Israelis like it if a group of cocksure crusaders suddenly turned up in their country determined to put an end to the age-old practice of male circumcision and set about denouncing the practitioners as barbaric baby-mutilators or worse? Well, we don't like it either.

At the end of the meeting, the local doctors, health-workers and teachers, the do-gooders who enter the middens and the villages to stamp out the abhorrent practice—quislings all—strut upon the stage and receive a standing ovation. Anyone would think they were war heroes. Then there is a great display of hugging, weeping and other sisterly emotion, as well as a mass exchange of *cartes de visites*.

Afterwards, we walk in silence along the corniche and watch the feluccas cross the river. Men and women lean together on the parapets waiting for the sun to sink between the hotels and the

227

palms on the far bank. The air is rosy. It is a time for old-fashioned romance, a mood that is certainly foreign to my narrow-minded companion.

'Mr Wassef,' she says, regarding the Nile in its twilit beauty, 'are there such things as *bateaux mouches* in Cairo?'

'Certainly,' I reply.

'In that case,' she says, 'I'd like to have dinner on one. Can you arrange it for me? Better yet, can you join me?'

I want to tell her what to do with her invitation but then I think: why not? My wife was in a foul mood when I left this morning, her tongue as sharp as horseradish. I am in no great hurry to see her again. So it is to spite my wife, rather than humour the Israeli, that I accede to the latter's request.

D o I need to tell you that the boat is full of tourists? Mainly ubiquitous Saudis and emigrés from America who have made their pile and want the suckers in the old country to know it. They prance around in their grave goods: gold chains about their necks and chunky bejewelled rings on their fingers, like tiny quoits of silver. The women are even more vulgar, and their children are inevitably overweight. The *Topaz* is truly a ship of fools; a ship whose only cargo is kitsch.

On a platform in the dining-room, a group of musicians in Hawaiian shirts are playing tunes that make me want to block my ears with beeswax. Why has the Israeli chosen this, of all places, to dine? Can it be that she wishes to humiliate me still further? To rub my nose in this gross parody of Egyptian-ness?

A waiter approaches our table and asks if we require anything to drink. 'Of course,' says the Israeli.

'Bring us a bottle of Cru des Ptolémées,' I say, 'the Pinot Blanc for preference.'

Meanwhile, we pile our plates with provisions from the buffet, scooping up mounds of humus, tahina, aubergine, wild rice, fish and more. The outlandish guitarists disappear to be replaced by local boys. We fill our bellies and befuddle our brains with an excess of food and wine. And all the while, the ship glides down the Nile, the moving buckle on a girdle of light. To my astonishment, I realize that I am beginning to enjoy myself.

Then the drumbeats grow more insistent, and a whirling dervish makes his entrance. He is dressed all in white, save for his skirts, which are as brightly coloured as a spinning-top. He rotates for thirty minutes, as if perpetual motion were his natural state. Slightly green, he staggers below stairs to be replaced by a belly-dancer, who comes wriggling out in a sequin-studded brassière and transparent pantaloons. 'Behold, the latter-day Eve,' says the woman from Israel, 'who knows but one thing: how to move provocatively. Whereas her counterpart, the latter-day Adam, is mobility personified. The first is a prisoner, the second is a free man.'

'Come, come,' I say, 'this is merely a floor show. Don't you think you are taking it a bit too seriously?'

At which point, the Israeli shatters the mood completely by gathering up her laptop and crying: 'Do you want me to show you the figures? For too long women have been denied the same rights and opportunities as men, with devastating consequences to our health and well-being. That injustice is the real reason for our presence in Cairo—gender equality, nay the *empowerment* of women!' Why can't she behave like a date? Why is she so determined to politicize everything, including belly-dancing?

Besides, she is completely wrong. Women in need of empowerment? Not in Cairo, nor in Jerusalem, I'll venture. Just watch the belly-dancer as she swerves from table to table. See how the cowed men grab their wives lest she plucks them from their chairs and forces them to perform publicly with her. Tell me, who is in the ascendancy here? The drums are now pounding faster and faster, and the dancer's hips are playing push-me-pull-you. She is so close I can hear her rapid breathing, feel the warmth of her flesh. She orbits around me like a heavenly body, until her gravitational pull begins to shift me in my seat. I am being sucked unwillingly into the maw of her dance.

For some reason, our struggle has claimed the attention of the entire room, which now fills with yells of encouragement. I sense that my resistance is at an end, that I will be lifted from my place by an all-conquering force. What is one more humiliation in an age of humiliations? I prepare to bow to the inevitable. At which point the Israeli also rises and says: 'Leave him, I'll dance with you instead.' The crowd don't care; any victim will suffice.

They clap on the beat as the Israeli starts to sway to the sinuous rhythms. Soon, the music is dictating all her movements, as though her will were nothing but a metronome. She is possessed by the music, by the siren sounds of Cairo, and spontaneously raises her T-shirt to expose her belly-button, which contains no jewel save a glittering droplet of sweat. For a few delirious moments, I become convinced that she will bare her breasts, and joyously anticipate the shame that sober reflection will bring. Why should I feel gratitude to a prissy madam who is—like all her kind—a slut at heart? By the end, the pair of them—the hypocrite and the object of her scorn—are moving in unison like Siamese twins.

'That wasn't the first time you've done that,' I say accusingly when she resumes her seat.

'I won't deny it,' she replies, gasping for breath. 'I took lessons and sometimes dance at home.'

'So what gives you the right to criticize someone who has no choice but to do it for a living?' I ask.

'For a start,' she replies, 'I was attacking society, not the woman; and second, I studied belly-dancing to facilitate childbirth, not to provoke men.'

This takes me by surprise. I suppose I had assumed that all the women at a conference on population control would at least be childless, if not outright lesbians.

'You have children?' I ask.

'Two,' she replies. 'Two boys aged five and nine.'

'Yet again the practice seems at variance with the preaching,' I say.

'Not at all,' she replies. 'We decided that it would be irresponsible to have more than two children. And so, after the birth of the second, we shut the stable door. My husband had a vasectomy.'

What is there left to say? I simply stare at her in amazement. This Amazon is more dangerous even than I suspected. Egyptian women are bad enough, but they have never yet, so far as I know, demanded the emasculation of their husbands.

Two days later, to Shafik's chagrin, I'm flying down to Luxor with Jane Fonda. To be sure, we are not alone. On the contrary, we are accompanied by the mustachioed Minister of Tourism himself, a gaggle of his grey-suited minions, hotel owners, airline officials, as well as a flamboyant array of local actors (among them the erstwhile star of *Mourning Becomes Electrolux*, who cruelly refuses to acknowledge my presence), not to mention a score or more of the delegates (including Little Miss Sourpuss from Jerusalem). Two air-conditioned coaches, flanked by black-coated outriders, transport us to the Winter Palace Hotel on the bank of the Nile.

A few tourists sit on the veranda, gingerly sipping brightly coloured fruit cordials and poring over maps of upper Egypt in search of unseen treasures. They look up in astonishment as our entourage sweeps past. A flunkey in a chocolate-brown jacket with gold buttons and braid fusses obsequiously around the Minister. It has been a long journey, and Jane Fonda is obviously uncomfortable.

'Hey,' she says to the flunkey, 'where's the restroom round here?'

'You have a choice,' he replies, gliding over the marble floor. 'Here we have the Continental Brasserie, for steak and chips; and, over there, the Oriental Terrace, where more traditional dishes are served.'

'The man is a numskull,' mutters the actress with the distended bladder. I seize my opportunity, almost without premeditation. 'Fool,' I cry, pushing the menial aside. 'Miss Fonda asked for a restroom, not a restaurant. Please,' I say, addressing the prima donna, 'allow me to guide you.'

'Why, thank you,' says Jane Fonda, walking with some haste. I calculate that I have no more than thirty seconds in which to sell my script.

'You may be surprised to learn this,' I say, 'but I am the man who wrote the most successful play of 1988. It ran for fifteen months on Cairo's equivalent of Broadway. The good news is that I have just completed a version for the big screen. A version written with you in mind. What do you say, Miss Fonda? Can I send it to you? Will you read it?' My Omar Sharif eyes

231

brim with tears, ready to overflow at the merest hint of an affirmative. A nod would suffice.

'Send it to my agent,' she replies, before disappearing into the ladies' room. At least she didn't say no.

When I return to the main corpus, I find that a middle-aged Englishman and his young daughter have engaged my Israeli in conversation. The girl is on the cusp of puberty, beauty in bud, but he looks devastated, as though he is convalescing from a heart attack, or worse. 'Tell me,' the man is saying, 'was that really Jane Fonda?'

'I think so,' the Israeli replies, as though a Hollywood star is unworthy of her attention.

'There's no doubt about it,' I say, butting in, 'that was indeed the one and only Jane Fonda.'

'Well I never,' says the Englishman, 'in Luxor of all places.'

'Daddy,' says his daughter, 'can you ask the man to get her autograph?'

'Ask him yourself,' I say, pinching her cheek. 'The man won't bite you.'

We leave the Winter Palace before dawn and troop down to the quayside, where we board a boat that will ferry us across the Nile. The Englishman and his daughter are already on board. They wave to the Israeli, who takes a seat beside them. I settle in behind. They must have continued their conversation after I retired last night, for a rapport has already been established, suggesting that intimacies of some sort have been exchanged.

'I dreamt of my wife last night,' says the Englishman quietly. 'She would have been so excited to be doing this.' He stops, looks around and absent-mindedly strokes his daughter's sun-bleached hair. 'She was a teacher, you know,' he continues, 'of history. I can picture her now, leaning on her desk, telling her kids the story of Howard Carter and the discovery of King Tut's tomb. I can see them, open-mouthed, as she describes how he found the first step, then fifteen more, then the doors, the last one with the unbroken seal. She was a great teacher. Knew how to hold a pause. When the kids could bear it no longer, she'd pretend she was looking through a keyhole and say: "I can see wonderful things.'" I yawn loudly. I have heard it all before. I am more interested in rubbing the sleep from my gummy eyes.

A slight breeze, no more than a warm exhalation, causes the boat's cotton canopy to shiver. In the greater canopy, the night shift is just ending. The full moon is retiring to the west bank, the land of the dead, where it will pack away our dreams and secret desires, the succubi and the incubi, the vampires and the ghosts, for another twelve hours. Meanwhile, the sun is clocking in above Luxor, the city of light, the city of the living, setting fire to the palms and minarets. This celestial exchange is reflected in the immaculate meniscus of the river, which is scattered with chevrons of mercury and flame. A few ibises glide over the surface, disappearing to the south, where the waters widen. The Nile is the heart of our country. More! More! It is the very pivot of the world, the meeting point of night and day, life and death, the quotidian and the dark side of humanity.

My meditation is rudely concluded by the noisy arrival of six black limousines and their attendant guardian angels, all of whom sport halos of blue light and carry Kalashnikovs. Chauffeurs appear and, heads bowed, open doors. Out steps Jane Fonda, followed by lesser luminaries, various ministers, unrecognizable dignitaries and—if my eyes do not deceive me—the president's wife. All ascend the gangplank, like the seraphim in Jacob's dream.

The principals aboard, the overture complete, grimy dark-skinned fellows cast off the ropes, and the boat commences its journey to the other world, on whose shores derelict hovels bask in the reflected glory of the rising sun, their windows glinting with false life.

The Englishman is bowled over by the Valley of the Kings. 'We were slaves in Egypt once,' he says, 'and now we are tourists.'

So he is another Jew; merely an ersatz Englander, a bit like me. The Israeli laughs. She, too, is impressed. What Jane Fonda makes of it, I cannot say. I glimpse her only in the distance, shielded from the elements (and the likes of me) by Japanese umbrellas and muscular bodyguards.

'Mr Wassef,' enquires the Englishman's daughter, 'when will you be getting her autograph?'

Here we stand beneath heaven's hot blue flame, on the outer

rim of a glowing honeycomb, each indentation filled with marvels, and all she can think about is the signature of an animated Barbie doll. I am tempted to slap her for insulting our ancient kingdom.

Wicked man, you will be thinking, hypocrite! Did you not put a greater value on her yea only yesterday? Ah, but that was self-interest, a different matter entirely; it was not Jane Fonda I cared about *per se*, only her power.

It is midday. In the fields, the fellahin loosen their *galabiyas* and watch with rumbling bellies as their wives advance towards them through the swaying rows of *berseem* or sugar cane with bowls of *melokhia* balanced upon their heads. These peasants may not own a bean and be blessed with the intellects of donkeys, but they have loyal women. My wife serve me lunch? I'm lucky if she throws it at me. As it happens, we are offered the self-same soup for our midday meal, though in somewhat different surroundings, and by waiters who do not carry the tureens on their heads.

The dusty plain that stands before the cliff-side temple of Hatshepsut is normally the province of the Polish National Academy of Sciences, but today it has been annexed by the Ministry of Tourism. Huge marquees, hundreds of metres in length, have been erected to provide shelter from the infernal sun. More discreet pavilions service baser requirements. Within the former, I feel like one of Pharaoh's charioteers who, having failed to catch Moses, finds himself at the bottom of the Red Sea. Here, sunshine is transformed by sumptuously coloured appliqués into cooling showers of saturated light that stain the face or fall straight upon the ochre ground, until it seems awash with red, yellow, blue and magenta. On either side, the banks of food swell and rise like coral reefs. Of course, there are fish; *samak Moussa* or sole, *loukoz* and *Sultan Ibrahim*, fried with *cousbareia* sauce.

It has become customary to serve *melokhia* at the start of such banquets because it is so unambiguously Egyptian; its unique mixture of indigenous leaf, garlic, oil and stock being deemed admirably patriotic. This version, being for the rich, is beefed up with fried minced meat and chicken balls.

After that, we are faced with a veritable wall of poultry and game. There is chicken with vinegar; chicken with pomegranate sauce; chicken with rhubarb; chicken with quinces; chicken with plum jelly; chicken with mulberries; chicken with chick peas, onion and cinnamon. There are fowls in sweet stew: with *fistakiyyeh* or pistachios, with *wardiyeh* or rose-hips, with hazelnuts and julep, or perhaps with purslane, which is called *sott alnoubeh* or the Nubian woman, after its black appearance. Chicken is ubiquitous, chicken is protean. Even the bread is stuffed with chicken. Otherwise there are pigeons and doves bursting with wild rice and pine kernels. After the birds come the eggs, great pyramids of eggs, *hamine* eggs, simmered for six hours with onion skins, until the whites have turned beige and the yolks a creamy yellow. As to vegetables . . . what else but *ful medames*, for is it not said: 'Beans have satisfied even the pharaohs'? They are scooped up with ladles from vast earthenware vessels, buried deep in hot ashes and deposited into pockets of pitta. There are fine wines, cold beers and colas for foreigners to guzzle, while good Muslims can sip rose-water syrup or tamarind juice. Couches and divans are provided for the satiated or the sleepy.

Needless to say, we were forced to read all the classic English texts at St George's: *Lorna Doone*, *Great Expectations*, *Prester John*, *King Solomon's Mines*, *The Children of the New Forest*, *Kim* and *Treasure Island*. Of course, I remember all the plots perfectly, but the only line that still sticks in my mind comes not from any of these, but from a letter Robert Louis Stevenson sent to his mother. 'An opera is far more real than real life to me,' he wrote. 'I wish that life was an opera. I should like to *live* in one.' Hear, hear! Egypt should not be a land of fellahin, haute bourgeoisie and bureaucrats, but a country of fat men and Farouks, of divas and Cleopatras, a place far larger than life, a vast stage dedicated to opera. There are precedents. Didn't the Khedive commission Verdi to write an opera to celebrate the opening of the Suez Canal? And aren't we all here, before the temple of Hatshepsut, waiting for *Aida* to commence? Now you know the truth. It wasn't Jane Fonda who drew me down to Luxor, it was the prospect of seeing my favourite opera. This may sound unconvincing, coming from a dramatist *manqué* with absurdist tendencies. All I can tell you is that my interest in the avant-garde was like love on the rebound; if I couldn't have my prima donna I wouldn't settle for a chorus girl, so I went to the other extreme and courted Miss Anorexia instead.

Spears of light pick out the colonnades of the temple and the reliefs carved on the walls within. The conductor takes his bow, the orchestra springs to life, a mighty crescendo shakes the desert floor, thereby—or so it seems—reanimating the ancient figures inside the temple. Anyway, people emerge slowly from between the columns, as if newly summoned from a millennial slumber. Five hundred singers and dancers, all dressed in the manner of the ancients, perhaps the very courtiers and soldiers who accompanied Queen Hatshepsut on her famous expedition to Punt. And surely that overweight mezzo-soprano is none other than the grotesquely fat wife of the local chieftain they found there. I sit spellbound and weep at the end when Aida and Radames (played by my friend—well, Shafik's friend—Hassan Kamy) sing their final duet, having been buried alive in a crypt by heartless priests. I observe that I am not the only one moved to tears as the great lament suffuses the night.

> *O terra, addio; addio, valle di pianti . . .*
> *Sogno di gaudio che in dolor svani*
> *Ah! noi si schiude il ciel e l'alme erranti*
> *Volano al raggio dell'eterno di.*

Oh Earth, farewell; farewell vale of tears . . .
Dream of joy which vanished into sorrow.
Heaven opens towards us, and our wandering souls
Fly fast towards the light of eternal day.

The Englishman is hugging his daughter. Both are crying.

Before the last tear has dried, the air is filled with a new noise, accompanied by an artificial wind which causes our shirts to billow and our curls to unfurl. Helicopters are circling overhead, stirring the fields of sugar cane with spatulas of light. You don't need to be head of the *Mukhabarat* to guess who they are looking for. *Aida* was produced in such an extravagant manner to persuade tourists that Upper Egypt is perfectly safe, so it would be a source of great embarrassment if a member of *Gema'a Islamiya* were suddenly to pop up from the greensward and assassinate Jane Fonda or any other guest. 'We've got to fight these so-called fundamentalists,' booms the Minister of Tourism, as we return intact to the east bank, to the land of the living. 'We can't let them destroy our economy.'

'**M**r Wassef, would you do me a great favour?' asks the lady with the laptop as we dip our croissants in morning coffee at the Winter Palace Hotel. 'The Englishman and his daughter intend to revisit the Valley of the Kings this morning. They have asked me to accompany them. I should like to go, but I am afraid that my acceptance will be wrongly interpreted. "Yesterday was for my wife," he said, "but today is for me." What do you think he meant by that, Mr Wassef?'

'I really don't know,' I say, slicing a fig, 'but I have heard that the bereaved often spout nonsense.'

'Perhaps you are right,' she replies, 'but I fear that I may have raised false expectations in him, which I have no intention of realizing. Anyway, Mr Wassef, I should be terribly grateful if you could help me out by coming along. Your very presence will be sufficient to short-circuit any embarrassing incidents.'

'As it happens my wife's uncle owns the Memnon Papyrus Museum across the river,' I say. 'He has produced some wall-hangings for my two boys which are, by his own account, absolute masterpieces. Being a conscientious father, I promised to collect them if the opportunity arose.' I take a spoonful of yoghurt. 'Apparently it has. Should you and your companions also stop there briefly and even make a few purchases—you can have your name written in hieroglyphics while you wait—I shall definitely find myself in my wife's good books when I return home.'

'You surprise me, Mr Wassef,' says the lady with the laptop, 'I really didn't see you as a family man.'

'If you will excuse me,' I say, rising from the table, 'I must make a telephone call. To alert my wife's uncle of our imminent arrival.'

The Englishman does indeed seem disappointed by my

presence, but he hides it well. Like me, he has been taught to dissemble by masters. His daughter, however, is unable to conceal her pique when I confess that I have not yet been able to obtain Jane Fonda's autograph. We are ambling along the corniche in the direction of the ferry. The sun has long since risen, and the river, a dazzling blue, seems to be spawning phosphorescent fish. A witches' brew of diesel and dung drifts over from the boulevard, sweetened *en route* by oleander, frangipani and jacaranda. The road is busy but uncannily quiet. Phaetons pulled by starving nags move slowly, mechanically, like half-wound clockwork toys. Even the cars seem to be drifting in dreamy slow motion. Rich tourists in crumpled linen suits and cotton frocks clutch their bottles of mineral water and mop their brows with spotted handkerchiefs, while local greybeards slump on benches beneath the palms like basking seals. Everyone seems overcome by lassitude, as though battling with the heat has worn them out. 'You know what,' says the Englishman, 'Luxor reminds me of Yalta or somewhere like it. Not that I've been there,' he adds. 'But I have read Chekhov.' That man again! Why can't anyone view our country through Egyptian eyes?

'Chekhov?' says his daughter. 'Isn't he that silly character in *Star Trek?*'

'I suspect your daddy's thinking of a different Chekhov,' I say, looking at the Israeli, 'a Russian writer who wrote some world-famous stories.'

Our driver is waiting for us on the opposite bank. I explain that there has been a slight change of plan. He shrugs. What's it to him? We set off in the direction of the Theban Hills. Within minutes, we have reached our first destination, the Colossi of Memnon: monstrous survivors from antiquity, who sit there like diners in a deserted restaurant, their gargantuan appetites forever unsatisfied. The driver steers the minibus into the car park. An elderly policeman with a huge moustache and the bearing of a sergeant-major leans against the window and extracts some baksheesh. 'According to Strabo, the northern colossus used to emit a soft, bell-like sound at dawn,' says the Englishman. 'The Greeks thought it was in mourning.'

'For what?' asks his daughter.

'For life, I suppose,' he replies. The man is obsessed!

The Israeli picks up her laptop, hoists it on her shoulder, then freezes like a wild animal that has been startled. 'What's that noise?' she asks. A good question! If it were winter, I'd say that hailstones were falling on the bus, but it is August, and there is not a cloud in the sky. Before I can produce an alternative hypothesis, the windscreen disintegrates, showering us with shards of glass. The little girl screams.

'Down!' cries the policeman. 'Everyone down on the floor.' He rolls under the bus. I look out of the window and observe three men in white robes running towards us across a brilliant green field of *berseem*. They are howling like berserkers and, far worse, brandishing Kalashnikovs.

I am mystified by my response, which is completely out of character. I do not run for my life. Instead, as the bullets begin to tear into the side of the vehicle, I instinctively fling myself upon the Israeli woman, interceding between her and mortal danger. Don't ask me why! Perhaps I am inspired by the Englishman, who is all but smothering his daughter. Or perhaps I am simply performing what man has been programmed to do in such circumstances. We dare not move; we hardly dare breathe; we feel as vulnerable as ears of wheat when the locusts come. In fact, I am still covering the lady with the laptop when the cop opens the door and announces that the would-be assassins have vanished.

'Is everyone all right?' he enquires.

I help the Israeli to her feet. She is unscathed, but there are two neat holes in her Toshiba. The machine dies quietly. No flashes as it reverts to its inanimate state, no hissing as the memory absconds. 'I have lost everything,' she wails, hugging the machine, 'every word I have written since I arrived in Egypt. My notes? Gone! My statistics? Gone! My new ideas? Gone! My . . . '

She is about to continue her lamentation when she sees the sight that has rendered the rest of us speechless. The Englishman is holding his daughter in his arms. A splinter of glass, the size of a playing card, is embedded in her forehead. Her face is white, save for a contour line of red around the wound, which looks like a mouth with a transparent tongue vulgarly on show.

'Oh, I must have done something terrible to deserve this,'

wails her father, 'but for the life of me, I cannot think what. After the funeral, my comforters assured me that the worst was over, but I knew better. I had the feeling that something like this would happen. I sensed that He was still holding my daughter hostage. I could almost hear him say, "One false move, and the kid gets it!"'

'Who are you talking about?' I say.

'God, of course,' he says, 'my enemy.'

'No,' I say, 'neither Jehovah nor Allah, but the latter's self-appointed agents on earth. In other words, some gentlemen from *Gema'a Islamiya.*'

Meanwhile, the Israeli raises the erstwhile laptop above her head and hurls it through the broken window, as Moses once cast aside the Ten Commandments. I note that her armpits are smooth and hairless. Ah, so she is not ideologically pure after all. Red with shame, she approaches the Englishman and his melancholy burden. 'I don't know what to say,' she mumbles, touching his arm.

He stands immobile, like some modern-day *pietà*. 'She's gone for ever,' he whispers, 'as dead as earth.'

The Israeli stares down at the girl's face. 'You're wrong!' she cries. 'She is not dead! She is in shock, for sure. But she is not dead. Look at the glass.' Sure enough, small beads of condensation trickle down its underside, as miraculous as the tears of the Virgin.

'If only you are right,' says the Englishman, 'then all my sorrows may yet be redeemed.'

The entire staff of the Memnon Papyrus Museum are lined up on the porch, my wife's uncle to the forefront. 'Do not worry!' he yells as, led by the driver, we stumble from the wreckage into the uncanny stillness of an otherwise ordinary day. 'Do not worry! I have informed the authorities. Help is already on the way.' Then he recognizes me and can barely contain his amazement. 'Yonnan, is it you?' he cries. 'Why are you here and not in Cairo?' He clasps a hand to his forehead. 'Allah protect me!' he moans, 'the boy has brought bad news.' He is an old man, his memory is not what it was. I remind him that I have come, as arranged, to collect the gifts for my sons. 'Of course,' he mutters. Still looking perplexed, he hugs me. 'Such a terrible thing, Yonnan,' he wails, 'and that it should happen outside my shop.'

The police also regard the incident as tactless, if not downright inconsiderate, coming so soon after *Aida*'s opening night. And, in the absence of the actual perpetrators, they are inclined to hold us responsible. 'Why did you not inform the local police of this excursion?' asks an officer accusingly. 'They would have ensured your safety. If you had only told them in advance, this poor girl would still be in the pink.' The aforementioned victim is surrounded by young men in dirty *galabiya*s, each of whom seems determined to pluck the splinter from her skull, as if she were the afflicted heroine of some fairy story and her father a rich king committed to rewarding the man who first awakens her. Anyway, the general consensus is that the glass should be removed as quickly as possible. The Englishman, however, has the casting vote. 'Let her be,' he commands, holding her tightly to his chest, 'the doctors will decide.'

It takes fifteen minutes for a helicopter to remove us from the land of the dead and deliver us to the halfway house they call the Luxor Hospital for Fevers. I can feel the Englishman's confidence in the local medicos begin to waver as soon as he sees the crudely painted sign at the hospital's entrance. It disappears altogether when we enter the building proper. This is no place for the living; it is limbo-land, and its inhabitants are the moribund and their lachrymose acolytes.

The hot and stinking corridor is chock-a-block with the latter; keening women in shabby burnouses. The Englishman sidesteps them with a finesse I haven't seen since I played rugger at St George's. Actually, he has no choice, given that he has chosen to keep pace with his daughter, now supine on a trolley, hanging on to her limp hand while a pair of scruffy porters wheel her at breakneck speed in the direction of the X-ray room. The purpose of the X-ray is to define the damage, to discern how deeply the glass has penetrated the brain. The question is this: are we now looking at the whole iceberg, or merely its tip?

If you have ever had the misfortune to travel with the lower classes on an Egyptian train, you will be familiar with the waiting-room. The place is filthy, the air foul. Crumpled packets of cigarettes litter the floor. Glasses of sweet tea stand half-finished on scratched tabletops. Some have been there so long, judging by the number of drowned flies, they are topped with black foam. Unwashed fellahin snooze horizontally on the benches, while their wives prepare food over little paraffin stoves. Worst of all are the children, verminous little brats who wail or run about like cockroaches. In a matter of moments, I am converted to the cause of population control, to the use of contraceptives, with especial emphasis upon abortion. So why am I still here with the groundlings? Why haven't I returned to my rightful place among the luminaries at the Winter Palace Hotel? What do I care about a foolish little girl whose only ambition in life seems to be the acquisition of Jane Fonda's autograph? What is the matter with me?

'She looks just like my wife,' says the Englishman, 'same fine features, same charming smile. To tell you the truth, when I saw her on the trolley outside the operating theatre, I thought she *was* my wife. I suppose you'd better call it *déjà vu* rather than mistaken identity.' He cannot keep quiet, let alone sit still. 'You see,' he continues, 'I've done all this before. At the beginning of the year—what's that, eight months ago?—I waited six hours while they cut a tumour the size of a tangerine out of my wife. Now it's my daughter's turn. Her doctor is very optimistic. He tells me that I'm not to worry. He assures me—in excellent English—that the X-rays are fine, that the injury is not as bad as it looks, that the glass can be extracted without fear of the consequences. A piece of cake, he calls it. My wife was also offered an excellent prognosis. A sixty per cent chance of a full recovery, which, believe me, is music to the ears of a person with cancer. Sure enough, she recovered well from the surgery. They had her on her feet within days. But shortly afterwards, things started to go wrong. The wound opened and wouldn't stop weeping. Her bowels ceased to function. Her belly distended. And one night, on the commode, she passed out. The nurses panicked. They got her back on the bed and fitted her up with an oxygen mask. That's how I found her; her bald head uncovered, her eyelids fluttering, her skin as white as a hard-boiled egg. The houseman came running—a woman from Hong Kong with all the humanity of a Red Guard; she shooed me away, examined my wife, then asked to see me in her office. "The pulse is strong, the heart is good," she said indifferently. "I don't think she is nearing the end." Dying? Who said anything about dying? My wife was supposed to be getting better, not dying. Later, other doctors succeeded in reassuring me, but I couldn't get those words out of my mind. Indeed, they proved prophetic; that episode turned out to be a dress rehearsal for the real thing. And now history is repeating itself.'

'You sound like one of those sick Jews who believes that it is his destiny to suffer, to be one of history's perennial victims,' snaps the Israeli. 'But I am here to tell you that it need not be so. Your wife died, and I sympathize. But it doesn't follow that your daughter will too.'

'I'm sorry if I'm letting the side down,' says the Englishman, 'but I wonder how rational you'd be if it was your daughter in there.'

'Point taken,' says the Israeli. 'In fact, my husband's probably going haywire right now if he's heard news of the attack and had no reassuring word from me on e-mail. You probably didn't notice, but my laptop was the other casualty of the attack.' She lowers her voice and addresses me in a manner that, in other circumstances, would be described as intimate. 'I'd telephone him,' she whispers, 'but I think my place is here for the moment. Just in case I'm wrong.'

'Give me the number,' I say, 'and I'll have my office contact him immediately.' She scribbles some figures on a scrap of paper which she hands to me. I pocket it and depart in search of a phone. When I return, she is all alone.

'Someone in a white coat appeared and led the Englishman away,' she explains.

'Tell me,' says my friend Shafik, lounging on a divan at the brand-new Café de Luxe, 'how was Luxor? Did you meet Jane Fonda?' He toys with some marzipan. 'Did you screw her? Come on, Yonnan, spill the beans.'

'Are you teasing me, Shafik?' I say. 'Or are you really an

ostrich? Surely there were a few lines in *Al-Ahram* about the ambush.'

'Not a dicky-bird, old chap,' he replies. 'According to our ace reporters, everything was as smooth as silk, not so much as a single shot fired in anger.'

I shrug. Obviously, the authorities, in their wisdom, decided that such a minor fracas, nothing more than an 'isolated incident', was hardly worth mentioning to the press. I am about to enlighten Shafik when a waiter approaches our table and won't go away. 'What does he want?' I ask. 'Don't worry he's not with the *Mukhabarat*,' laughs Shafik. So I commence my narrative.

Meanwhile, the dextrous waiter drops a lump of wax into a coffee-pot, which he places on a portable stove. 'That's the ambergris,' says Shafik. 'When it is melted, he will pour in the coffee. Then he will fumigate our cups with smouldering embers of mastic.'

'Anyway,' I say, 'the girl survived the operation. Afterwards, her father was very keen to fly her back to England, or even Israel, but the British Consul insisted that there were cheaper options. "The private hospitals in Cairo are perfectly adequate," he said. In the end, she was transferred to the El Fayrouz Clinic in Giza. For some reason, I chose to accompany the Englishman and the Israeli when they moved the girl, perhaps because I was in no hurry to return home. The girl travelled in an ambulance, of course. We shared a taxi. The driver took us the long way, over the Sixth of October Bridge. Did he do it maliciously, knowing that one of his passengers was an Israeli? If so, he hit the wrong target. The Englishman, not the Israeli, reacted. "The sixth of October 1973, that's a day I'll never forget," he mused. "In the afternoon, a friend comes running around—have I heard the news? The Egyptians have crossed the Suez Canal. The Syrians are swarming over the Golan Heights. The situation is desperate. A few moments later, the phone rings. A woman friend. She is at a party in York. Would I like to join her? It's Yom Kippur, I'm in London and I'm worried about Israel's survival, but I say yes. Yes! Yes! As soon as the fast ends, I shoot up the motorway. I arrive in York just before midnight. She is clearly pleased to see me. We embrace. We talk. Hold hands. Kiss. Smoke marijuana.

And make love. To you, this bridge may commemorate a war, but for me, it is a reminder of the first time I made love to my wife." Poor fellow! The whole world is a memorandum that his beloved once existed and that he has lost her.'

'What a story!' exclaims Shafik. 'Does it have a happy ending? Will the girl recover? Will the hero get his proper reward? I trust that the lady in question has already demonstrated her gratitude.'

'The girl is still unconscious,' I reply, 'but not in a coma, the doctors insist, just deeply asleep. As for the Israeli, she hasn't even said thank you.'

'The ungrateful bitch,' says Shafik.

At last, the waiter departs. Shafik sips the fragrant brew. 'Apparently, the owner went to Japan and fell in love with the tea ceremony they have over there,' he explains. 'Upon returning, she resolved to establish an equivalent in Egypt. What do you think?'

'The tourists will love it,' I say, 'but I cannot see Naguib Mahfouz becoming a regular.'

Now it is Shafik's turn to surprise me. 'Haven't you heard?' he says, putting down his coffee-cup. 'Mahfouz is in hospital.'

'Since when?' I say.

'Since yesterday,' replies Shafik. 'He was walking home from one of his haunts when he was accosted by a group of fanatics, one of whom stabbed him in the neck.'

The news shocks me more than the attempt on my own life (which had the merit of being impersonal). What sort of country is it if our greatest writer cannot walk the streets in safety? Maybe the Israeli was right when she said that the war was no longer between Jew and Arab, but between progressives and fundamentalists.

The conference ends, and the delegates pack their bags. I return to my post at the Institute of Translation. I am there, slouched over my desk, when the Israeli unexpectedly telephones. Needless to say, we do not have individual receivers, so it is our taskmaster who takes the call. 'Keep it brief,' he hisses.

'Good news,' says the Israeli. 'The girl has woken up.'

245

'Wonderful,' I say (and, what's more, I mean it).
'She is asking for you,' continues the Israeli.
'For me?' I say.
'Yes,' comes the reply. 'She wants to know whether you managed to obtain Jane Fonda's autograph.'
'It was the last thing on my mind,' I say.
'No matter,' says the Israeli. 'I have a plan.'

The co-conspirators meet at lunchtime in the lobby of the El Fayrouz Clinic, mingling with its 152 resident professors and consultants. 'What do you think of this?' asks the Israeli. She hands me a piece of card. Written on it are the words: TO A BRAVE LITTLE GIRL, WITH LOVE FROM YOUR FRIEND, JANE FONDA.
'You are a genius,' I cry. 'How did you get it?'
'Well,' says the Israeli, looking pleased with herself, 'I remembered that Jane Fonda had sent a letter of solidarity to every delegate at the conference. So it was just a matter of unearthing the original and copying the signature.' She places the two side by side.
'Brilliant,' I say. 'Even Jane Fonda couldn't tell them apart.'
Nor, Allah be praised, can the girl. 'Mr Wassef,' she says, 'how can I thank you?'
'By getting better,' I say, kissing the plaster on her forehead, 'and by remembering that many more Egyptians wished you well than did you harm.' The Englishman beams and shakes my hand.
'That girl made me ashamed,' says the Israeli as we step out on to Gamal Salem Street. 'She sheds tears of gratitude for a forgery, while I haven't even thanked you properly for a genuine act of courage. It is possible that you saved my life, Mr Wassef. The least I can do in return is to buy you dinner at my hotel. Not tonight. Tonight I am dining with the Englishman. Perhaps tomorrow?'

'Yesterday was an extraordinary day,' announces the Israeli as she sips her ice-cold vodka. 'Just before sunset, the Englishman knocked on my door—we have adjoining rooms— and asked if I would care to accompany him to the pyramids. You can see them from our hotel bedrooms, but they are further away than they look. So we took a taxi. It was dusk when we arrived, and all the tourists had departed, but not the guides. "You must have a guide," said one, more persistent than most. "They insist. No entry without. You want camel? You want horse? I give you very quiet horse." We followed obediently, not knowing better. The stables stank of dung. Those horses that were not tethered were being whipped. Everyone had whips. If they had no horses to whip, they whipped the air. Our mounts looked half-starved. "Off you go," commanded their owner, throwing stones at their flanks, "tally ho!" They trotted up the hill, wheezing like asthmatics. We felt guilty to be adding to their burdens.' She finishes her vodka and orders another. I ask for a whisky. The Israeli looks at me quizzically. 'So you are not such a good Muslim after all,' she says. 'The flesh is weak,' I reply, 'especially if the spirit is strong.'

'The whole place now belonged to the locals,' she continues. 'Wild youths galloped their emaciated nags across the dunes, while their elders led the camels to wherever camels go at night. First the sky was pink, then pale blue, then a darker blue, as if the heavens were slowly freezing over. Whole families unrolled rugs and squatted at the base of the pyramids, where they prepared and ate their supper. What can I say? It was a magnificent sight. It stirred my blood. The Englishman, however, was very quiet. "A penny for your thoughts," I said. "I was thinking about the last time I kissed my wife," he said. I leaned across and patted his thigh, which was the best I could do in the circumstances. Actually I wanted to hug the poor man, to restore him to the present, so that he too could partake of the extraordinary atmosphere. But he was lost in some distant cancer ward.

'"It was the last Friday of her life," he said. "By then, the pain had become unbearable, and she was sedated most of the time. Not exactly asleep, but not entirely conscious either. On that day, alarming new symptoms began to appear. She became paranoid, imagined that everyone in the ward was plotting against her. She got angry if I tried to speak. 'Hush,' she would say, 'can't you see I'm listening?' Things got worse very rapidly. She began talking to herself. Nonsense, gibberish. Even more upsetting was the look of terror that haunted her eyes. You are familiar with the phrase, scared out of her wits? Well, I was looking at its personification. Hitherto, I had always been able to calm her, but not that Friday. She had moved beyond my reach. So she lay there in her bed, a living skeleton with a quivering jaw and horror-struck eyes, obsessively rolling the sheet between her fingers. Then suddenly, just as I was about to withdraw, she puckered her lips and, curling her arm around my neck, pulled my face towards hers. It was our last living embrace." He paused and peeped at my face, as if he were checking upon the effectiveness of his words, to see whether a few more touches were required to bring tears to my eyes—which, as it happens, were dry.

'"She died the following Wednesday," he continued, "having lapsed into a coma during the weekend. As usual, I took our daughter to see her after school. I can still hear her anguished yelp as she leant over the bed, 'Look at Mummy's hands!'

'"A nurse told us that her circulation was beginning to break down. In desperation, my little girl grabbed her mother's hands and began to rub them between her own. Sure enough, the purple blotches disappeared, and their proper pigment was restored. But they wouldn't stay pink for long. So she rubbed them again and refused to stop. My wife, of course, was completely oblivious to this life-and-death struggle. Her eyes were open, but they saw nothing. I couldn't let it continue. Come, I said, gently pulling my daughter away, let's go to the cafeteria—I'll buy you a Coke. When we returned, a few minutes later, the curtains were drawn around my wife's bed." He looked at me again. This time, I was weeping. I couldn't swear to it, but it seemed to me that there was a guilty smirk on his face.'

The Israeli downs her second vodka and orders a third.

'After dinner, we retired to the hotel terrace,' she continues. 'We could see the outlines of the pyramids in the distance, but alas, their spell was broken by a Las Vegas cabaret. The Dreamgirls, shapely women clad only in black waistcoats and fishnet tights, were dancing energetically to recordings such as 'Strangers in the Night' and songs from *Cabaret*. Egypt was put to flight by the razzmatazz, and so were we.

'I awoke in the early hours to see a huge moon, apparently balanced on the apex of the largest pyramid, like the all-seeing eye on the reverse of a dollar bill. I arose like a sleepwalker, pulled on a T-shirt and walked out on to the balcony. The Englishman was already there—perhaps he never went to bed—also moonstruck. The air was warm and full of strange noises—indefinable sounds, among which I recognized only the call of the faithful to prayer, the crowing of cocks, the barking of dogs. "This is magic," I said. The Englishman moved towards me, so that only the low glass partition separated us. "I'd call it gorgeous," he said. His body seemed tense, expectant; his eyes were full of longing. Of course, I knew what he wanted me to do. He wanted me to hook him with my arm, just as his dying wife had done, and kiss him on the mouth. But I could not do it. I am a married woman. At the same time, I was naked beneath my T-shirt and could feel the intimate caresses of the pungent air. If only the Englishman had summoned up the courage and made *aliya* to my balcony, I would have succumbed to his embrace and the night. Instead, we stood silently for an hour or more, not even touching, while the descending moon rolled down the side of the pyramid like a silver ball.

'A few hours later, we had breakfast together. He told me that he had just experienced a terrible nightmare. He had seen Michael Holroyd wearing a black robe like a burnous. In his hand, he held a bloody butcher's knife. "What can it mean?" he asked. I said that first I would have to know this Michael Holroyd. He said that he was a famous British biographer. "Beats me," I said. Can you understand it, Mr Wassef?'

Well, I am only the Egyptian, not Joseph the soothsayer, but even so, I think I can make sense of it. The Englishman feels guilty, as well he might. He sees himself as a biographer, viz. a character assassin. And, like the figure in his dream, who received a fortune for his biography of George Bernard Shaw, he hopes to profit from his act of betrayal. Who is the Englishman betraying? His late wife, naturally. He probably doesn't even realize it himself, except in the realm of dreams, but that's what he is doing. He kids himself that he is a suffering soul, but deep down he knows that he is a calculating bastard. Why, even I would think twice about using the death of my wife as an aid to seducing another woman. 'Beats me, too,' I say.

'Mr Wassef,' says the Israeli, a little tipsily, 'may I ask you another question?'

'Be my guest,' I say.

'We try so hard,' she says. 'We don't expect you to love us, but can't you at least make the effort to like us?'

I am not nick-named El Sayed for nothing. The Englishman may have hesitated at the first hurdle, but tonight I am ready to o'erleap the Suez Canal. 'Shall we take a stroll?' I say.

We are walking in the hotel garden. 'Oh, Mr Wassef,' giggles the Israeli, linking her arm in mine, 'I feel a little light-headed.' I stop, look at her with all the sincerity I can muster and, as if overwhelmed by the night-scented jasmine, embrace her. At first, her body registers surprise, then it slowly relaxes, and her lips part, allowing my tongue the access it desires. Now is the moment of abandonment, the time to speak freely: 'Let's go up to your room,' I say *sotto voce*.

'You must forgive the mess, Mr Wassef,' she says.

'My name is Yonnan,' I say.

'Yonnan,' she echoes, 'Yonnan, Yonnan,' again and again, as though trying to memorize a difficult foreign word. She strokes my cheek. 'Please do not jump to any false conclusions, Yonnan,' she says. 'I have never done anything like this before; I have always been a faithful wife.' She begins to tell me about her marriage, her husband's career, her children and her own job at the university. A familiar litany! It seems that Israeli women are no different from all other women. Counterfeit a little respect, and they are yours!

'For two thousand years or more, Jews everywhere recited the prayer "Next year in Jersualem",' she says, while unbuttoning her blouse. 'Now that seed has come to fruition; we inhabit the city. But it is an earthly city, built not of dreams but of limestone. Do not misunderstand me, Mr Wassef; I think the creation of our state is little short of miraculous. Even so, it is not quite what we had in mind. We are still not at peace with ourselves, let alone our neighbours.' She begins to unclasp her brassière.

'My husband is a good man,' she continues 'albeit, I regret to say, with a blind spot towards the Arabs, and our marriage is a strong one. But it is not quite what I had in mind for myself. I adore my two children. Never doubt that. Should you ever threaten them, Mr Wassef, I would shoot you without hesitation. Yet even they are not quite what I had in mind. I hate myself for it, but if their school reports are less than excellent, if their conversation falls short of sparkling, I am disappointed. Yes, as each day starts with the morning dew, so does disappointment cling to my life. Why am I opening my soul to you, Mr Wassef? Is their something in your character that draws me out? You are handsome and you are charming, but I am a grown woman—a feminist, even—who harbours no secret desire for the Sheikh of Araby.'

Pretending to listen, I walk across the room—it is indeed in a state, underwear and other intimate apparel littering the floor, as though her suitcase were a seed pod that had ripened and burst asunder—and lift a mango from the fruit bowl. Picking up the knife, I cut myself a slice. 'Would you rather that I went?' I enquire.

Never before has anyone given themselves to me so completely, so enthusiastically. The lady with the laptop writhes beneath me, groans, digs her nails into my back, squeals, sweats, and finally, flinging her arms out wide, calls upon her god to witness her transports of delight. Afterwards she says, 'Please don't think badly of me.'

I sigh and kiss her on the breast. 'You were magnificent,' I say.

'I don't mean as a lover,' she says, 'I mean as a woman.'

So I flatter her and cajole her and generally tell her what she wants to hear. However, I do not tell her what she needs to know, which is that my condom, unable to withstand the ferocious passion of an uncircumcised female, has ruptured *in medias res*.

'You are mocking me,' says the Israeli.

'No,' I lie, 'I am smiling because I am happy.' Actually, I am relishing the delicious irony of this bluestocking returning from a conference on population control with a bellyful of Egyptian sperm. I can already hear Shafik's guffaw as I recount the details of my latest conquest.

And then, as the imam said they would, the heavens open. For a few days, we are all Venetians as the monsoon turns our streets into rivers. Further to the south, it is much worse. Floods wash away some sleepers, which causes a train to derail. This, in turn, crashes into an oil depot, which ignites and destroys a village called Dronka. 'It was like winds of fire coming down the mountain,' says a survivor. Another survivor is a baby boy found floating, like Moses, on a makeshift raft of straw. Recovering in hospital, Naguib Mahfouz condemns the fanatics who put him there: 'I pray to God to make the police victorious over terrorism and to purify Egypt from this evil.' Shafik assures me that he is expected to make a full recovery. In return, I tell Shafik about my over-enthusiastic coupling with the Israeli. However, his applause does not provide me with the anticipated satisfaction. On the contrary, I feel unclean. Nor can I stop thinking about the Israeli. I keep seeing her troubled face and hearing the words, 'Please don't think badly of me.' I wonder whether she really is pregnant. Soon I have become as single-minded as the Englishman; everything reminds me of the Israeli, even my own wife. As a result, I resolve to treat her more kindly.

'Why don't you ever empty your pockets?' she grumbles, handing me some scraps of paper gleaned from soiled trousers destined for the laundry. 'Thank you, my dear,' I reply, rather than curse her for her nosiness, and am rewarded with the rediscovery of my lover's e-mail address. I use it as soon as I arrive at the office, concocting a message with the aid of a newly acquired Hebrew dictionary. *Rachel, ani ohev otach.* Rachel, I love you.

Why am I doing this? What do I hope to gain? All I know is that this is only the beginning, and that the end is far, far away.

At night, I go out and watch the sky. The rain has cleared the air, and the stars seem to shine with a renewed vigour. Somewhere, amid that glorious firmament, is the satellite which transmits my daily mantra, my hope for the future. I search the heavens for that molecular green light. It is there, of that I am certain, even though I have yet to see it.

For Pamela

HAROLD PINTER
GIRLS

Harold Pinter

I read this short story in a magazine where a girl student goes into her professor's office and sits at his desk and passes him a note which he opens and which reads: 'Girls like to be spanked.' But I've lost it. I've lost the magazine. I can't find it. And I can't remember what happened next. I don't even know whether the story was fiction or fact. It may have been an autobiographical fragment. But from whose point of view was the story told? The professor's or the girl's? I don't know. I can't remember. The blinding ignorance I am now experiencing is the clearest and cleanest road to madness. What I want to know is quite simple. Was she spanked? If, that is, she was including herself in her all-embracing proposition. If she was including herself in her all-embracing proposition, did she, personally, benefit from it? Was she, not to put too fine a point on it, one of those girls? Was she, or is she, one of those girls who, according to her account, like to be spanked? If that was the case, did it happen? Did it happen in the professor's office, on the professor's desk? Or not? And what about the professor? What did he make of it all? What kind of professor was he, anyway? What was his discipline? Did he subject the assertion (girls like to be spanked) to serious critical scrutiny? Did he find it a dubious generalization or, at any rate, did he set out to verify it? Did he, in other words, put it to the test? Did he, for example, in other words, say: 'OK. Lie on my desk, bottom up, face averted, and let us both determine whether there is substance to this assertion or not'? Or did he simply warn the student, in the interests of science, to tread warily for evermore, in the perilous field of assertion?

The trouble is, I can't find the magazine. I've lost it. And I've no idea how the story—or the autobiographical fragment—developed. Did they fall in love? Did they marry? Did they give birth to lots of little animals?

A man or woman or both must have written this piece about a girl who walks into her professor's office and sits at his desk and passes him a note which he opens and which reads: 'Girls like to be spanked.' But I don't know his or her name; I don't know the author's identity. And I simply don't know whether the girl was in fact spanked, there and then, without further ado, in the professor's office, on his desk, or at any other time, on someone else's desk, here, there, everywhere, all the time, on the hour, religiously, tenderly, fervently, ceaselessly, for ever and for ever and for ever. But it's also possible that she wasn't talking about herself. She might not necessarily have meant that *she* liked to be spanked. She may just have been talking about other girls, girls she didn't even know, millions of girls she hadn't even met, would never meet, millions of girls she hadn't in fact ever actually heard of, millions and billions of girls on the other side of the world who, in her view, liked, simply, without beating about the bush, to be spanked. Or on the other hand she may have been talking about other girls, girls born at Cockfosters or studying American Literature at the University of East Anglia, who had actually told her personally, in breathtaking spasms of spectacular candour, that they, when all was said but nothing yet done, liked, when the chips were down, nothing better than to be spanked. In other words, her assertion (girls like to be spanked) might have been the climax of a long, deep, thoroughly researched course of study she had undertaken honourably and had honourably concluded.

I love her. I love her so much. I think she's a wonderful woman. I saw her once. She turned and smiled. She looked at me and smiled. Then she wiggled to a cab in the cab rank. She gave instructions to the cab driver, opened the door, got in, closed the door, glanced at me for the last time through the window and the cab drove off and I never saw her again.

NOTES ON CONTRIBUTORS

CAROLINE ALEXANDER has a doctorate in classics from Columbia University. She is the author of *One Dry Season* and *The Way to Xanadu*. Thirteen years ago, she taught remedial English to the Florida State football team. *Battle's End*, her account of what became of the players, will be published in the United States by Knopf in November.

ANDREA ASHWORTH was born in Manchester in 1969 and educated at Oxford, where she is now Junior Dean at Hertford College. 'Our Mother's New Man' is from a book in progress which draws on her childhood.

EDWARD BLISHEN, formerly a teacher, is a writer, broadcaster and the author of thirteen volumes of autobiography, of which *Everything Must Go*, he fears, will be the final volume. In 1981, he won the J.R. Ackerley Prize for Autobiography.

DOUGLAS BROOKER is a writer and photographer based in Pasadena, California. He is currently working on a book of photographs of 'less than wholesome' women in Los Angeles.

LINDSEY HILSUM is a freelance journalist who has covered Africa for the past twelve years. She contributes regularly to the *Observer* and BBC Radio 4.

CLAIRE MESSUD was born in the United States in 1966, and educated at Yale and Cambridge. Her first novel, *When the World was Steady*, is published in paperback by Granta Books.

BLAKE MORRISON is the author of *And when did you last see your father?* He is currently writing a book about children, to be published next year by Granta Books.

HAROLD PINTER's previous contribution to *Granta*, 'The New World Order', appeared in issue 37. His plays include *The Caretaker, The Birthday Party, Betrayal, No Man's Land, Old Times, Party Time* and, most recently, *Moonlight*.

GITTA SERENY is the author of *The Invisible Children, The Case of Mary Bell, Into that Darkness* and *Albert Speer: His Battle with Truth* which is published in September by Picador in the UK and Knopf in the United States.

CLIVE SINCLAIR's collected stories *For Good or Evil* are published by Penguin, as is his most recent novel, *Augustus Rex*. His new collection of stories will be published early next year.

JOHN SWEENEY writes for the *Observer*. He is currently working on a comic novel about Bosnia.